Give us a neg!...

...A trawl through the sporting archive of Swindon's picture agency...

Richard Wintle
Calyx Picture Agency

The Hobnob Press

First published in the United Kingdom in 2022
by The Hobnob Press, 8 Lock Warehouse, Severn Road, Gloucester GL1 2GA
www.hobnobpress.co.uk
© Richard Wintle 2022
Calyx Picture Agency   www.calyxpix.com
The Author hereby asserts his moral rights to be identified as the Author of the Work.
All rights reserved. No part of this publication may be reproduced, stored in a retrieval system, or transmitted in any form or by any means, electronic, mechanical, photocopying, recording or otherwise, without the prior permission of the publisher and copyright holder.
British Library Cataloguing in Publication Data
A catalogue record for this book is available from the British Library
ISBN 978-1-914407-27-7

Dedication

To my very patient wife Pat, without whose help this book wouldn't have happened, and Sarah and Guy, and Ross and Sally who helped us both through the pandemic.

I thank you all.

I apologise in advance for all those sports that I have missed out of this book, but there are only a finite number of pages and, to tell the stories of the events, I have had to make the decision to put some sports in abeyance for future books.

Richard Wintle was born in 1951 in Gloucester England. Richard moved from the Worcestershire village of Bredon (made famous by John Moore in the Brensham trilogy) to the Gloucestershire town of Dursley in 1959 where he became interested in the art of photography when he was given a Brownie 127 camera as a birthday present on his 9th birthday.

While attending the local secondary modern school he had his first experience of having a picture published when the local weekly paper, the *Dursley Gazette* used and paid for two images of the school's CSE science project; to build a hot air balloon and fly it. The two images of the balloon in flight set the destination for the budding photographer with a determination to have more published at national and international level.

While in Dursley he supplied the *Gloucester Citizen* and *Western Daily Press* newspapers with local stories, while honing his media photographic skills.

A move from Dursley to a job in the Science department at Brunel Technical College (now the City of Bristol College and where the BBC filmed Casualty before moving the production to Cardiff) and another move to the CF Mott College of Education in Liverpool as Education Technician followed.

In Liverpool one of the technicians was a former *Daily Express* photographer who mentored Richard resulting in a chance photograph of youth crossing the M57 at Knowsley appearing in the Manchester edition of the *Daily Mail*.

The first national picture gave a turbo boost to getting more and better pictures published.

Calyx was set up after an eight year employment at Raychem in Dorcan Swindon, six years of which were spent in the Marketing department travelling the world setting up exhibitions and doing the marketing department's pictures.

Richard and his team have supplied images of local and national news events to the world's media and between 1999 and 2012 he was the only video cameraman to follow the royal family in a freelance capacity, with his footage being used in television news and documentaries throughout the world.

Now in semi-retirement, it gives him a chance to reflect and gather together the 2 million film images, and the 2 million images stored in digital files, into an archive which tells the story of local news for the 40 years he has taken pictures in Swindon.

As a press photographer I take pictures of life; and, as an archivist of pictures, I store life's stories. Stories that quite often have a theme; stories, some happy some sad. Some stories amaze people and some deflate egos.

Most stories have a beginning, middle and end, and with many picture stories the start is a long way from the end in time; sometime years.

In wading through my archive and selection images that are sport related, I have found links between stories and Swindon that never existed at the time I took them.

Here are a few links that my research has thrown up, along with images from the forty-plus years of Swindon history that I and my colleagues have recorded.

Many of the pictures have been published nationally and even internationally, so these stories are about Swindon's national image, as well as of local interest.

Some of the images have succumbed to the rigors of the press industry, where a quick turnround sometimes damages the negatives, so please excuse some of the marks on the pictures. I have tried to remove most of them in that infamous photo management software, but some damage is irreparable.

To add to the headache of technological advances that forty years of photography has seen come and go; in 2000 there was a massive revolution in media photography, when we went from film to the digital capture of images. This change gave us a problem, in as much as storage of film is easy and very cheap, digital archiving however requires a lot of digital storage and work on the meta-data, and this costs quite a lot in both time and money.

We opted for storage on writable CD and DVD discs, as hard drives were in there infancy and very expensive. CDs and DVDs, we were told, were indestructible and would last forever, you could eat your dinner off them and they would still work. This turned out to be a slight exaggeration on behalf of the CD production companies: they don't!!

From 2000 until about 2007, many of the discs I used for storage have degraded and in some cases are totally unreadable, hence there are some gaps in the archive.

Some of the missing images I have managed to retrieve from the agencies that syndicate my work, but others I just have to write off.

To compile this book I have taken information from our archive, as well as from many websites and encyclopedias, and have credited them in the copy.

I hope you enjoy the meanderings of a crazy press photographer as much as that photographer has enjoyed the journey of compiling this missive.

My journey has taken a twist, well more of a jolt I'd say.

In 2018 I was diagnosed with a rare cancer: they call it the secret cancer as it creeps up on you and hides itself as another ailment. Mine was as asthma. That cancer is Neuroendocrine Cancer and I hope to raise awareness of the cancer through this book and any talks I give as a result of this tome.

The prognosis of my particular type of Neuroendocrine Cancer is good, well as good as it can be, as it's the typical type, the lesser and least aggressive of the four types, on my lungs. Recently some famous names have made headlines, having succumbed to the more virulent form in the Pancreas; they are Steve Jobs and Aretha Franklin. BBC political Editor Nick Robinson has Neuroendocrine tumours on his lungs too.

Rare yes; about 4000 people in the UK are diagnosed with some form of Neuroendocrine Cancer each year, that's about 40 people in a million.

Neuroendocrine cancer is a term used to cover a group of cancers that start in Neuroendocrine cells. These cancers may also be referred to as NETs, NECs, NENs or even Carcinoids.

I will be donating £1 of every book sold to the Neuroendocrine Cancer UK charity.

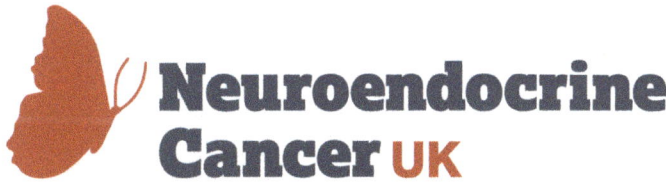

(Formerly NET Patient Foundation)

The thing about press photography that amuses me is the speed that's needed to get your picture into the picture desks for it to be considered for use, and how the photographers panic to achieve this aim.

Time and time again the snappers dash to their computers to send pictures off faster than the opposition's photographers.

But, as I have discovered over the years, timing and quality is as important as speed when it comes to getting pictures used; as I experienced when Swindon Town beat Wigan Athletic in the FA Cup in 2012.

Under their enigmatic manager Paolo Di Canio, Swindon played Wigan at the County Ground and came out 2-1 winners with a goal by Matt Richie on the hour.

Di Canio celebrated, as only Di Canio can; rushing up the touchline while screaming his joy at the turn of events finishing just a few metres from me.

Great picture, I thought, and carried on taking shots of the game. Meanwhile, the specialist football photographers grabbed their computers to send images of the goal to their desks.

The game ended, and Di Canio celebrated with the players; turning to acknowledge the fans, before vanishing down the tunnel to the reception.

I went back to the office to send my material, better late than never I thought, as the time approached six o'clock.

After photographing occasions like that; the next day you buy all the national papers to check to see if any of your images have made it into the pages.

The Sunday papers almost require a trolley to transport them, with all their supplements and junk literature, but I sat down and ploughed through them, with no sign of any of my pictures appearing in print.

I left the heavies till last as they tend to use their own photographers or images from one of the big agencies like Getty or Press Association, but, when I eventually came to the *Sunday Telegraph* and took out the sports supplement, there was one of those OMG moments.

My image of Di Canio almost-filled the front page!

For accounting purposes we had to talk to the picture desk on the Tuesday to get order numbers for used pictures, and I said to the picture editor, "You used that well", to which he replied, "Yes, a good picture, and it landed at the same time the sports desk were calling for a picture of Di Canio, so we looked no further."

The picture desks receive many tens of thousands of pictures of football on a Saturday afternoon from all four football leagues, so to time your images' arrival on the desk is pure luck, but sometimes speed is not the only answer to getting them used...

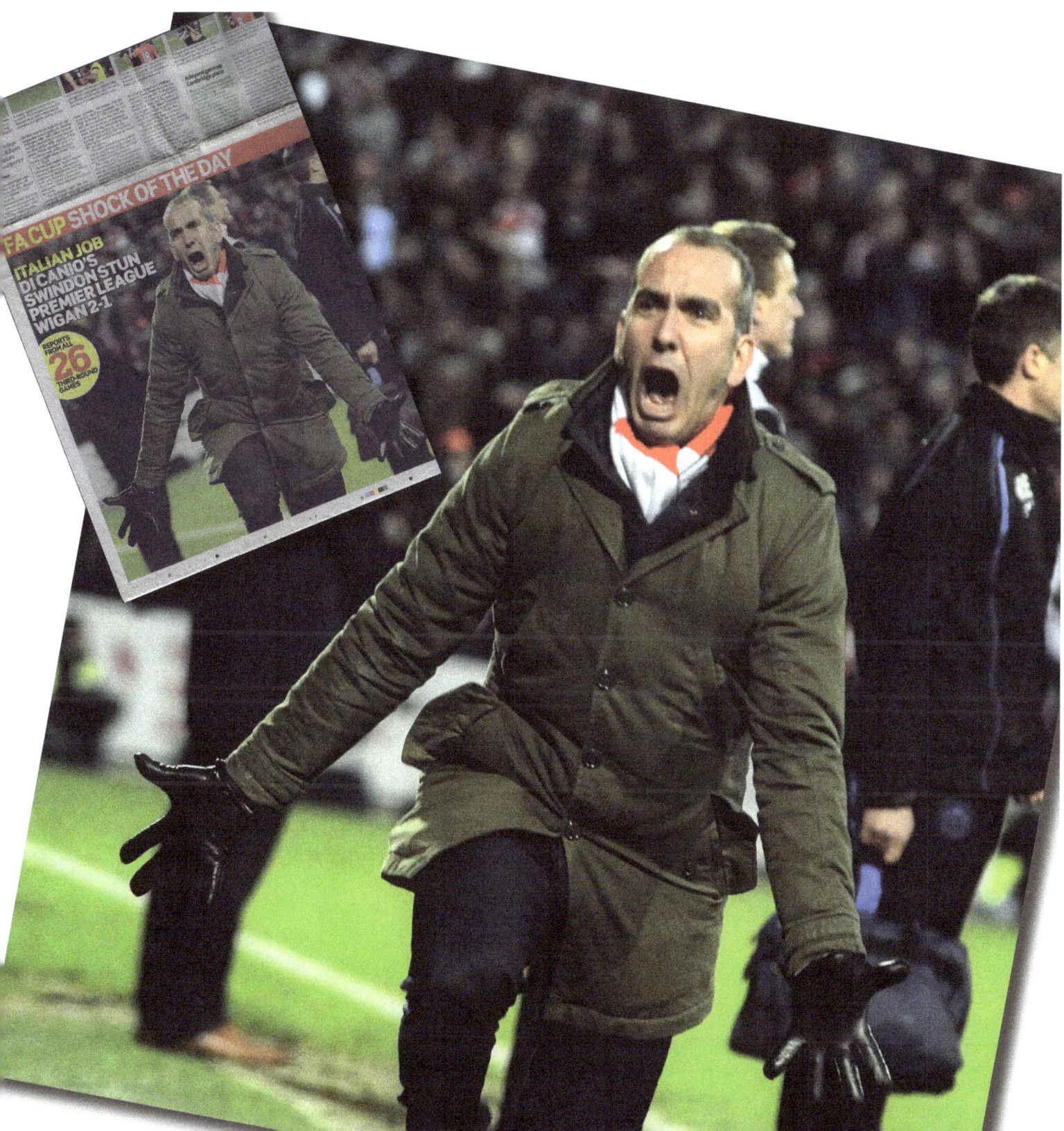

...Press photography is a specialist genre in the art of photography. Basically we are the Jack of all trades and masters of none, except press photography.

There are studio, wedding, food and fashion genres among many others in the photographic world; all specialist subjects requiring specialist knowledge to be proficient in that environment. As press photographers we are expected to be able to cover all those fields and be adequately professional with the results.

Within press photography there are specialist fields too: features, news, social, paparazzi and sport to name but a few; again, we are expected to cross over into these fields seamlessly.

Many good press photographers however come unstuck when it comes to photographing sport, as it is possibly the most difficult field to be proficient in.

You have to follow the sport to be able to anticipate where things are going to happen next, and have the equipment to do the job, such as suitable cameras and lenses, hence you have specialist snappers in cricket, football, ice hockey, gymnastic, equestrian; the list goes on and on.

In my time behind the camera I have photographed many sports and loved most of them, but never specialised in one; well maybe football, which I have covered for four decades, and Jet Ski racing which I covered for a few years in the late eighties and early nineties.

All the other sports I have been associated with are as a press photographer...

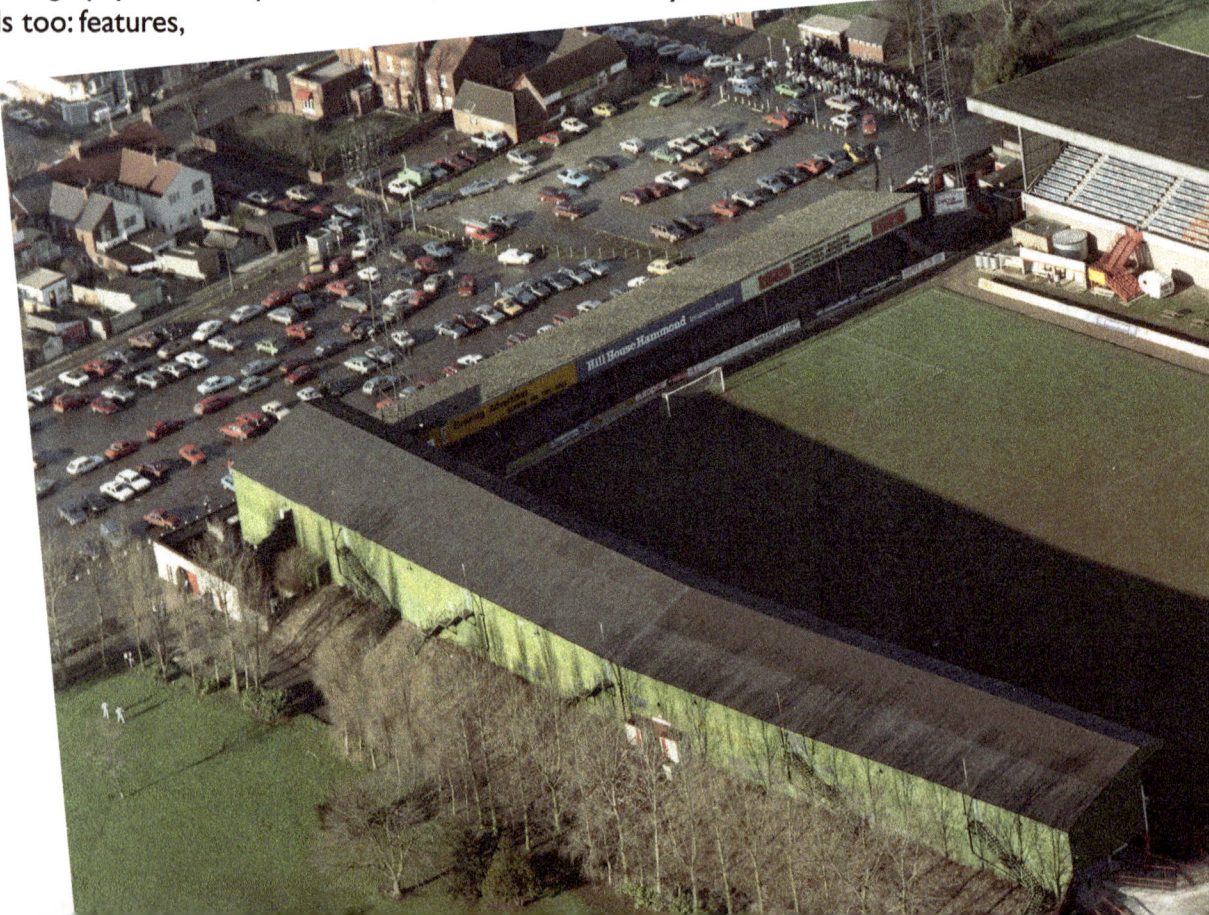

...My association with Swindon Town Football Club started at school in the Gloucestershire market town of Dursley, where there was a two-way split with the sport-minded boys. One half supported Bristol City and the other half Bristol Rovers.

I didn't like either side, but as with most school battles I was forced to name a local team. By chance my father was a teacher there and one of his colleagues supported Swindon. He had a season ticket for the Stratton Bank and invited dad to go to a game.

My late father was of Welsh mining stock from the Rhonda Valley, and not into football, but preferred rugby; so suggested I go instead, as I played for the school first team and would enjoy the experience much more than he would.

The game was Swindon Town v Queen's Park Rangers, I don't remember the score, but what I do remember is that it was played in very heavy rain. The pitch was, in the modern game, unplayable, but the match went ahead and the main attention was on the two forwards, Swindon's legend Don Rogers and QPR's legendary Rodney Marsh.

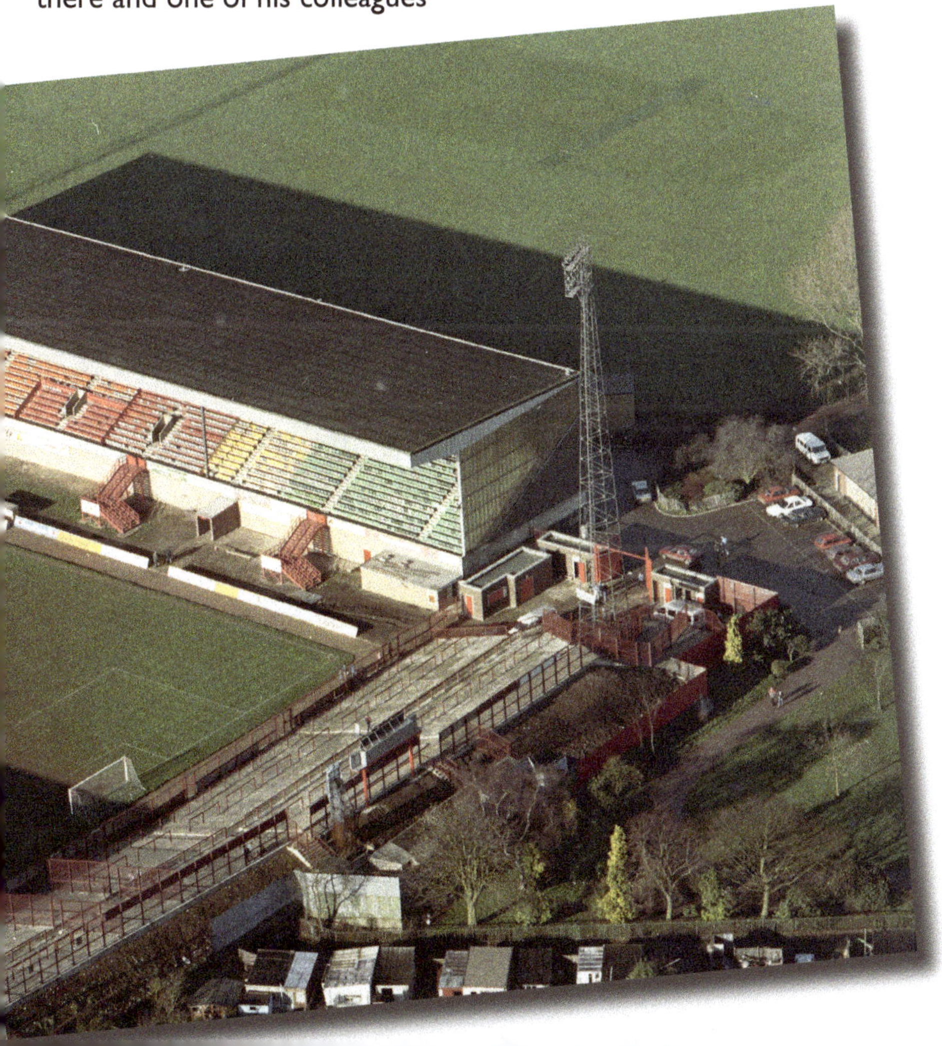

What hit me at the end of the match was that Marsh was covered in mud and Don Rogers was almost as clean as he had emerged from the dressing room.

That game cemented Swindon Town as my local team, so it was, with some pleasure, that when I started to photograph football after turning to photography full time it was Swindon I was photographing.

It's somewhat ironic that if I was growing up in Dursley in this era the local team would be Forest Green Rovers, who I feel support for now. Their ground (at the time of writing) is in Nailsworth less than ten miles from where I lived, so that, at a local derby, I see both my teams in action and see myself as a neutral...

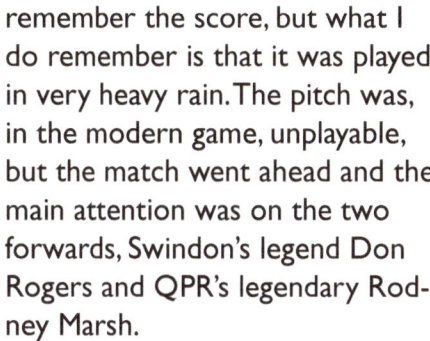

..I started my Swindon Town sojourn when the late Don Beard, my predecessor as a freelance, retired and the national newspapers were looking for a Swindon contact to cover the games. This was because the local paper photographers were unable to supply images from the games.

In those days Swindon were in the lowly Division Four, so not many pictures were ordered of the games, but that was to change in dramatic style.

New sponsors demanded a high profile manager, and on 23rd July 1984 former Manchester United star Lou Macari was brought in to fill the role. Macari brought with him former United goalkeeper Harry Gregg as his number two.

The Macari Swindon story is quite well published, but the sacking by Chairman of the Board, Maurice Earle, of both Macari and Gregg on Good Friday, 5 April 1985 brought protests and even saw the unlikely sight of Lou Macari seated in the Arkells' stand watching Swindon at home to Southend the next day.

As I revealed in a previous book, about that time I had forked out to purchase a rather expensive 300mm F2.8 lens, which I had used during the covering of a protest at the Railworks where it enabled me to get an exclusive picture of a noose being raised above the crowd.

The lens this time gave me another exclusive, that of Macari in the stand watching the game while he was sacked.

Exclusive; as the local paper photographer only had a short focus lens which was no good for the crowd shot but worked well for the action images of the game...

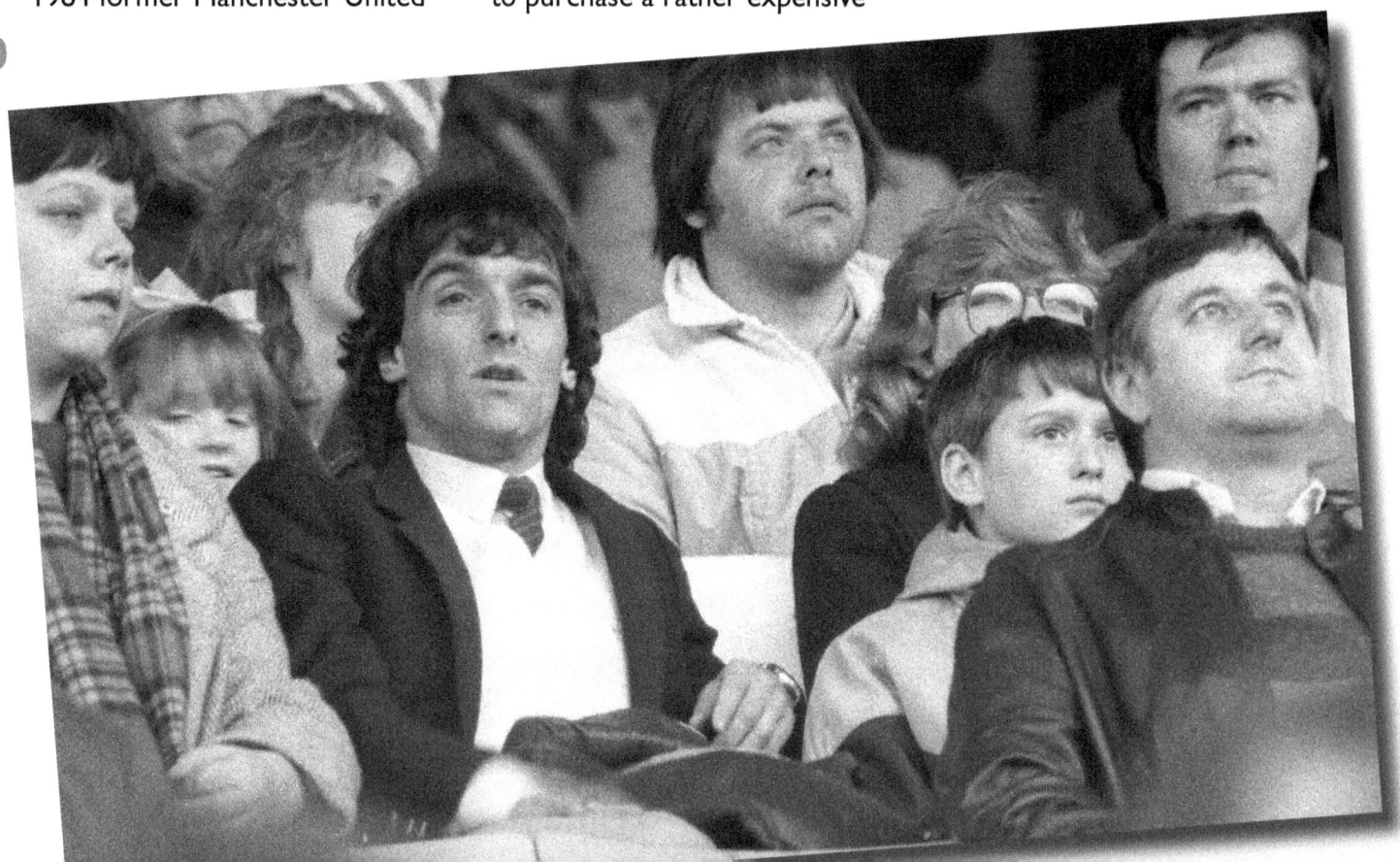

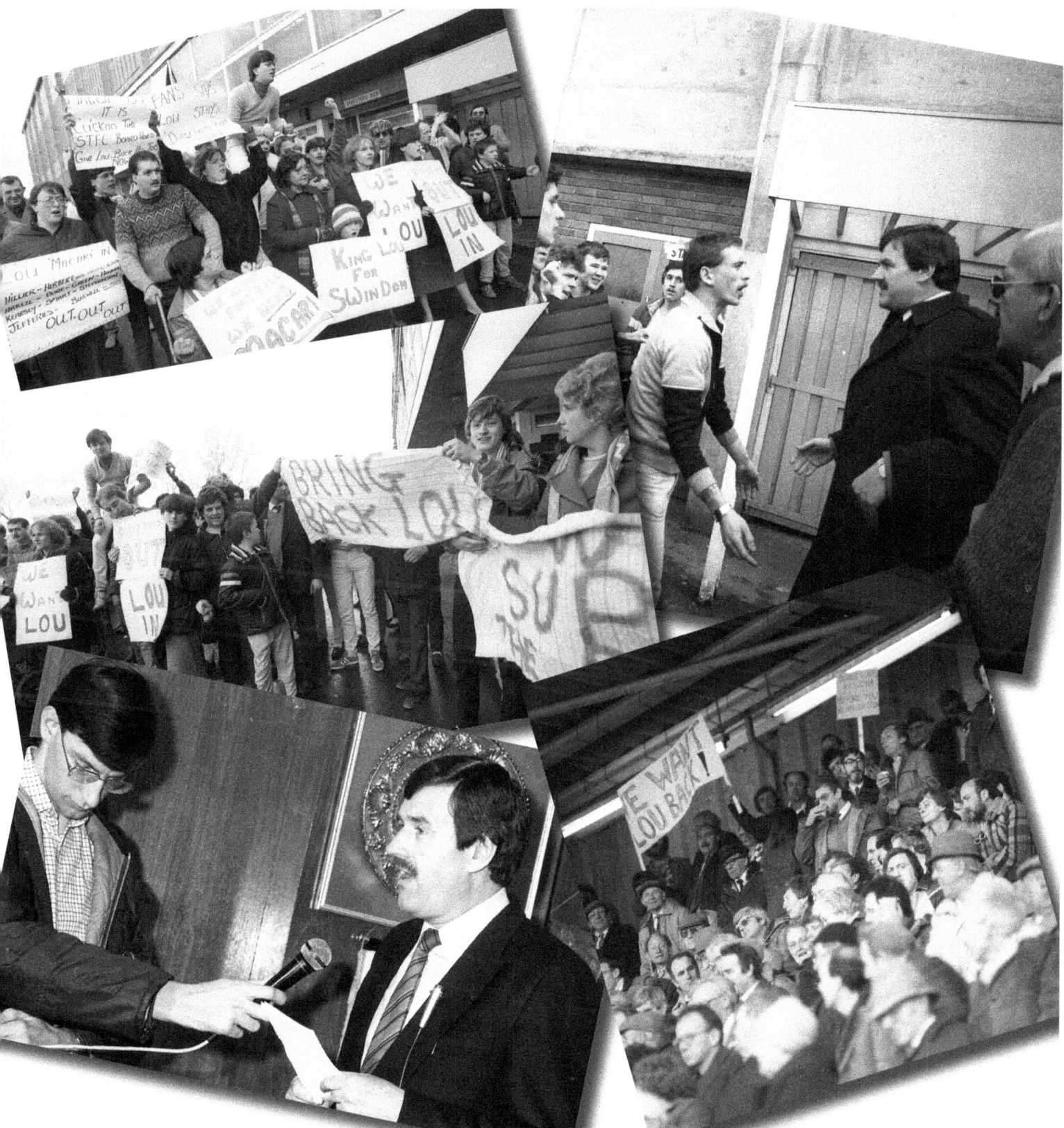

...On the day after the double sacking took place, a very lonely looking Harry Gregg was seen outside the ground while Macari was inside.

The fans protested to Brian Hillier who in due course reinstated Macari; who went on to get a double promotion, but that brings more stories...

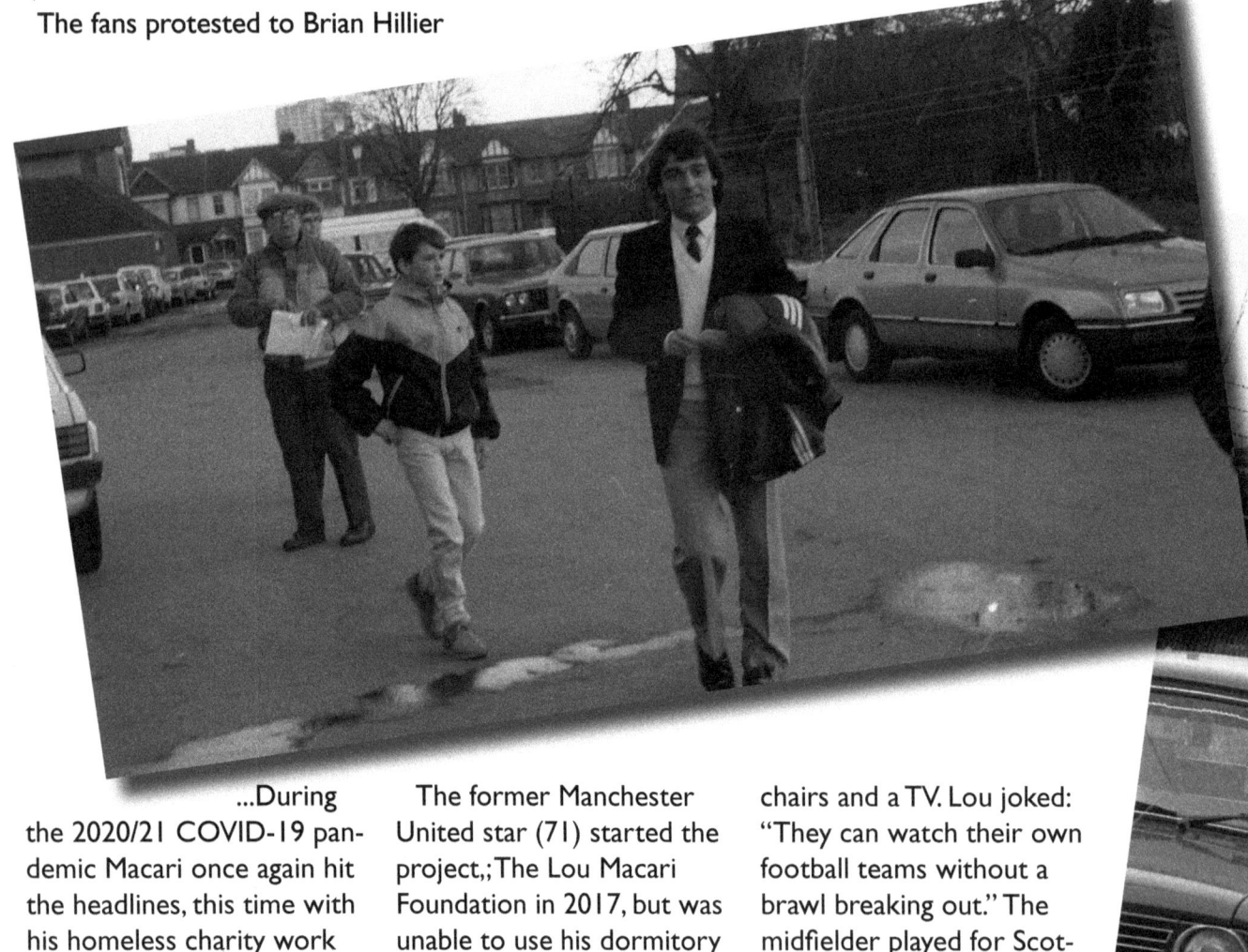

...During the 2020/21 COVID-19 pandemic Macari once again hit the headlines, this time with his homeless charity work in Stoke-on-Trent where he has helped dozens of homeless people get back on their feet by turning 46 luxury glamping pods into individual shelters, in a warehouse the size of a football pitch.

The former Manchester United star (71) started the project,; The Lou Macari Foundation in 2017, but was unable to use his dormitory style shelter when Covid hit.

By chance he discovered a glamping site and used the pod concept to fill the warehouse with pods.

Each pod is 15ft x 7.5ft and has a bed, table and chairs and a TV. Lou joked: "They can watch their own football teams without a brawl breaking out." The midfielder played for Scotland in the 1978 World Cup and later managed clubs including Celtic and Stoke and of course Swindon Town...

...I think it's time I explained the title of this tome "Give us a Neg" or "Ganzing".

Sports photographers, and football snappers in particular, are very cliquey, and they work together as a pack even though they work for different papers. Sports picture editors, like any other picture editors, demand the best picture of an incident.

Football pitches are about 110 meters by 75 meters, so for one person to cover the whole pitch topographically is almost impossible, hence you select the arc that best suits your brief, i.e. Swindon attack. By doing this you can miss out on an incident or goal at the other end of the pitch. It therefore follows that the best picture of an incident is not always out of your camera; so, to get out of trouble, the photographers borrow negatives (or now files) and submit them, hence; "Give us a Negative."

The problem comes when the photographer whose byline is on the picture can be seen in the image on the other side of the pitch...

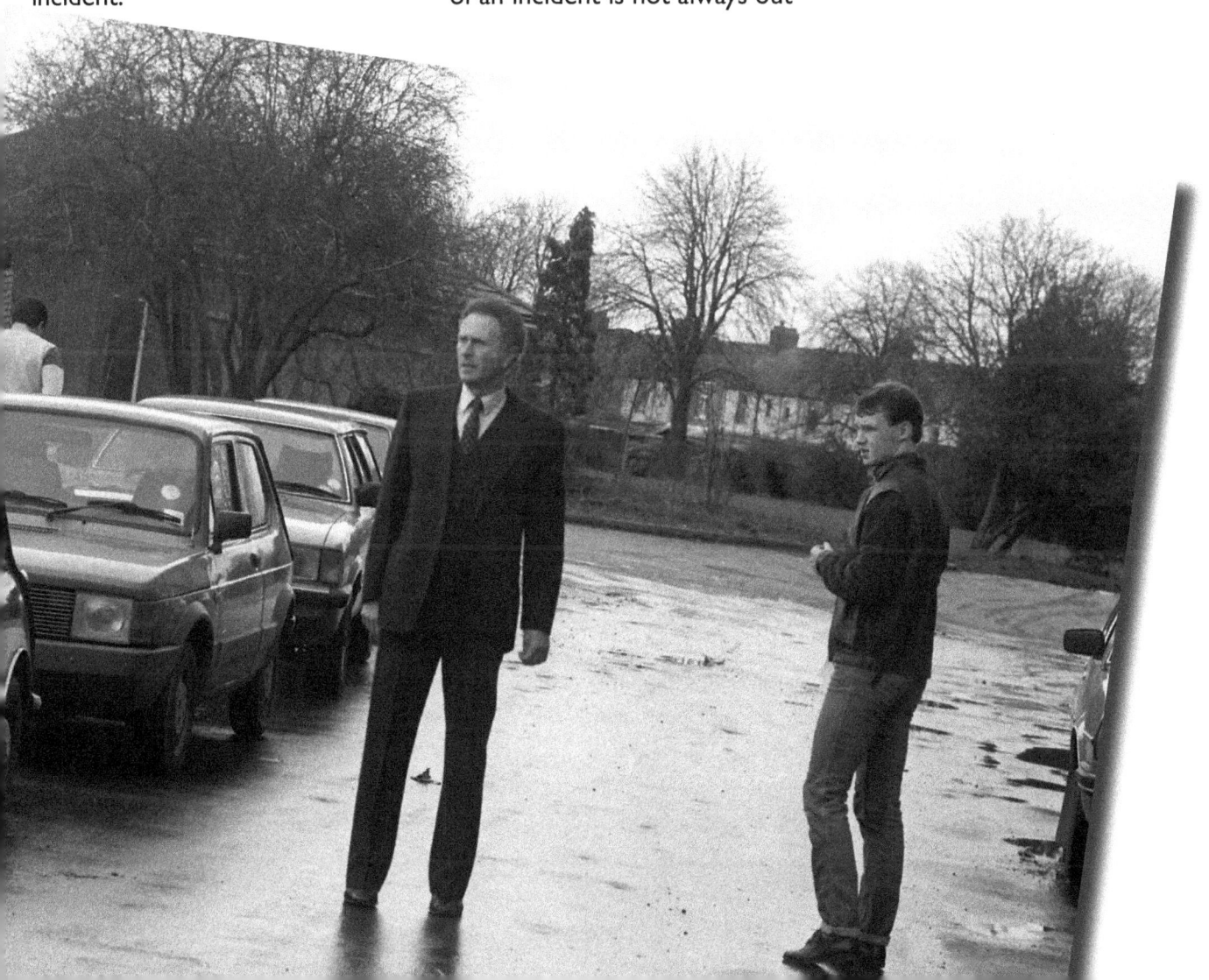

...Macari was a Manchester United star, but the giant club fell into the Second Division and called on the services of Alex Ferguson to get them out of trouble.

Ferguson's first game as United's manager was at the old Manor Ground in Oxford, where there was a press pack gathered for the match. With a certain Robert Maxwell seated in the Oxford Chairman's seat in the stand, Ferguson took his seat in the away dugout and watched his team struggle.

I was photographing for the *Daily Star*, as I frequently did cover the Oxford games for them, but on this occasion there were many more photographers in attendance and one shot was inevitable as the pack laid out on the ground all taking pictures of Alex Ferguson rather than the game.

The image that the *Star* used taught me not to rely on the single exposure setting on the camera, but use the motor-wind on continuous high speed setting, as the resulting image was in the middle of a series of frames, and the chances of capturing it as a single frame was remote.

The image hit the back page...

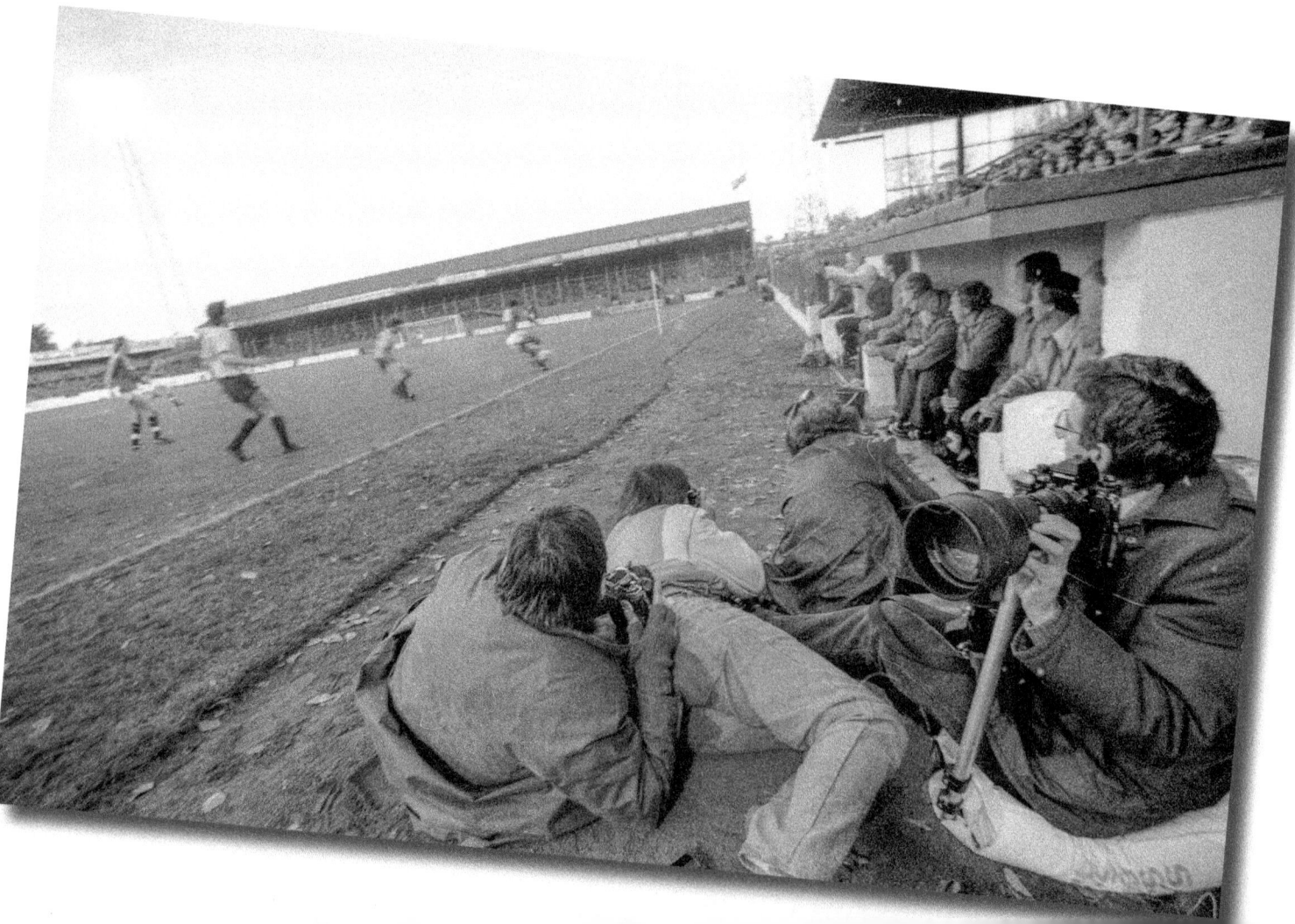

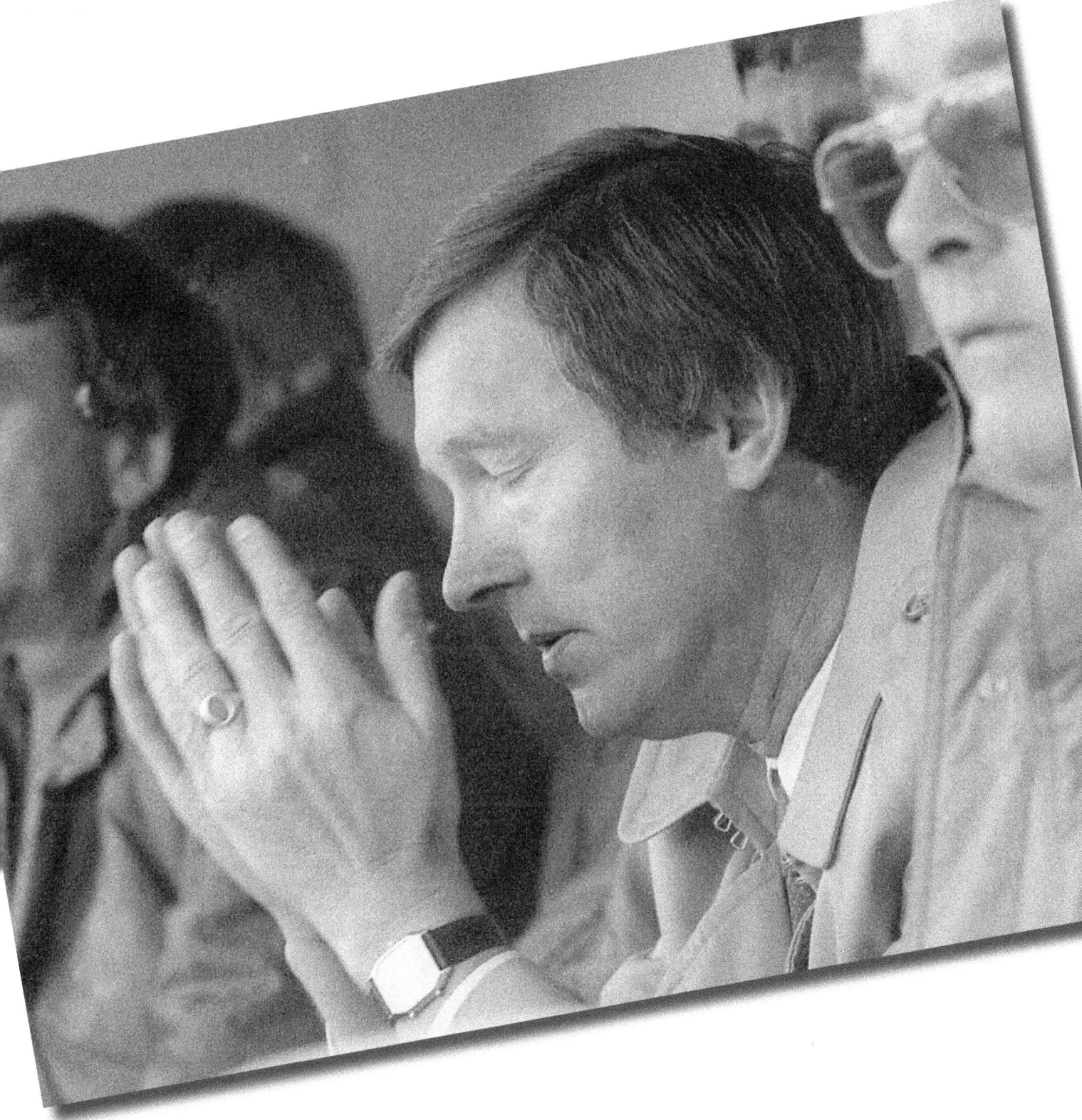

...Sir Alex Ferguson has a string of race horses and the Swindon locality is studded with world-famous stables which, over the years, have produced some famous winners such as Bob Champion and Aldiniti, who won the Grand National on 4th April 1981 while recovering from testicular cancer, after being given a 30% chance of surviving and three to four months to live.

Aldiniti was trained by Josh Gifford in his yard at Findon, West Sussex,

Bob's home and stable was at Ufcott alongside the Wroughton Airfield where he and wife Jo lived with son Michael.

I did a feature on them in 1985 and followed them after that, with one story that hit the the front page of a tabloid...

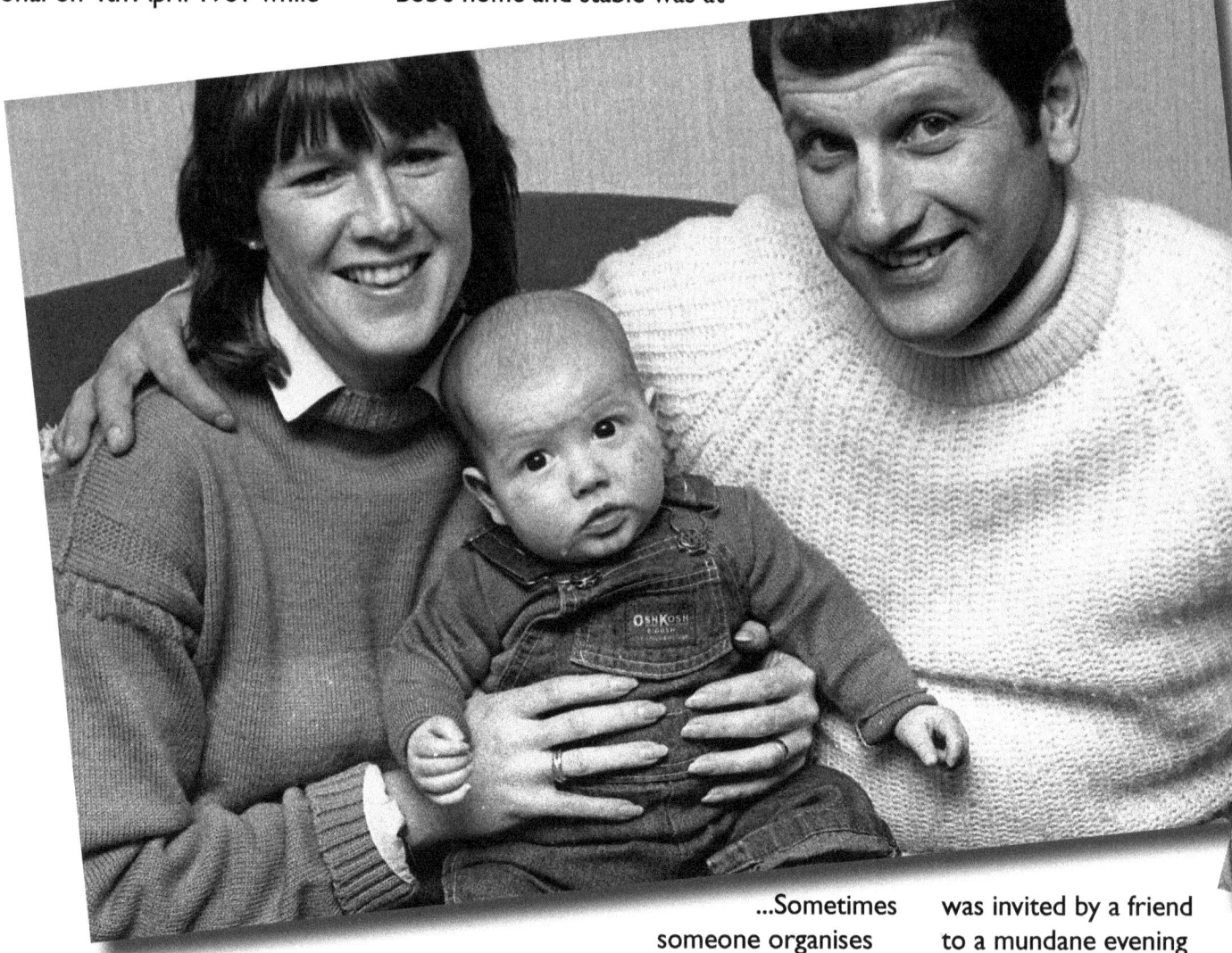

...Sometimes someone organises your luck for you, as was the case when I was invited by a friend to a mundane evening out in the British Rail Social Club...

...and you look from where you are sitting and see at the next table the Grand National winner Bob Champion and wife Jo enjoying a private evening, supposedly away from the limelight!

I am sure the evening was arranged specifically so that I would be there and get the picture, as the host had an interest in racing and was a friend of Bob's. I will, I fear, never know for sure...

Needless to say, images finished up on film in my trusty Nikon, and the pictures and story were tagged as Exclusive on the front page of the Sun.

Bob now heads up the world renown cancer charity.

He was appointed Commander of the Order of the British Empire (CBE) in the 2021 New Year Honours for services to prostate and testicular cancer research...

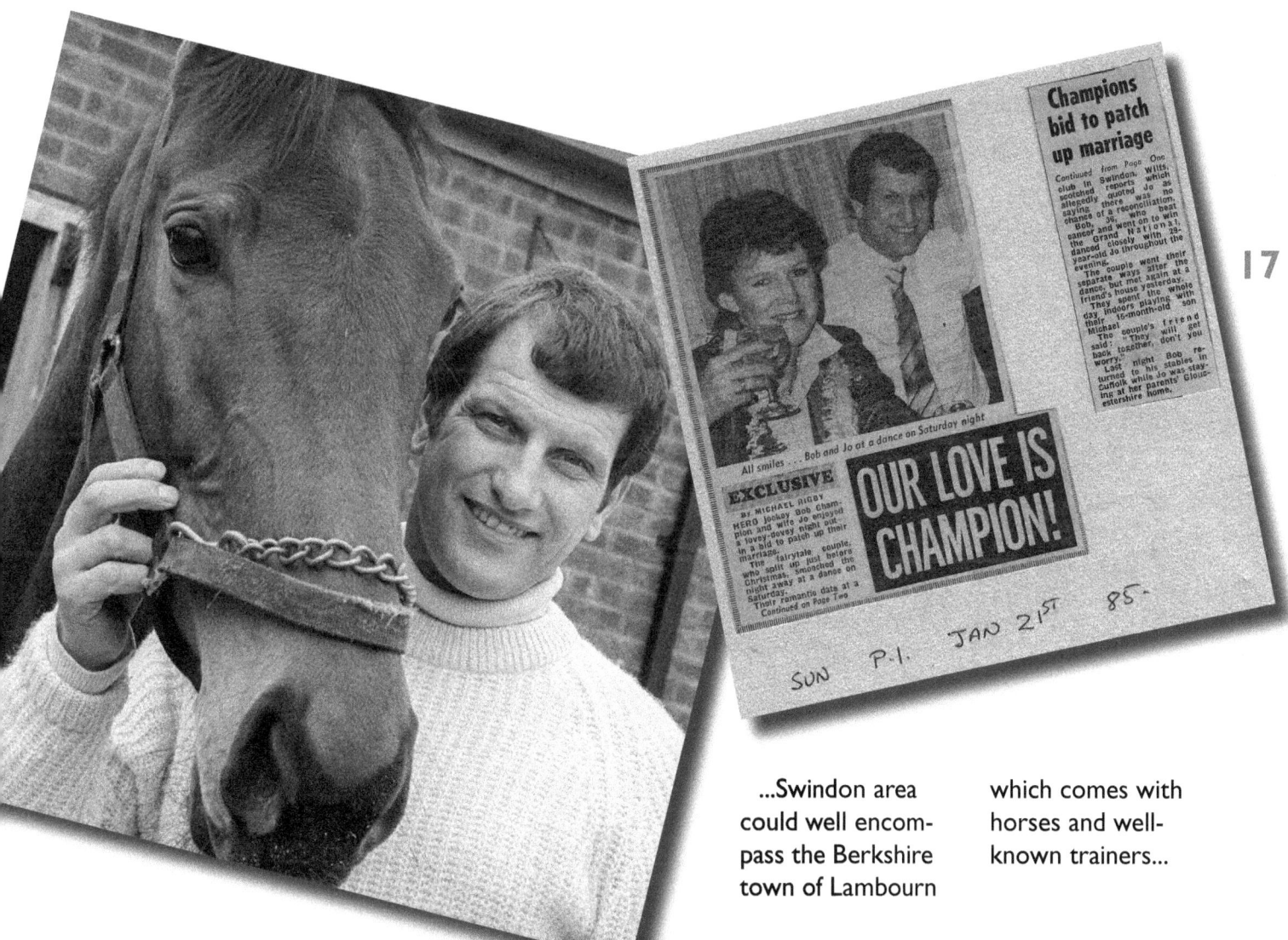

...Swindon area could well encompass the Berkshire town of Lambourn which comes with horses and well-known trainers...

...and, as trainers go, Jenny Pitman is up there with the greatest as her entry in the 1983 Grand National, Corbiere, held off the Irish-trained Greasepaint to win the race by three quarters of a length.

This victory made her the first female trainer to win the Grand National...

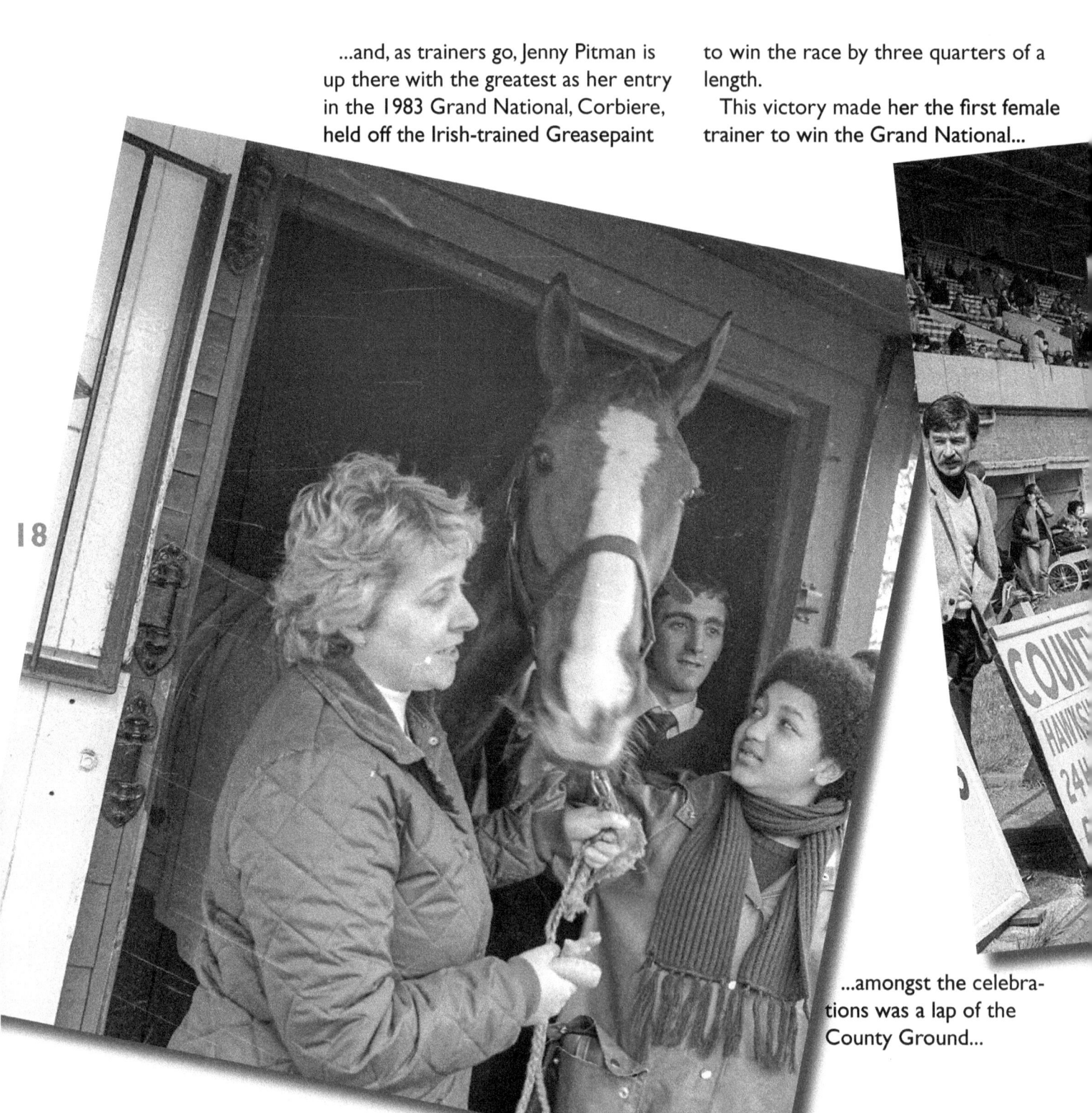

...amongst the celebrations was a lap of the County Ground...

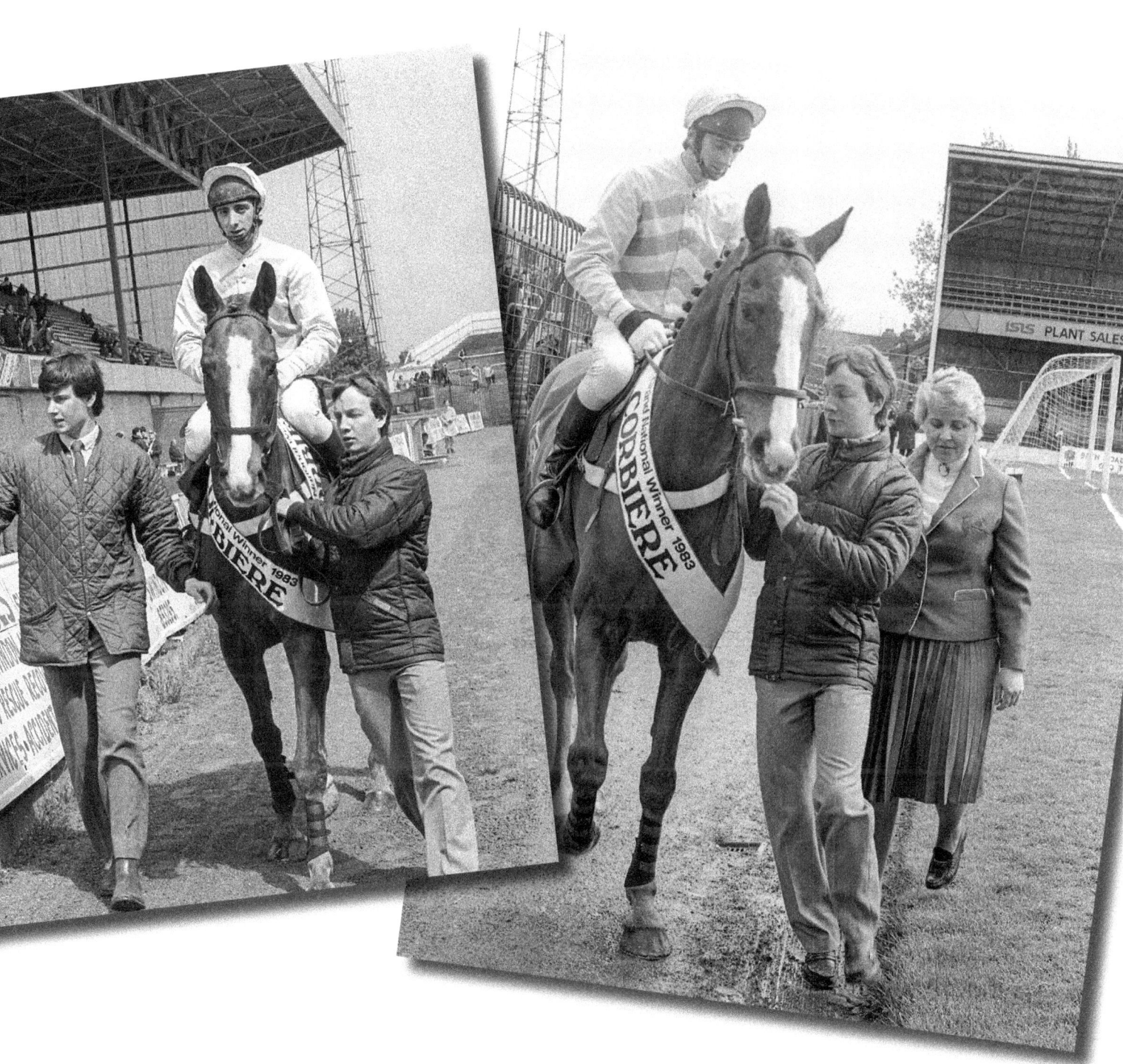

...In 1995 Jenny completed the double, winning the Grand National with Royal Athlete.

Royal Athlete was among those worthy of respect, but considered out of form, with a starting price of 40/1. Irish jockey Jason Titley was in the saddle and he romped home in a time of nine minutes and 4.1 seconds with a seven lengths lead.

The next day Lambourn turned out to celebrate the win...

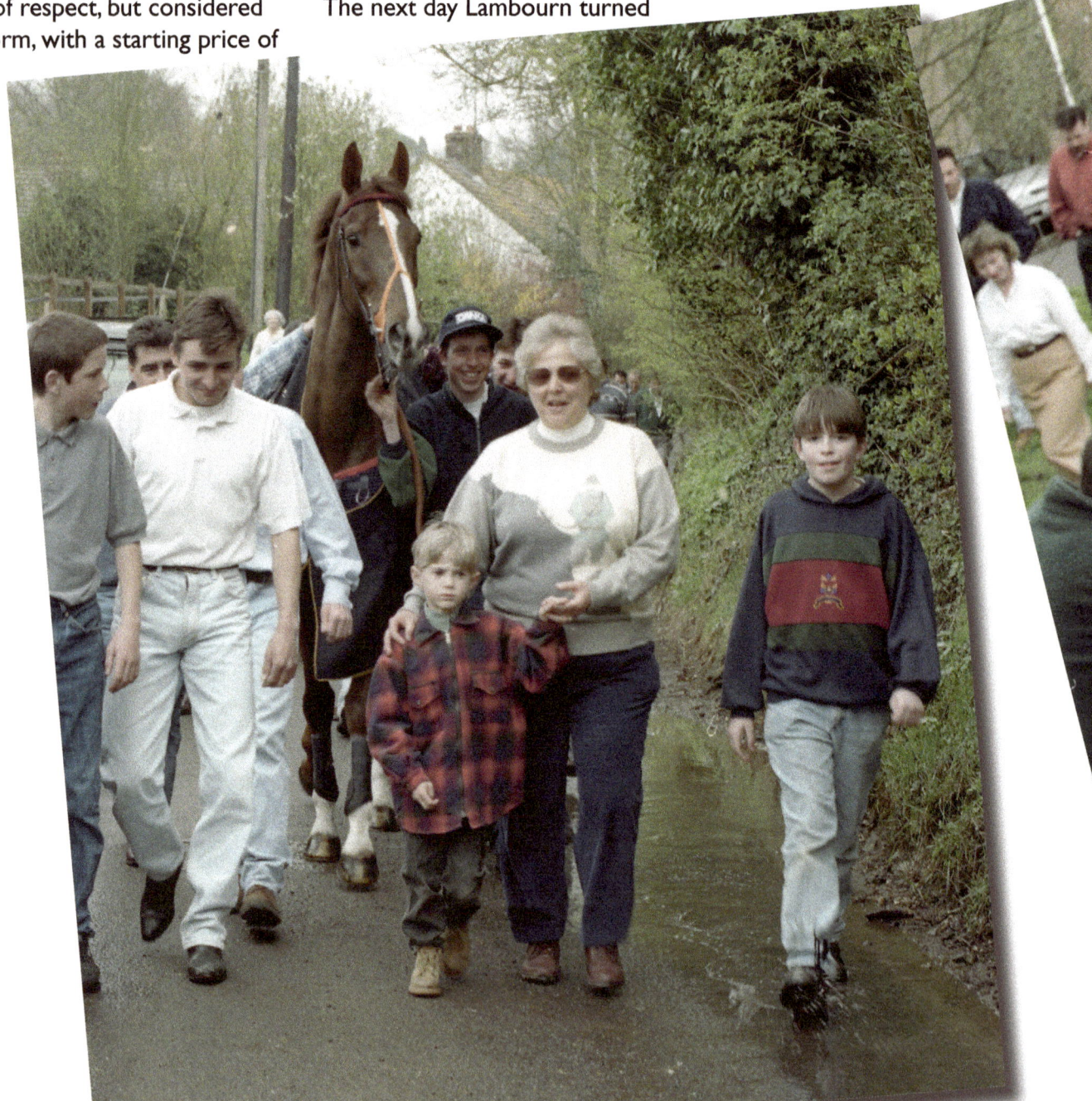

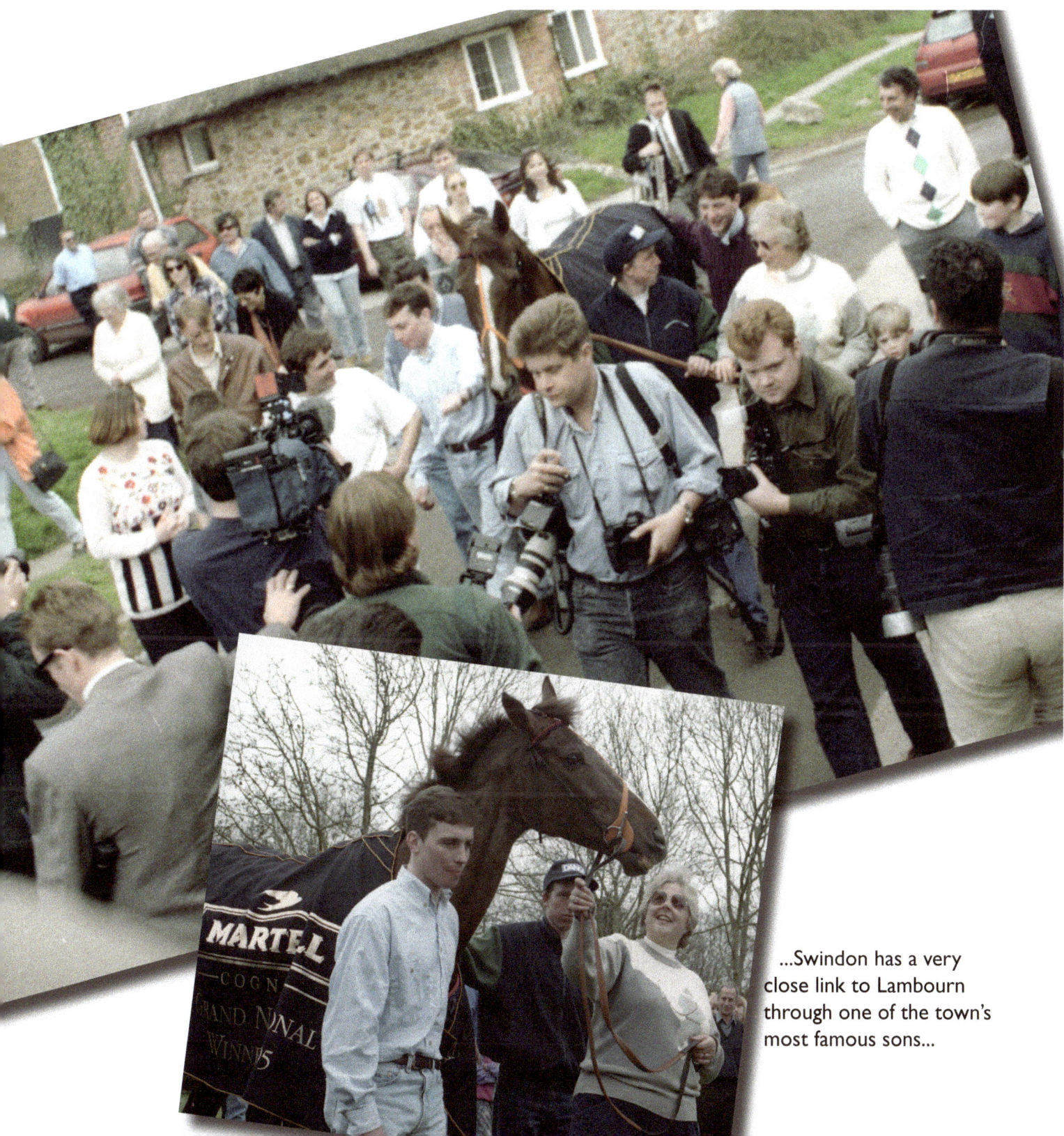

...Swindon has a very close link to Lambourn through one of the town's most famous sons...

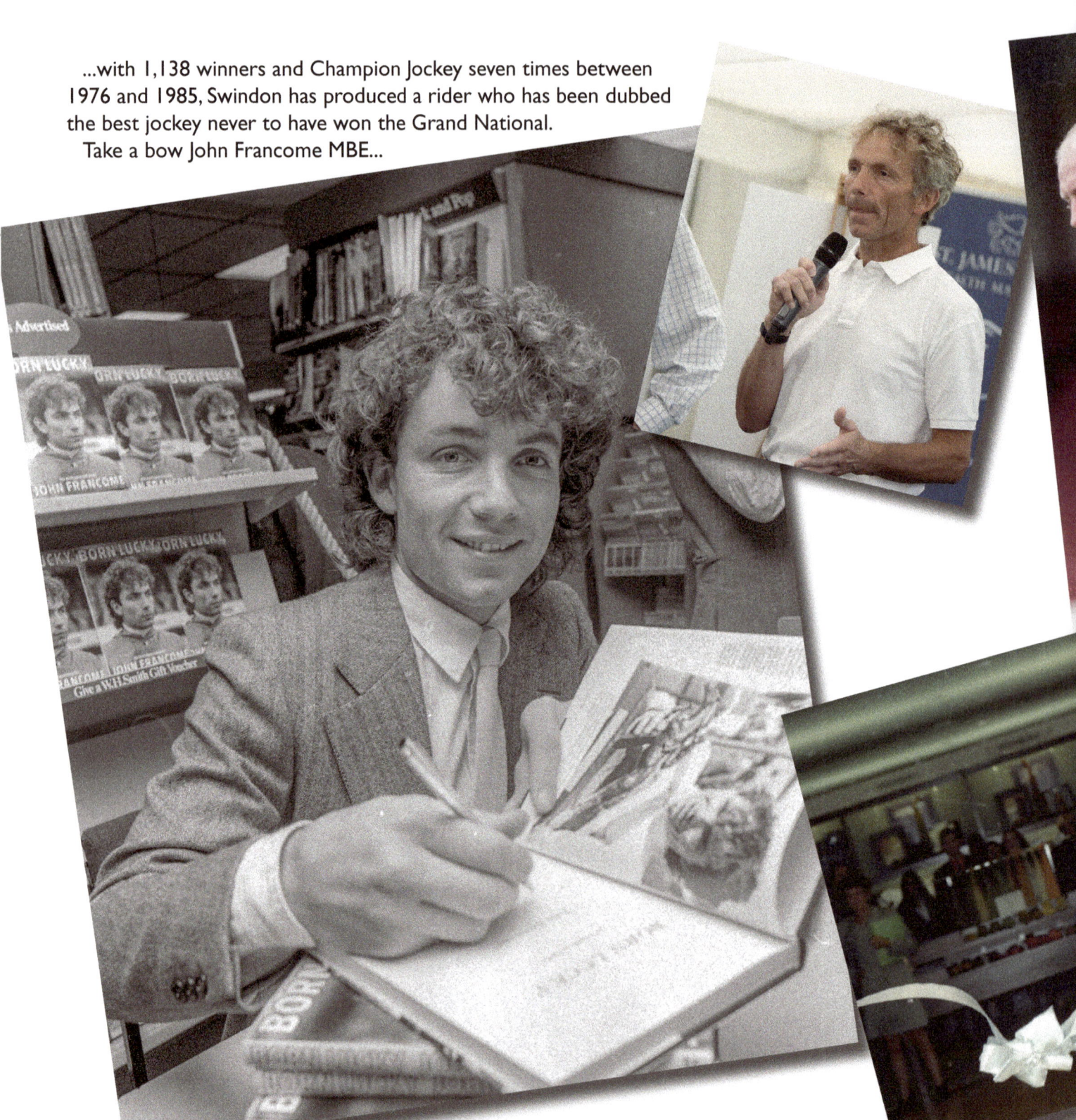

...with 1,138 winners and Champion Jockey seven times between 1976 and 1985, Swindon has produced a rider who has been dubbed the best jockey never to have won the Grand National.
Take a bow John Francome MBE...

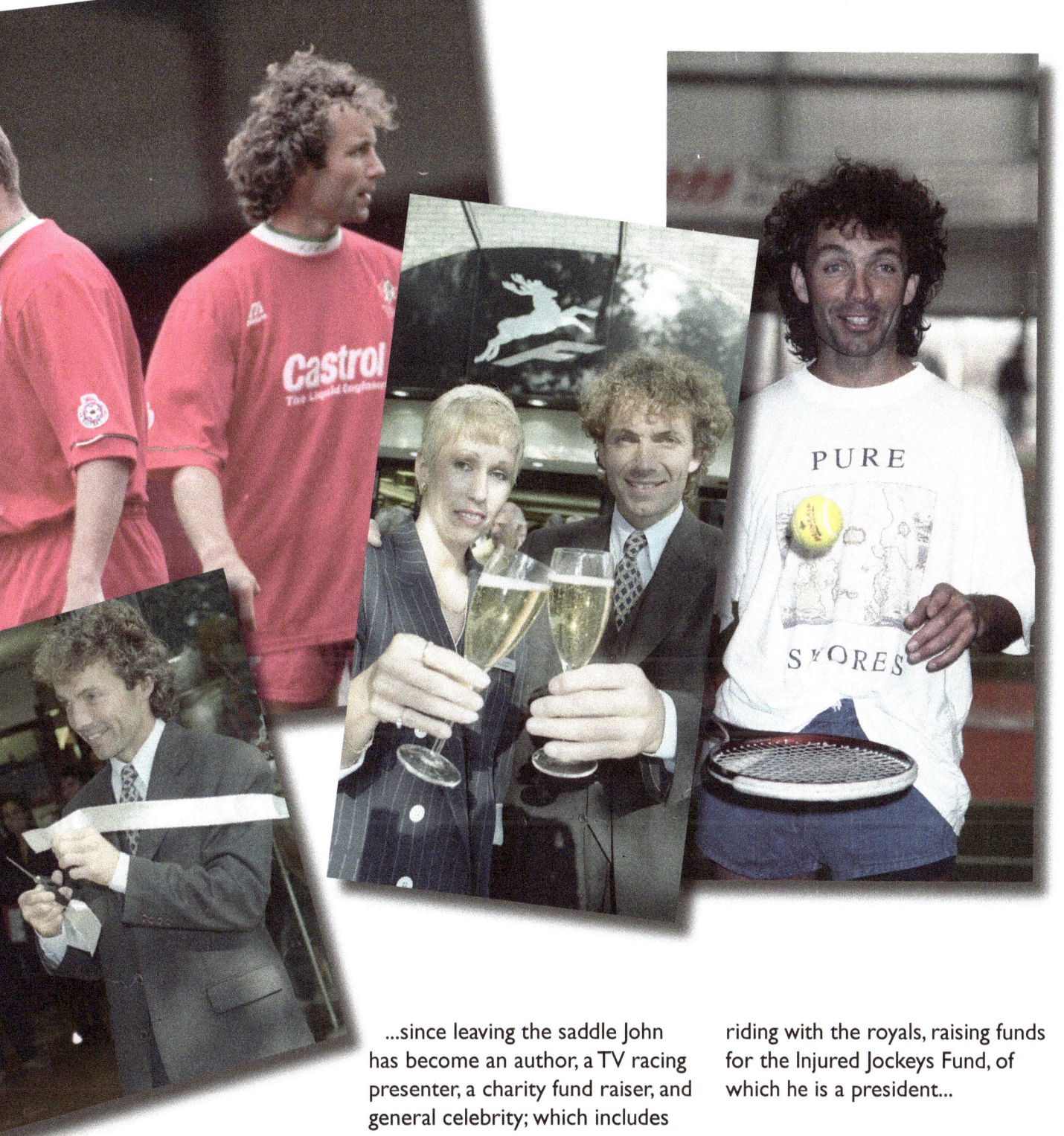

...since leaving the saddle John has become an author, a TV racing presenter, a charity fund raiser, and general celebrity; which includes riding with the royals, raising funds for the Injured Jockeys Fund, of which he is a president...

...John competed against Zara Phillips in an Eventers v Jockeys event at the Barbury Castle Horse Trials....

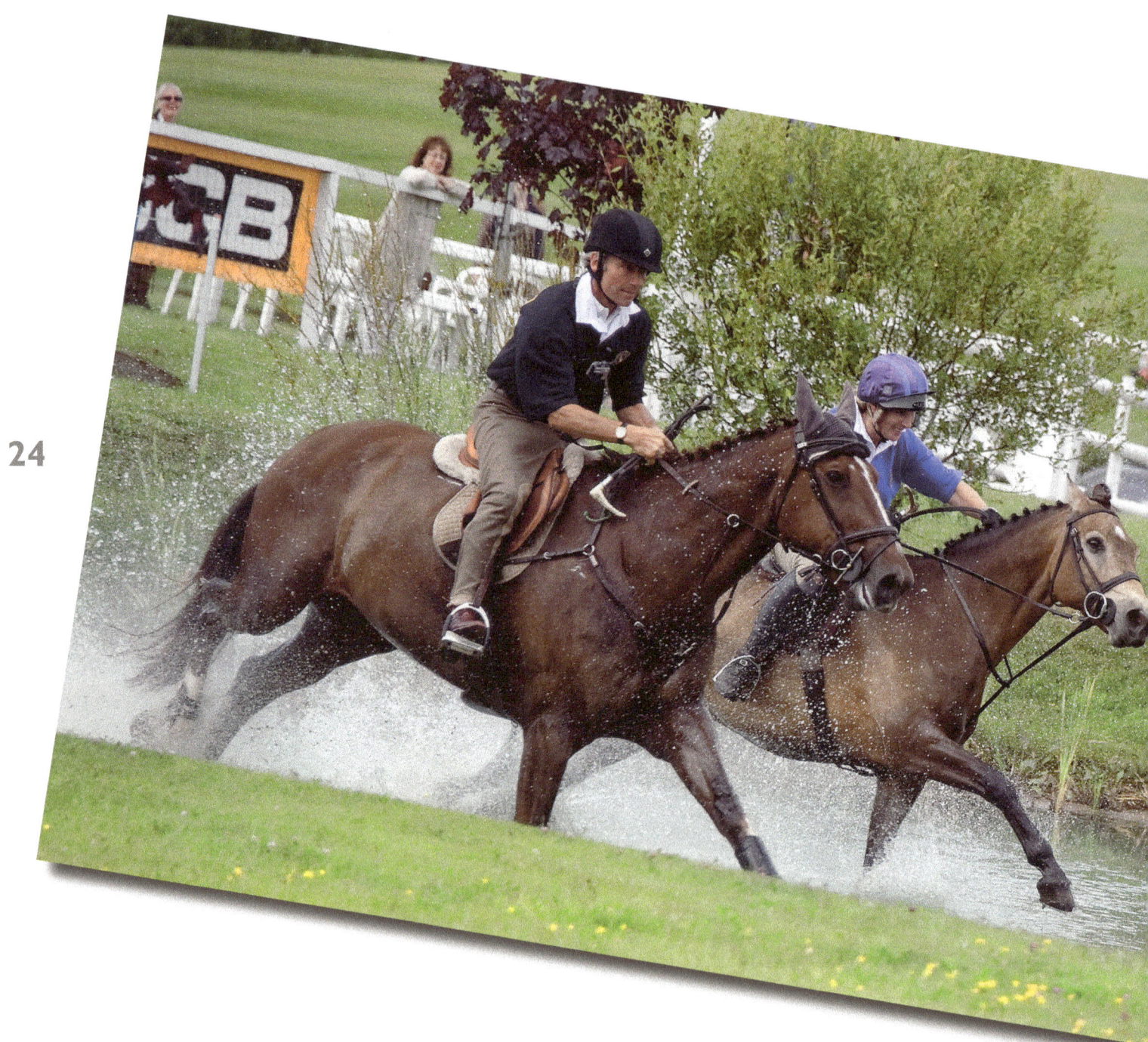

...Zara's involvement with the Injured Jockey's Fund goes back to the turn of the millennium when she gathered a team of eventers to take on a team of jockeys for a bike polo match during the Rundle Cup fixture at Tidworth. Included in the teams were Princes William and Harry.

I filmed the event on the old fashioned SD television digital format, and these images are frame grabs from that footage.

As the match finished, a TV crew from the then TVS/Meridian turned up and missed all the fun, so my footage was broadcast all over the world as exclusive!

The commentator for that event was none other than Channel 4 racing's John Francome, who became the president of the fund in 2012 and is still a Vice Patron...

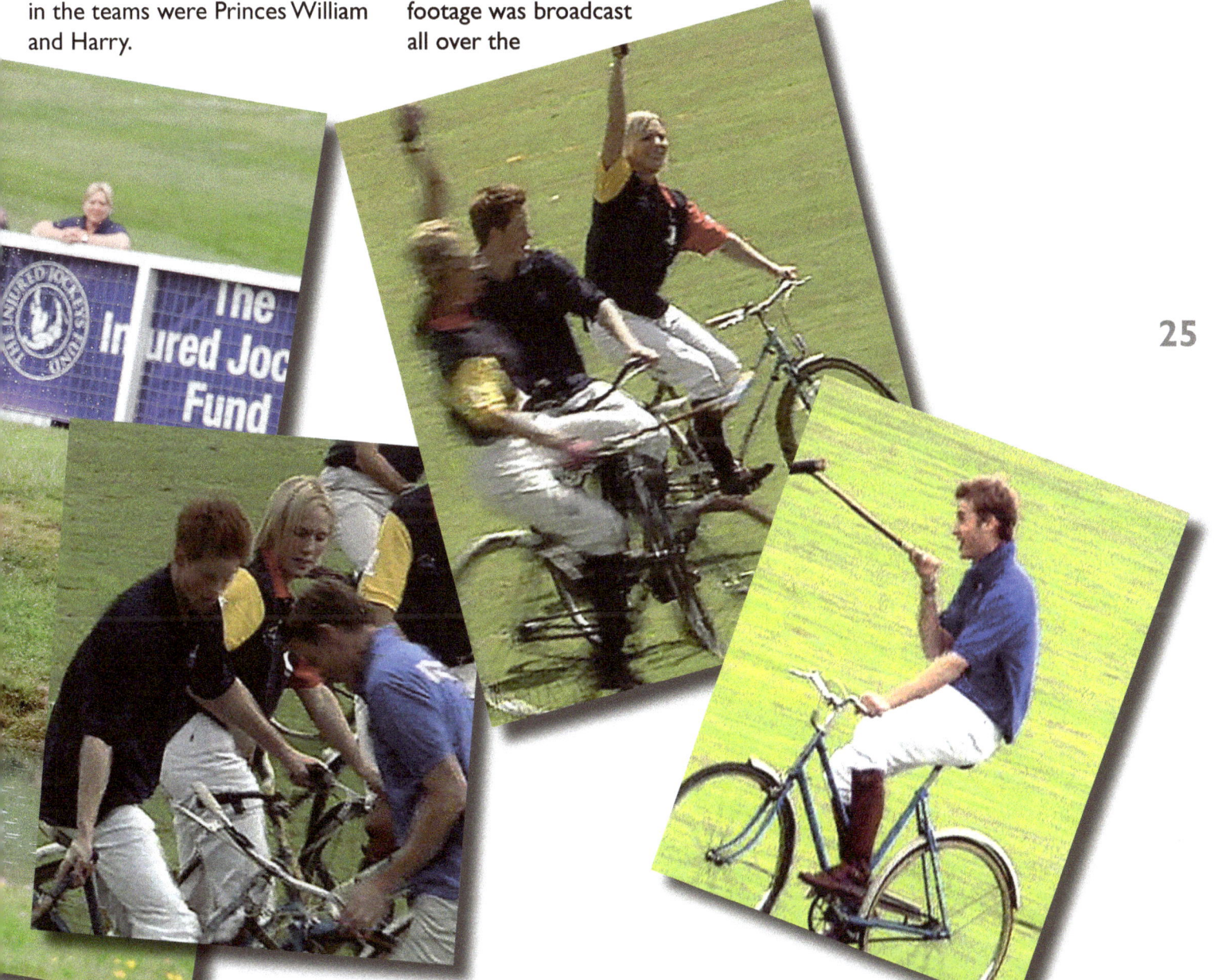

... but Zara isn't a stranger to sport in Swindon as, when she was at Cheltenham Ladies College, she was in their hockey team which took on a Swindon team...

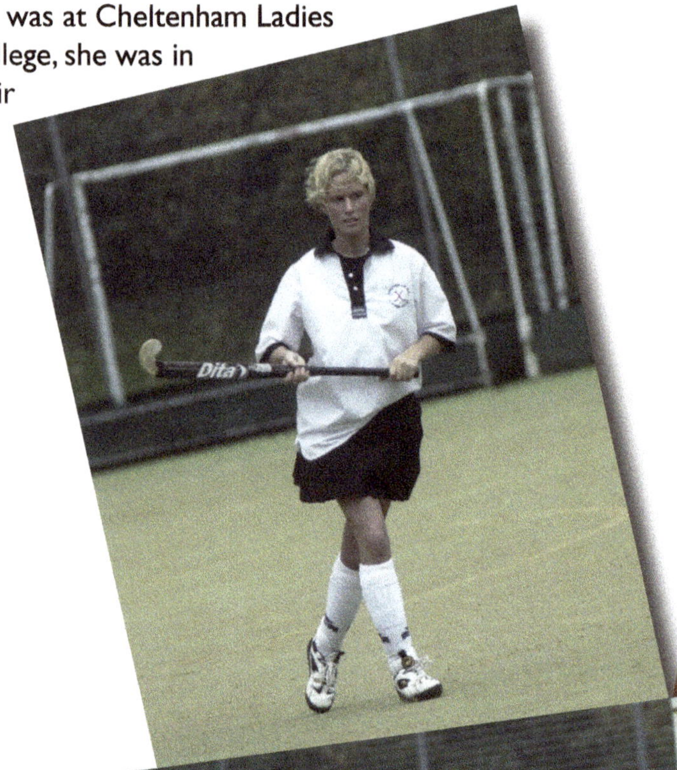

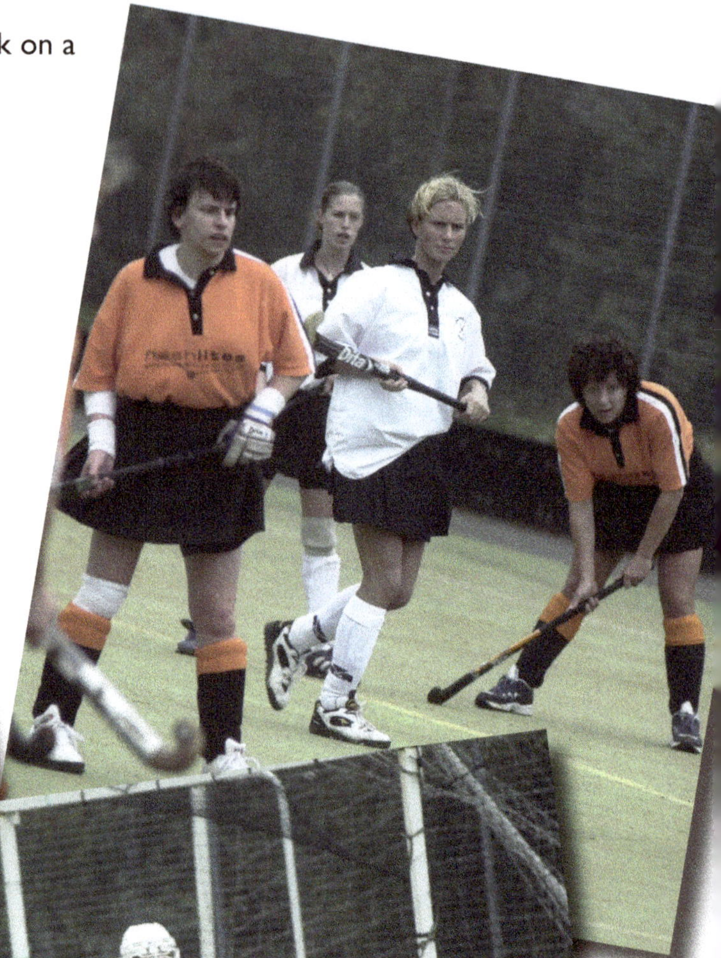

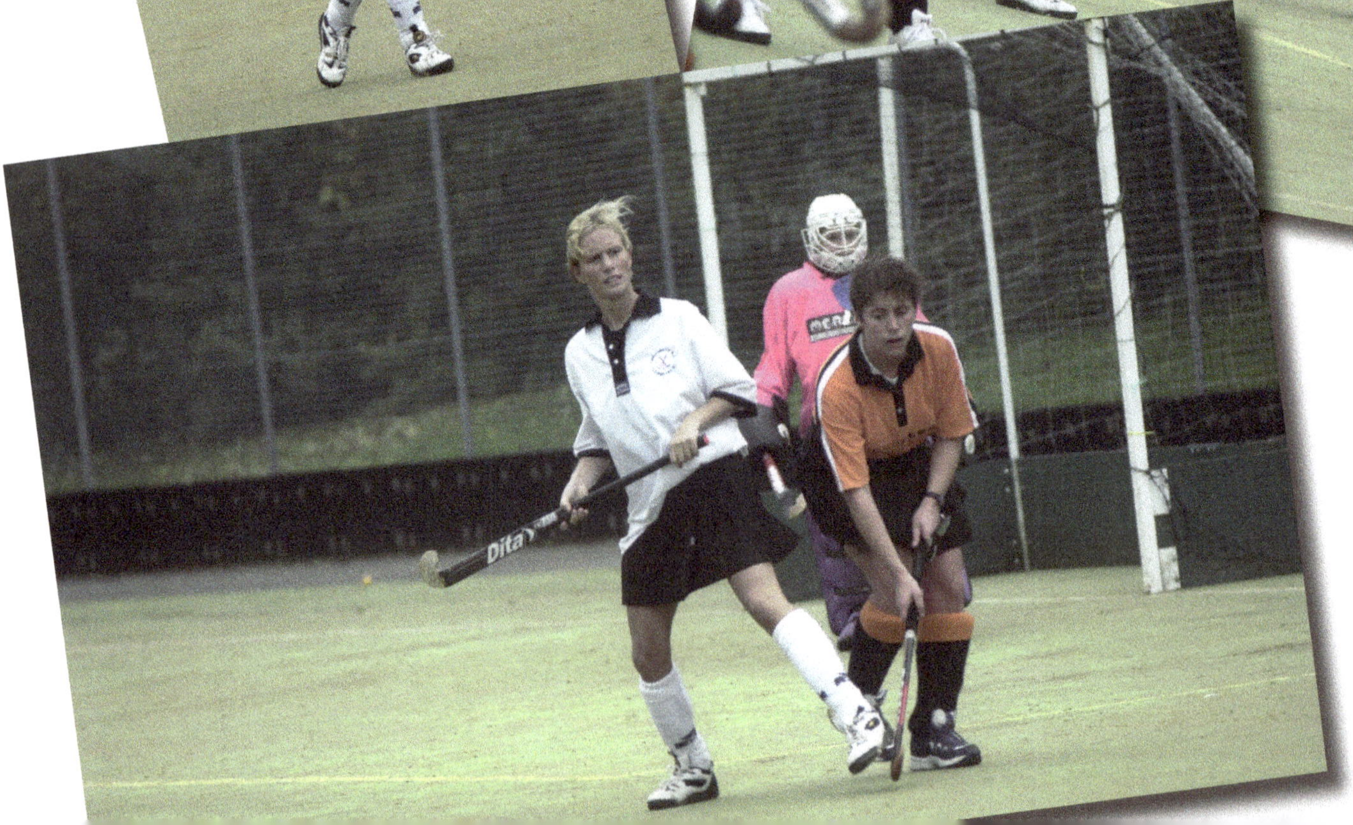

...Zara played her hockey on an all-weather pitch at Greendown, now Lydiard Park Academy, which at the time had one of the best pitches in the town.

Just down the road is the Link Centre and Swindon's Ice Arena where hockey is played too, only on ice.

The story of photographing Swindon's Ice hockey is a tale of a changing environment.

My first pictures are taken on a pushed black and white film under very poor lighting, and the most recent on a modern chipped camera with digital lighting.

When we pushed the film it was a way to compensate for poor lighting.

A film is given a speed rating which equates to the film's sensitivity to light. There are two standards, ASA which the arithmetic scale, and ISO which is the logarithmic scale. Modern digital cameras retain the ISO scale.

So, to push a film, you expose it for a higher ASA value or underexpose it. For example, you take a film rated at 400 ASA and expose it at what would be 1600 ASA or +2 f.stops on the lens and compensate in the processing.

In the developer you would normally give it say six minutes but, as you have underexposed by 50%, you double the development time to 12 minutes. Film manufacturers provide a very detailed chart that gives all the accurate times for developing film at a variety of different speeds.

The results tended to be contrasty and grainy so the exposure had to very accurate and made on the mid-tones of the subject. Ice hockey was particularly difficult as you had very white ice over most of the image and dark figures silhouetted on it, so the first attempts were a bit hit and miss.

Modern cameras have done away with the excitement of this part of photography and the joy of seeing if your maths, and in many cases experience, had paid off...

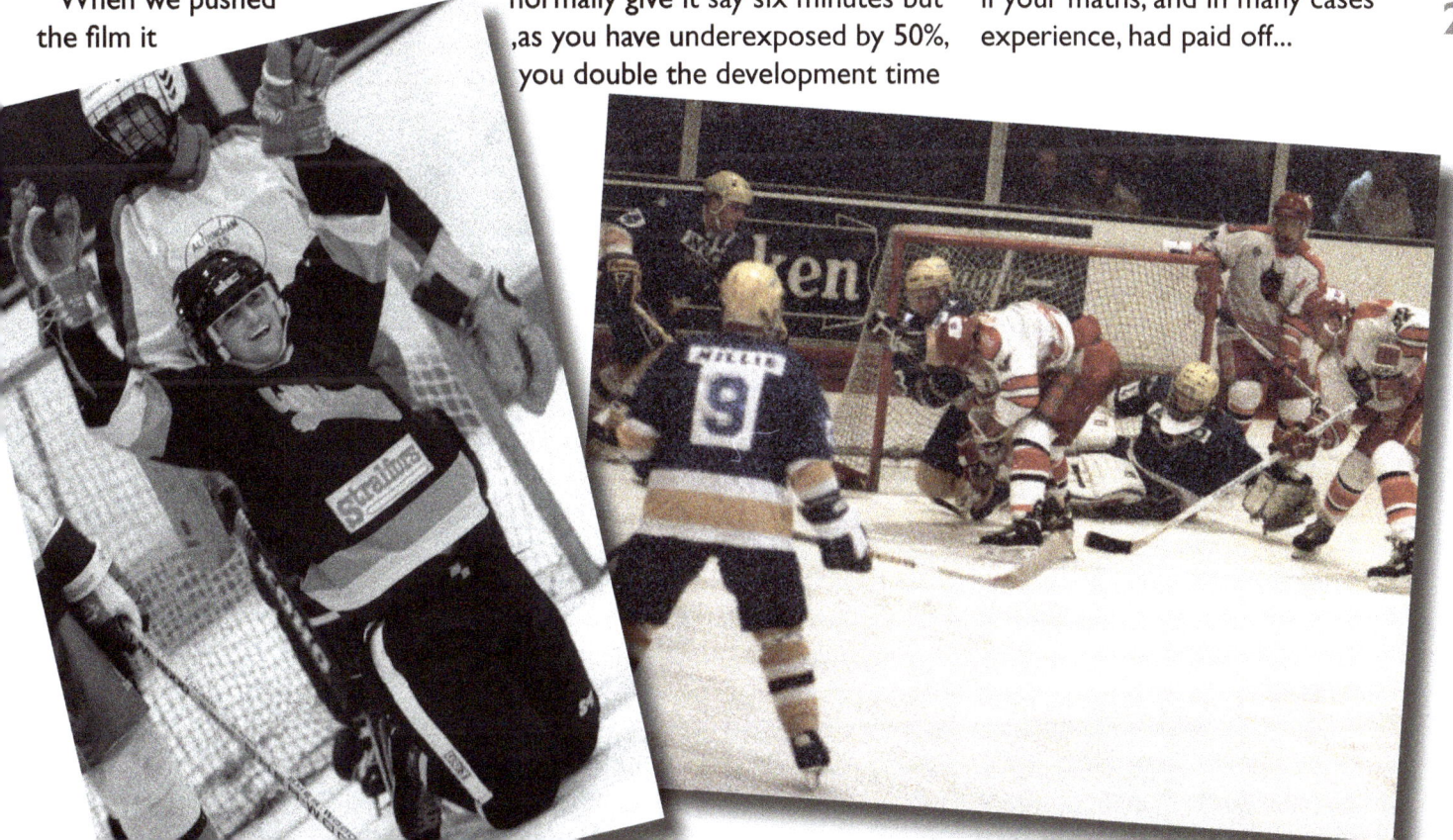

...Along with the odd lighting there is the problem of photographing through the glass that surrounds the rink.

The several millimetres thickness of glass gives several problems to any snapper. For instance you get reflections from the lights around the outside of the rink from the automatic food and drink dispensers. Then glass also refracts the image, giving multiple images, and is not optical photographic quality so has slight distortions in it.

You overcome these problems by holding the lens hard up against the glass at an angle of 90° to the glass. This causes the glass to act as a filter as if it was on the front of the lens.

In holding the lens close to the glass at as near to right angles as we can, means that you can only photograph the largest area of the rink from the corners.

The glass also has to be clean, particularly as the players splash ice onto the surface when stopping and turning quickly, so frequent visits by the rink crew is useful.

Taking all that into account I think, over the years, we haven't done too badly with the pictures we have taken...

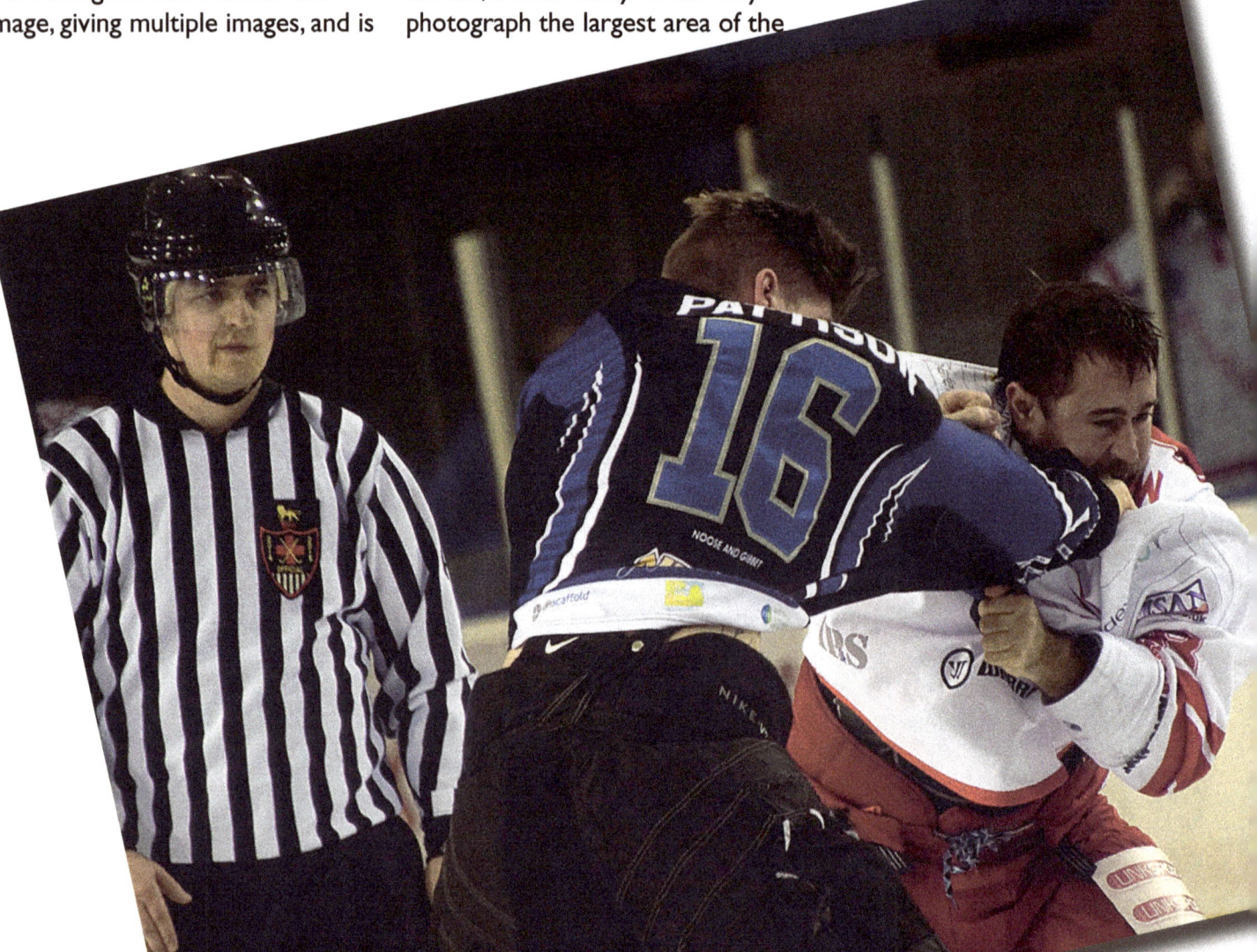

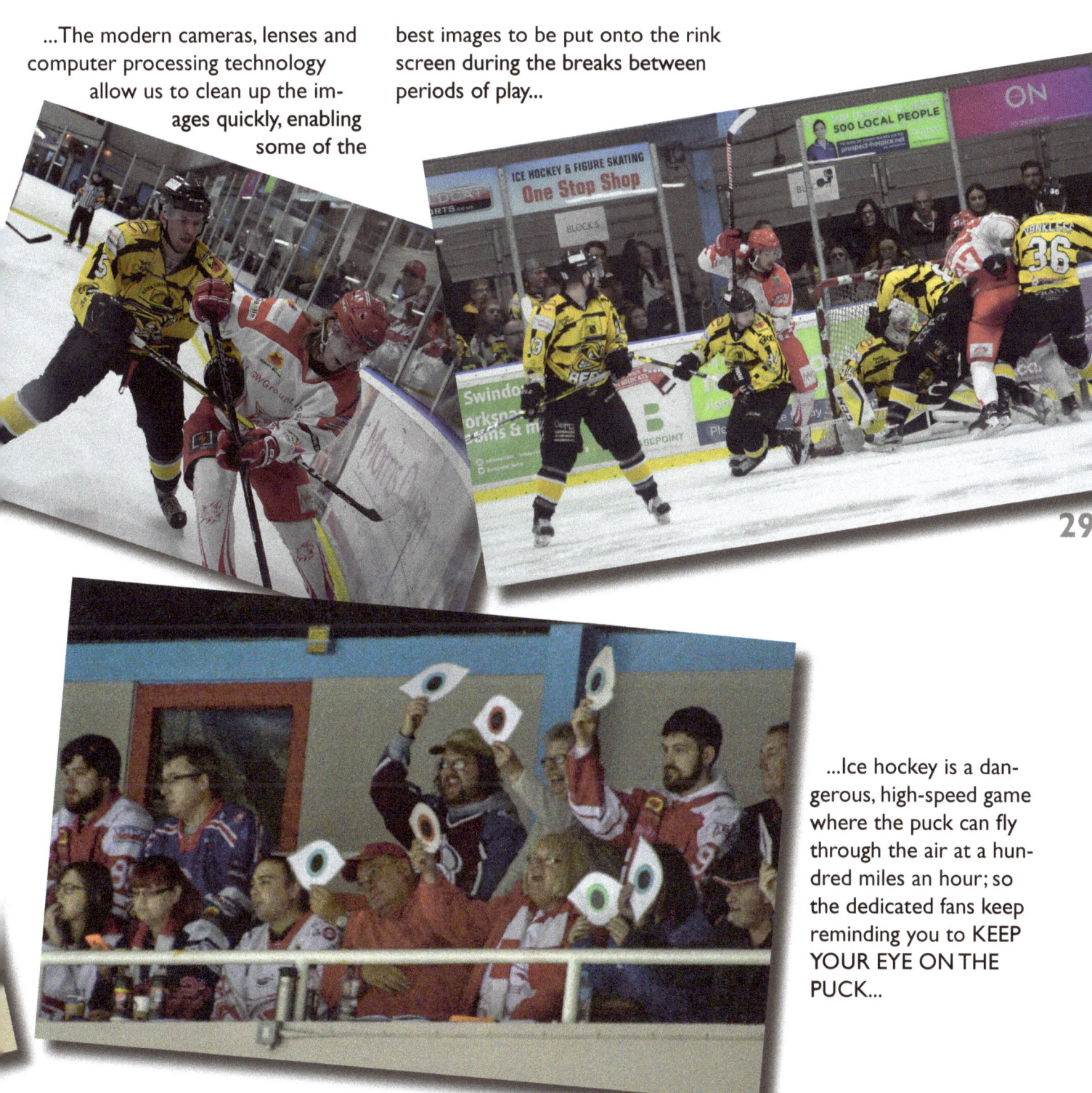

...The modern cameras, lenses and computer processing technology allow us to clean up the images quickly, enabling some of the best images to be put onto the rink screen during the breaks between periods of play...

...Ice hockey is a dangerous, high-speed game where the puck can fly through the air at a hundred miles an hour; so the dedicated fans keep reminding you to KEEP YOUR EYE ON THE PUCK...

...The Wildcats attract many loyal followers and play most matches to an almost full house. Fans include England's favourite farmer BBC Countryfile presenter Adam Henson, and Singer Phoebe Maddison who starred in an audition for The Voice Kids, performed in front of judges Will.i.am, Pixie Lott and Danny from the band Mcfly....

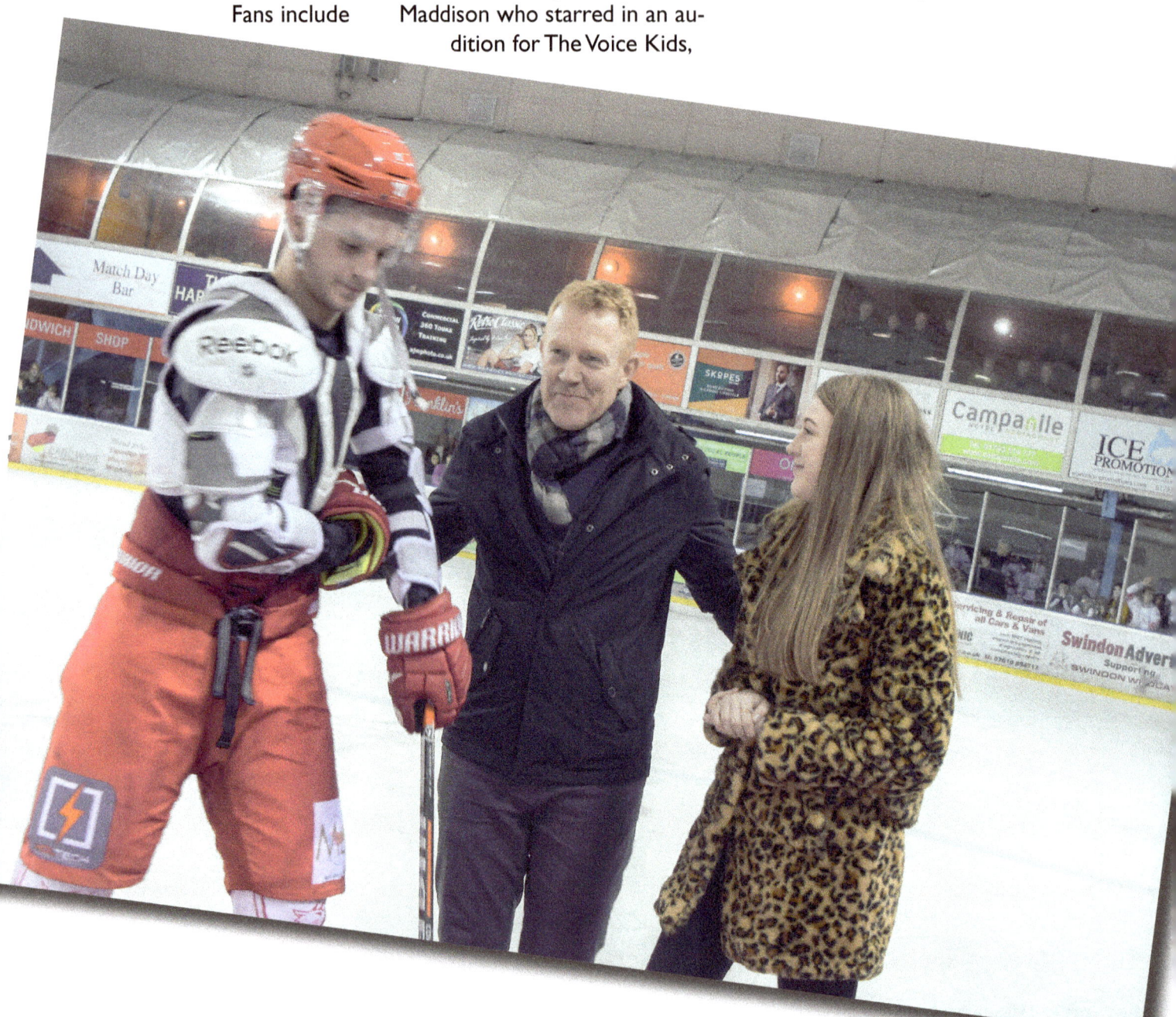

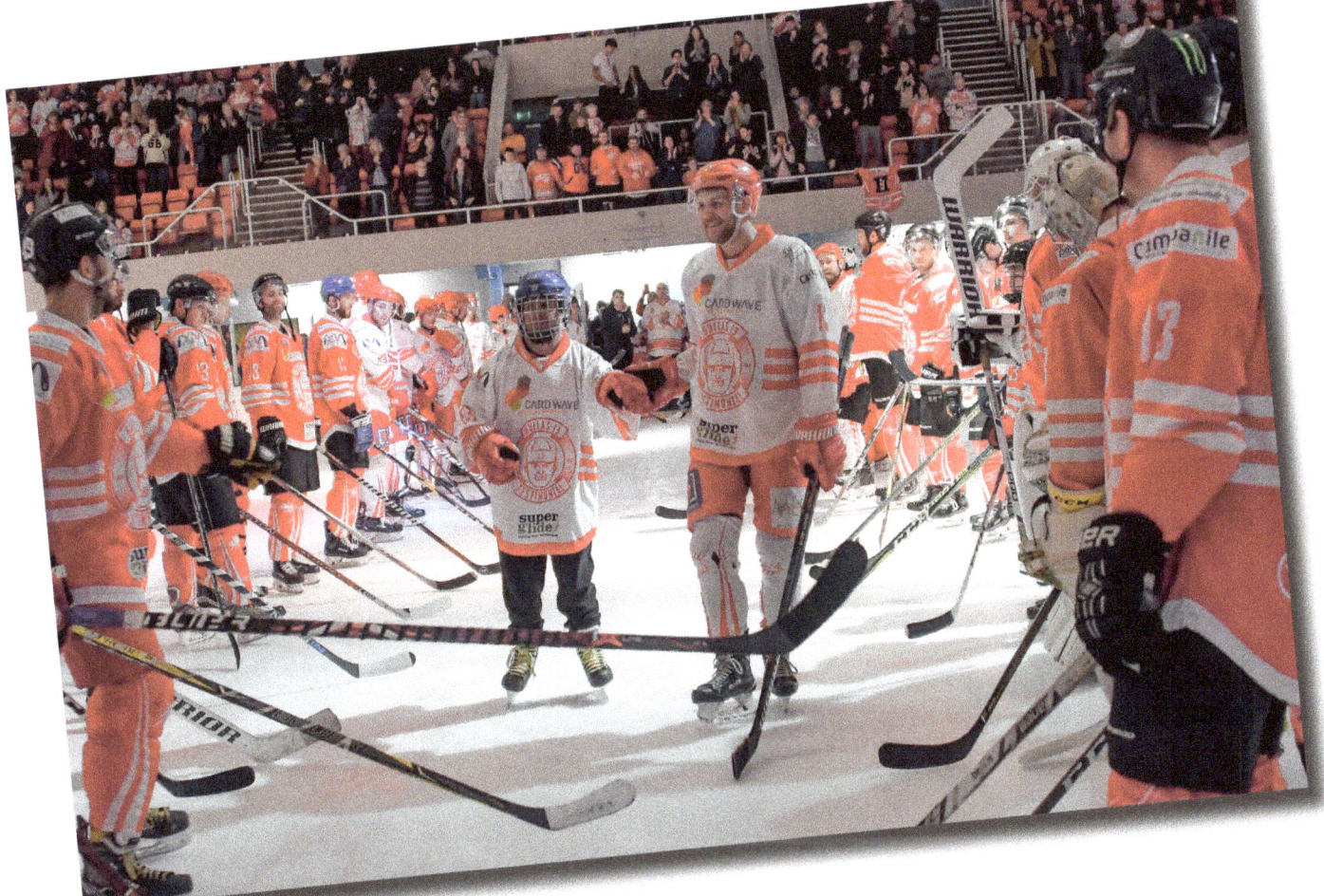

...Swindon as a town, and north Wiltshire in general, has a lack of the five main sports, which are: senior league football, elite rugby, county cricket, championship golf and horse racing.

In the absence of any major sport, with the exception of football, for rugby you have to go to Bath, Bristol or Gloucester; county cricket, Bristol; championship golf is occasionally played at Bowood; and you have to go to Salisbury, Newbury, or Bath for the horse racing..

At the time of writing this book, Swindon's senior football club is in the Championship Division 2, or, three divisions from the premier league, with Swindon's second club, Supermarine, several divisions lower.

Swindon Wildcats Ice hockey team are in the second national league, with the Speedway team in the national elite setup.

It's understandable then that we don't get much national recognition for the sports in Swindon.

One picture editor on one occasion said about a Jet-ski picture I had taken of two skis colliding in mid air, "It's a wonderful picture, but as no-one was hurt it's not news, and it's not in the mainstream sports, so where do I put it in the paper?"...

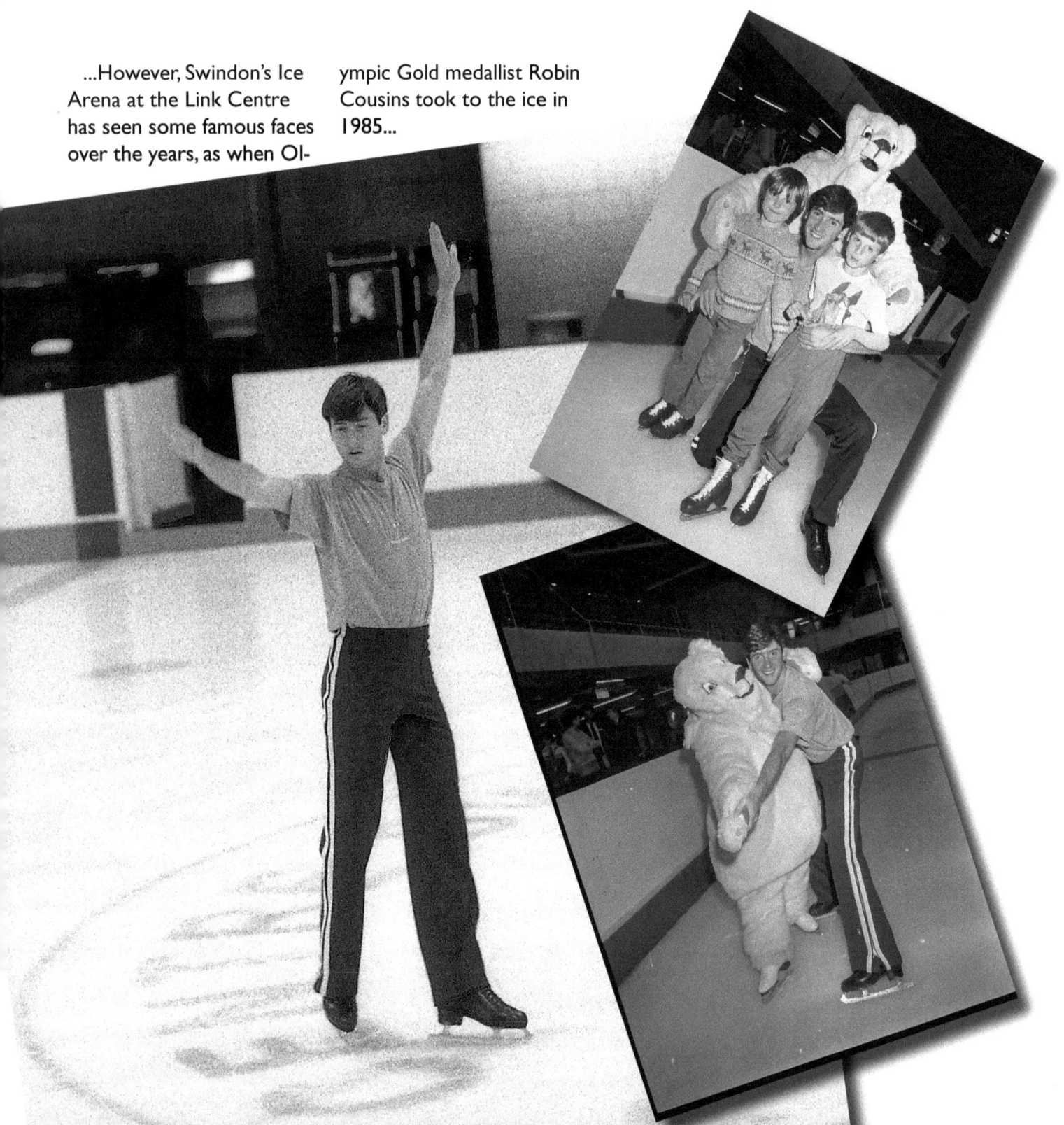

...However, Swindon's Ice Arena at the Link Centre has seen some famous faces over the years, as when Olympic Gold medallist Robin Cousins took to the ice in 1985...

...Football legend David Seaman and his wife, professional skater Frankie Poultney, stopped by the Ice Rink to meet up with Swindon's skating British Champions Christopher Boyadji and Zoe Jones...

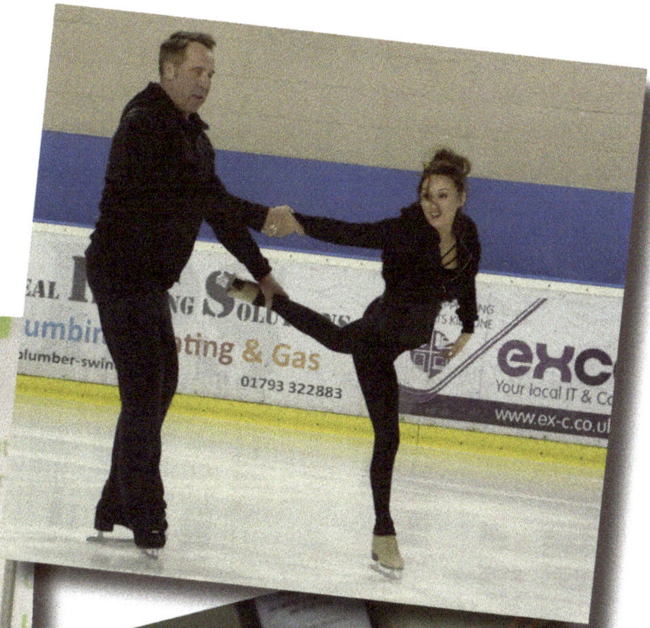

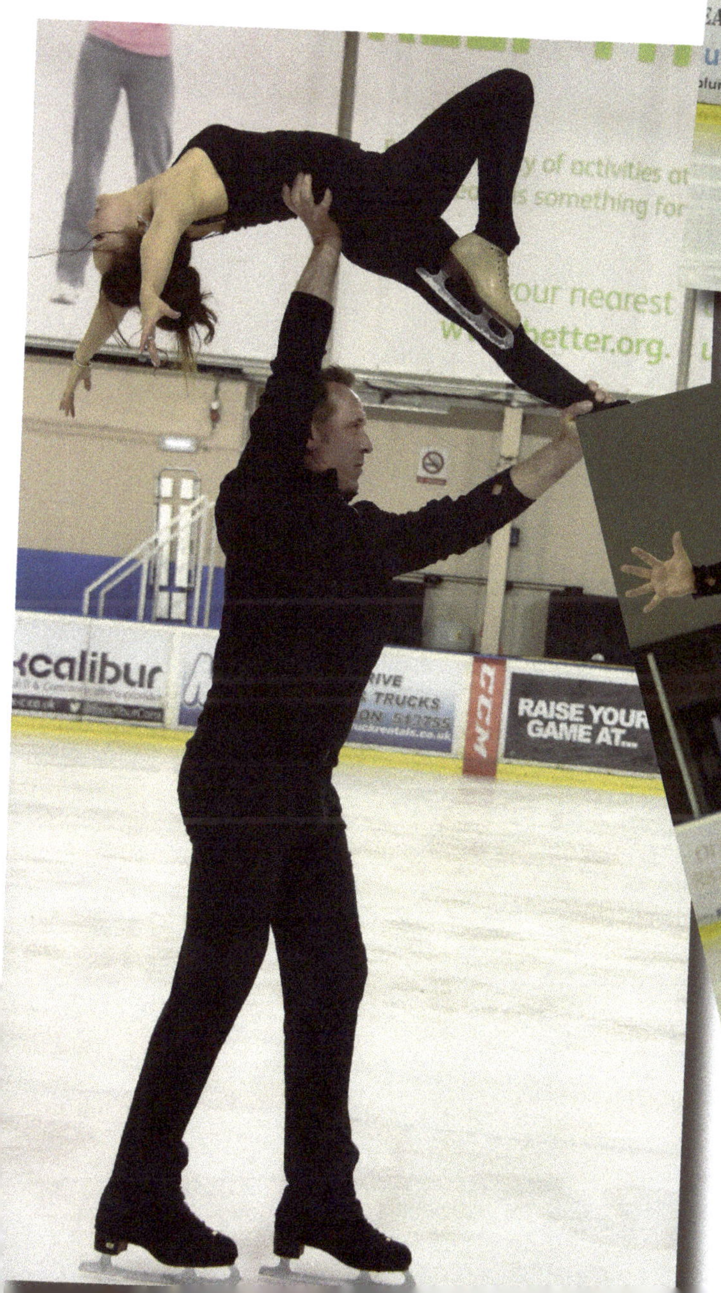

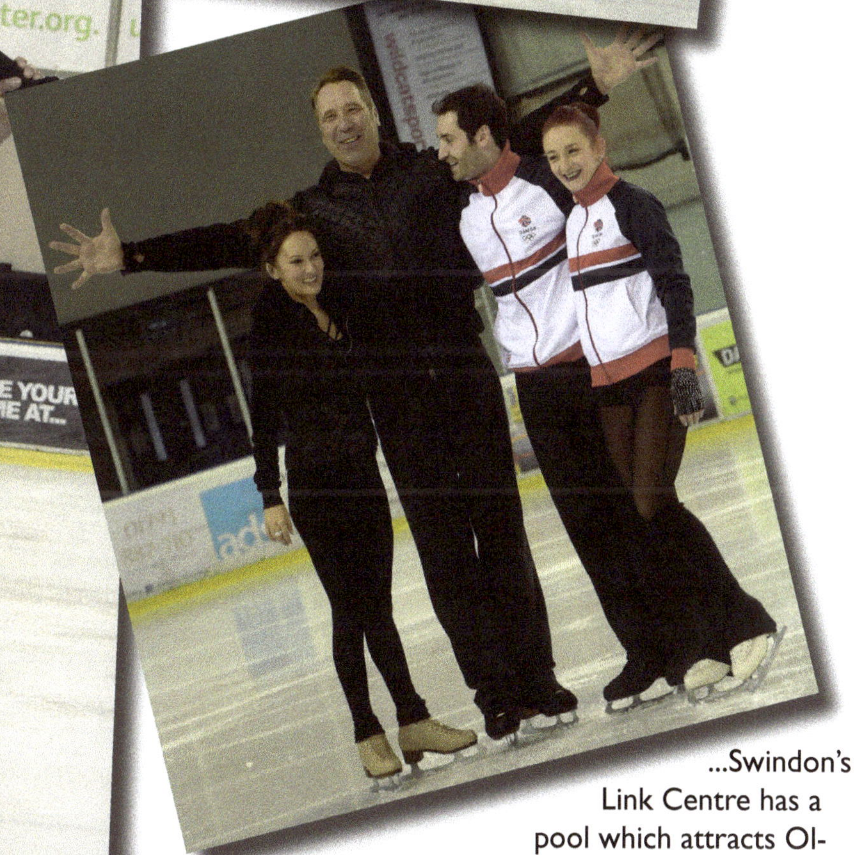

...Swindon's Link Centre has a pool which attracts Olympic heroes too...

...Over in the Link Centre pool Swindon Tigersharks train, and the club has produced an Olympic champion in the person of Jazz Carling.

In Sept 2016 Jazz made an emotional returned to the centre with her two medals to show the club and was given VIP treatment...

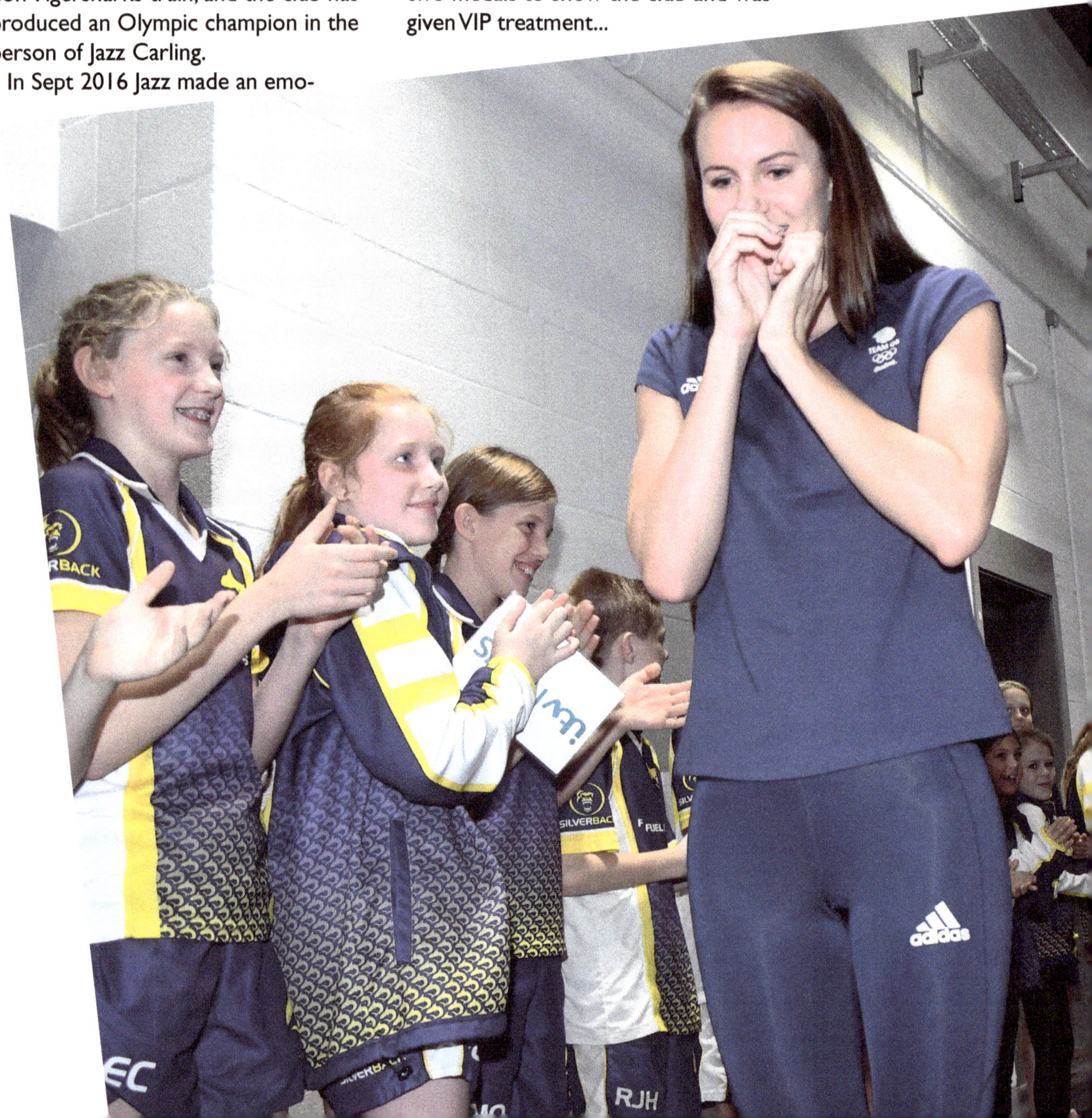

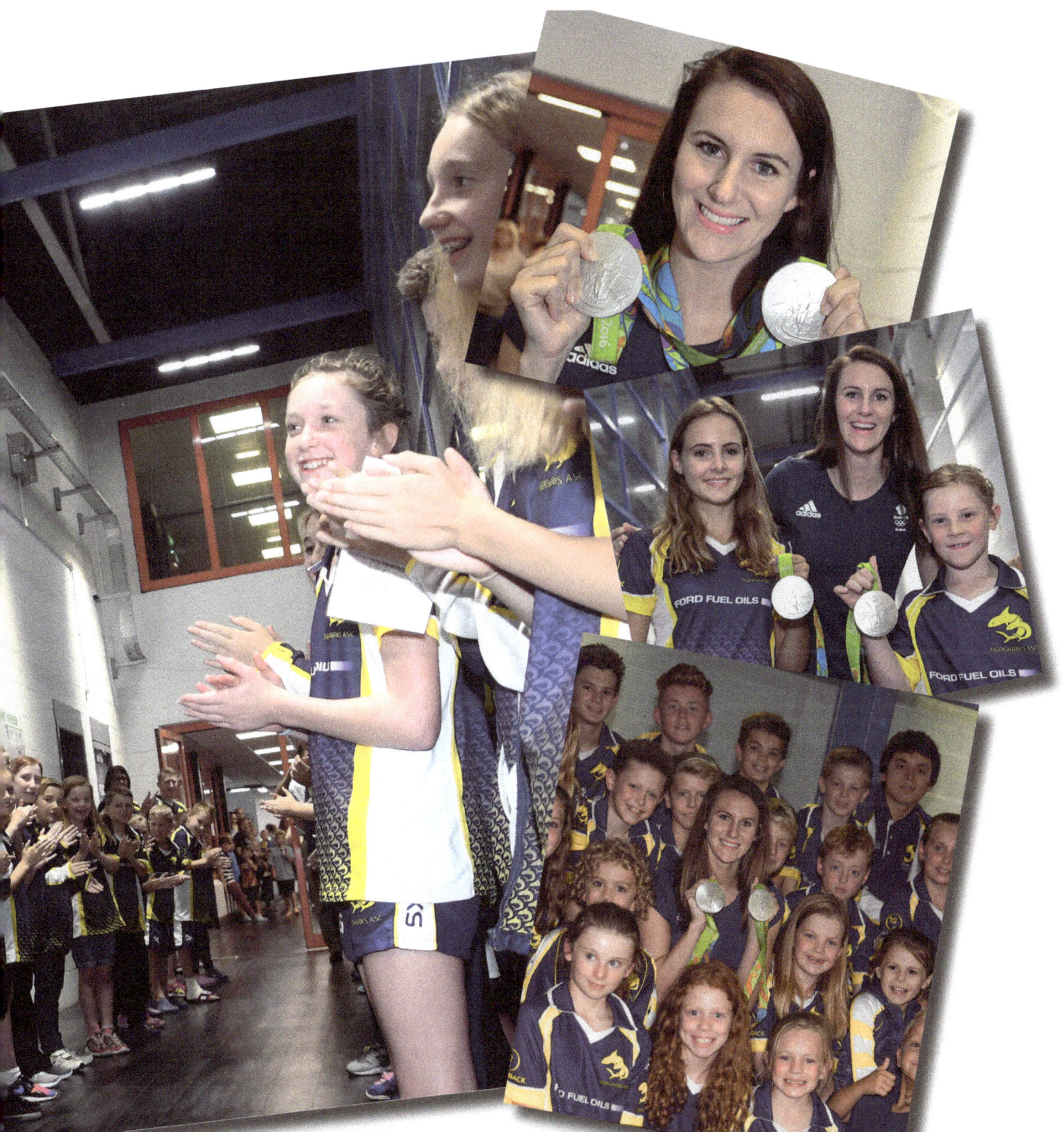

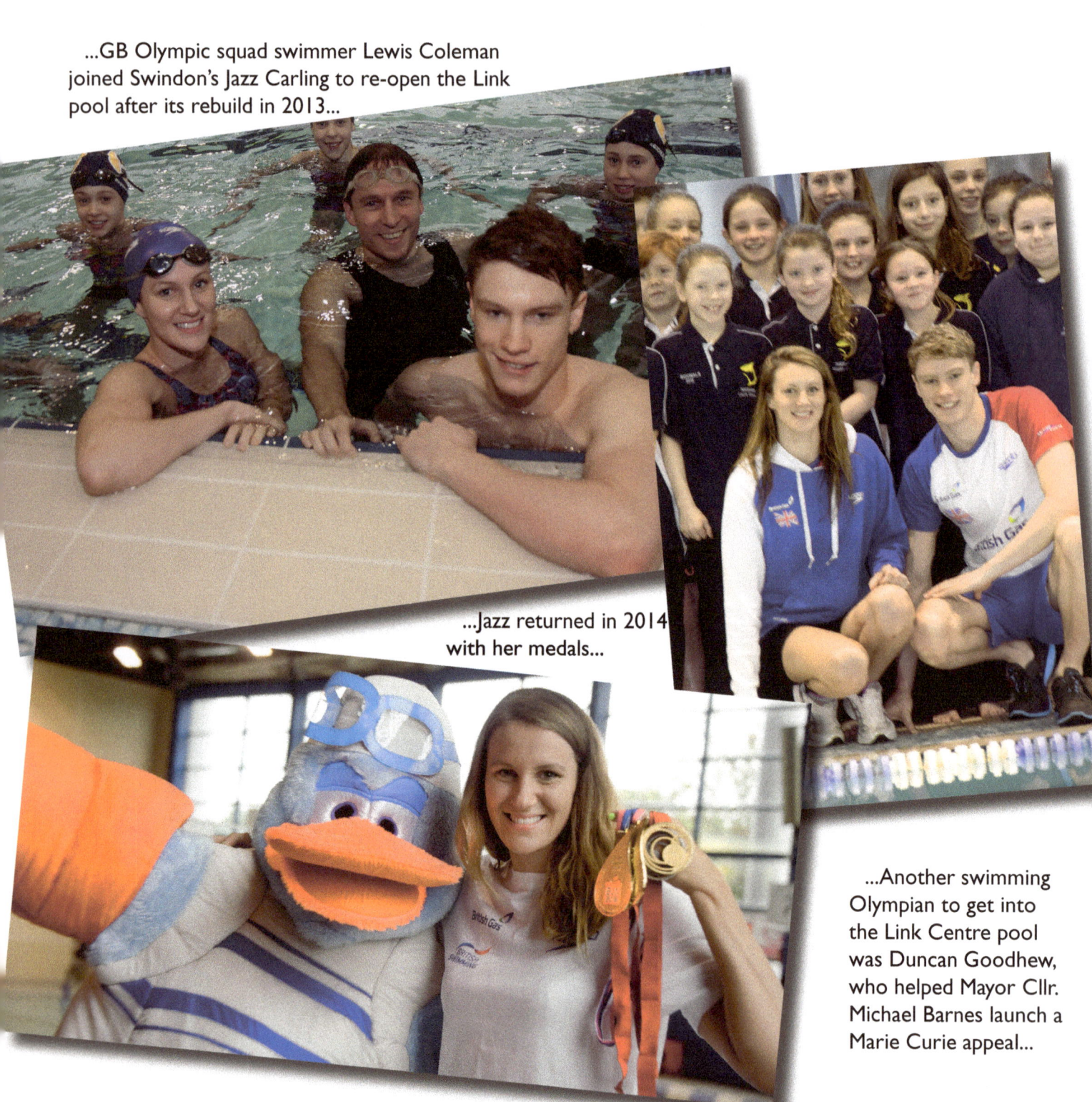

...GB Olympic squad swimmer Lewis Coleman joined Swindon's Jazz Carling to re-open the Link pool after its rebuild in 2013...

...Jazz returned in 2014 with her medals...

...Another swimming Olympian to get into the Link Centre pool was Duncan Goodhew, who helped Mayor Cllr. Michael Barnes launch a Marie Curie appeal...

...Technology is a wonderful thing; when it works!

When someone like Duncan Goodhew arrives at a pool to launch an appeal there is a major local press call. When he was at the Link pool there were quite a few press, including the local ITV News, ITV West Country, with a good friend of mine filming the swimmer in action and being interviewed.

Everything was going to plan when the cameraman went into panic mode as he discovered his GoPro® (a matchbox-sized solid state camera designed for all conditions including underwater filming) had a flat battery.

I was at that time experimenting with an Olympus camera that was advertised as being indestructible, and had the ability to shoot moving pictures, luckily I had

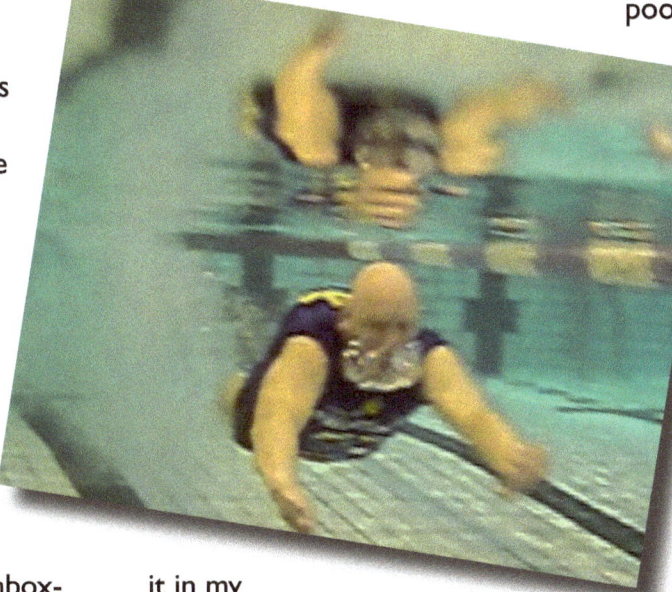

it in my camera bag. I offered it to the crew, explaining that the quality wasn't that of full broadcast and they still took up the offer. Goodhew was about to dive into the pool with some other swimmers and took the lane nearest us. With the crew filming from the poolside, I started the camera and held it under the water at arms length pointing it the general direction of where Duncan Goodhew would enter the water.

He dived in and swam a length of the pool with the poolside cameras trained on him. I pulled the camera out of the pool and reviewed the footage which was acceptable. The chip was removed from my camera, and the footage downloaded onto the crews laptop.

Watching the local news that evening, there was my footage.

Duncan being the ultimate professional he is, repeated the dive so that I could get the still images...

...The Link pool was opened by Olympian Sharon Davies in 1992 with a charity swim for a homeless charity.

Taking photographs can throw up some challenges though, especially with flash photography in the days of film, as the flash was not completely controlled digitally by the camera as it is today, but by an optical metering system within the camera.

Taking ladies in lightweight swimsuits is one of the challenges, as it made the suits transparent...

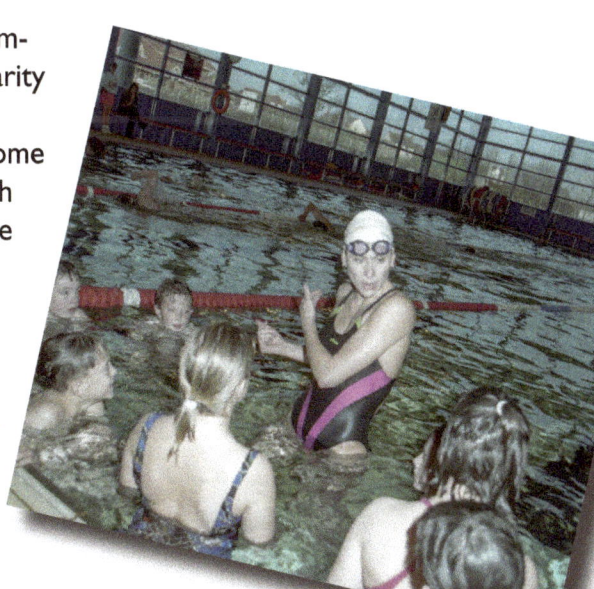

...Some Swindon sports men and women have made it on to national media after retiring from their sports, most notably Chris Kamera who played for Swindon Town at two different times.

Since retiring from football, where he both played and managed, he has made a career on television as a football pundit, presenter and panel show celebrity. He is also seen in quite a few advertisements too...

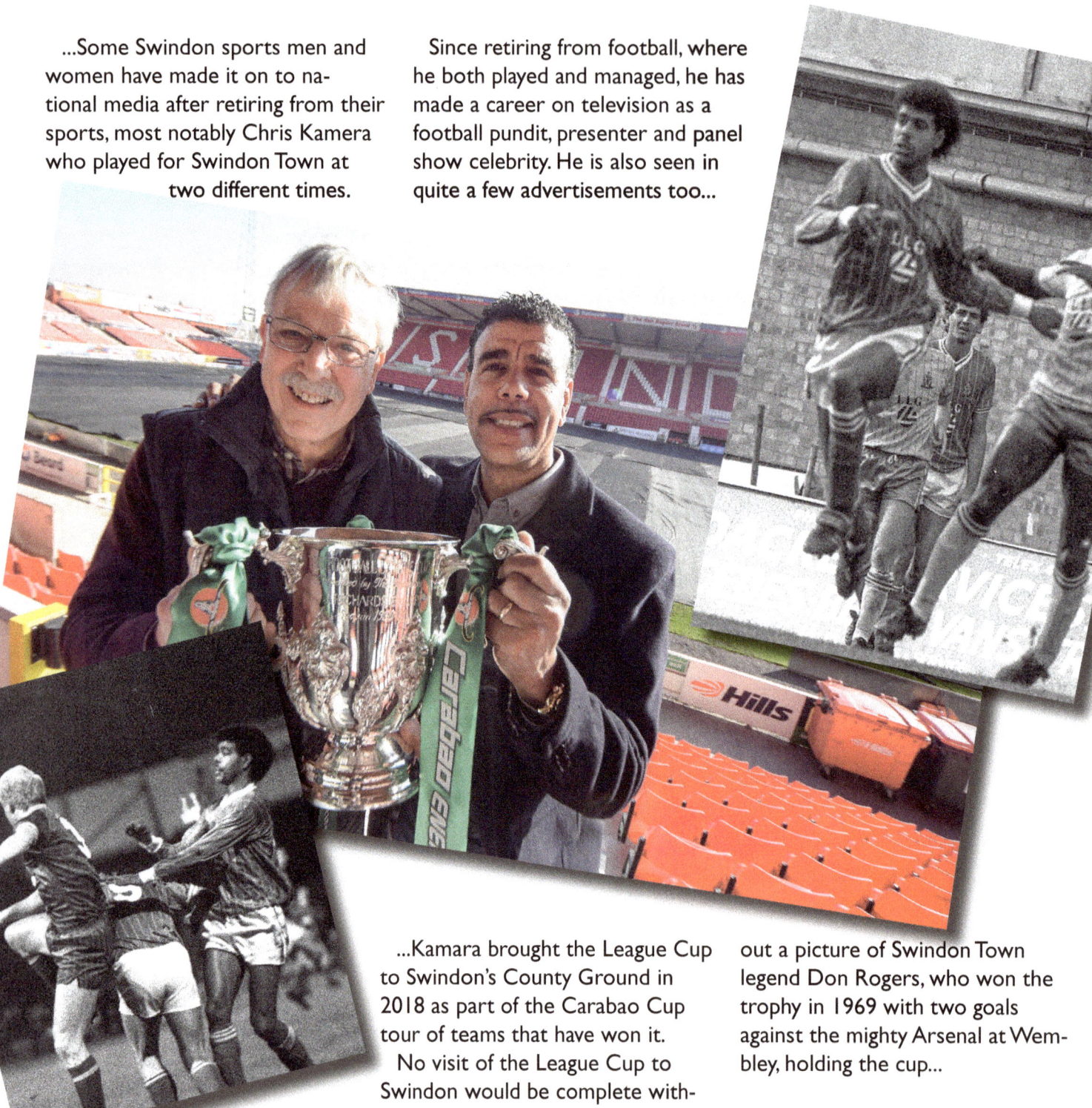

...Kamara brought the League Cup to Swindon's County Ground in 2018 as part of the Carabao Cup tour of teams that have won it.

No visit of the League Cup to Swindon would be complete without a picture of Swindon Town legend Don Rogers, who won the trophy in 1969 with two goals against the mighty Arsenal at Wembley, holding the cup...

...Among other Swindon players who have made it include Sam Parkin, who has gone on to National sport radio via our own BBC Wiltshire Radio, Steve White, and Dave Hockaday.

The most recent town player joining the media is former Swindon Town keeper Phil Smith...

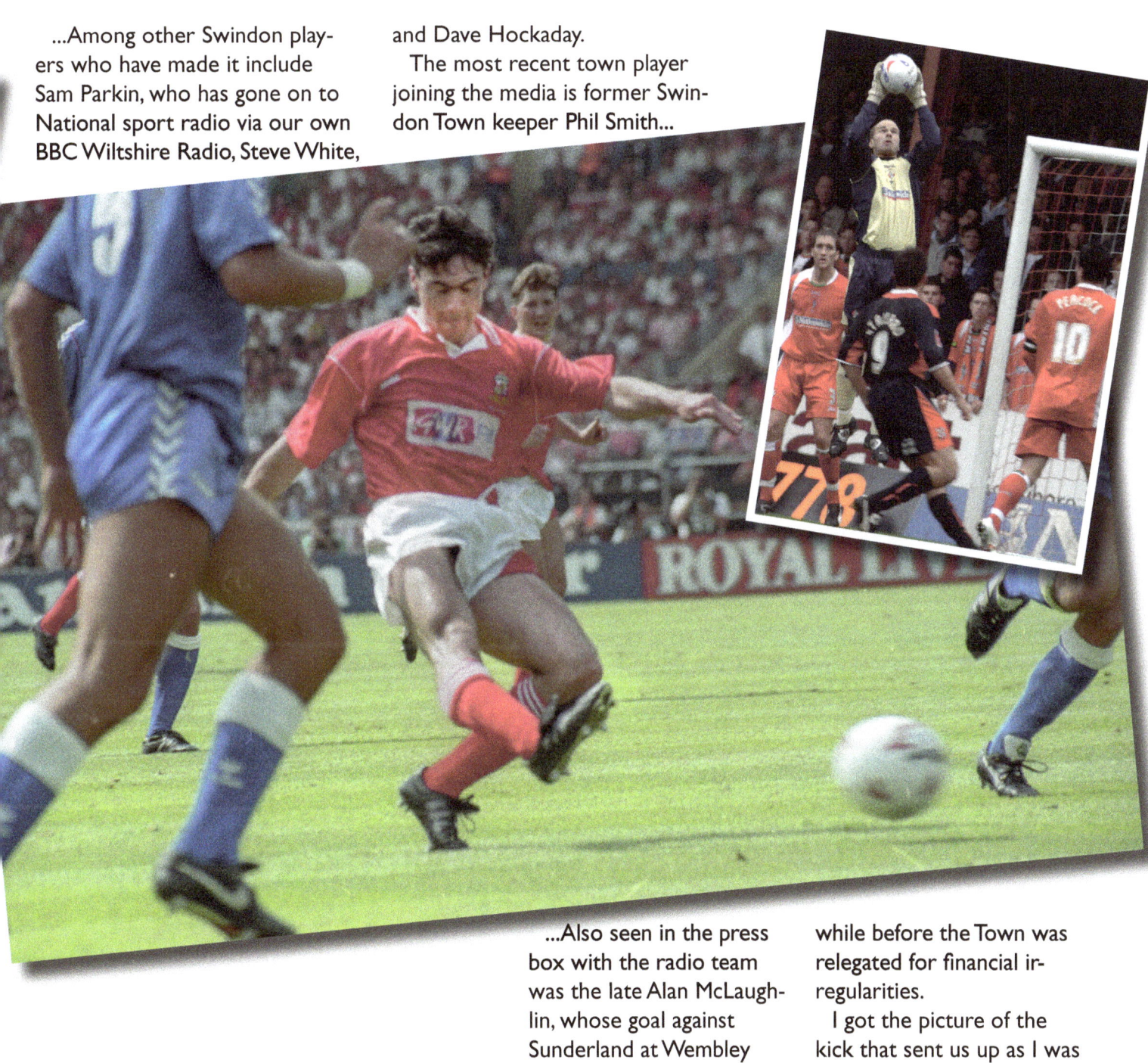

...Also seen in the press box with the radio team was the late Alan McLaughlin, whose goal against Sunderland at Wembley took us into the Premier League, albeit for a short while before the Town was relegated for financial irregularities.

I got the picture of the kick that sent us up as I was lucky enough to be on the left-hand side of the goal...

...Swindon Town favourite Sam Parkin moved into the media on returning to the area after retiring from the sport, having completed the 2013/4 season at Exeter.

He now is one of three former professional footballers who host a podcast called Hanging Up The Boots (HUTB). The podcast features a special guest every episode.

Parkin has presented for BBC Radio Wiltshire and has provided media content for his former clubs Swindon Town and Chelsea.

More recently he is to be heard regularly on BBC Radio London as a co-commentator, and seen as a TV pundit on the free-to-air EFL round-up show on the Quest channel...

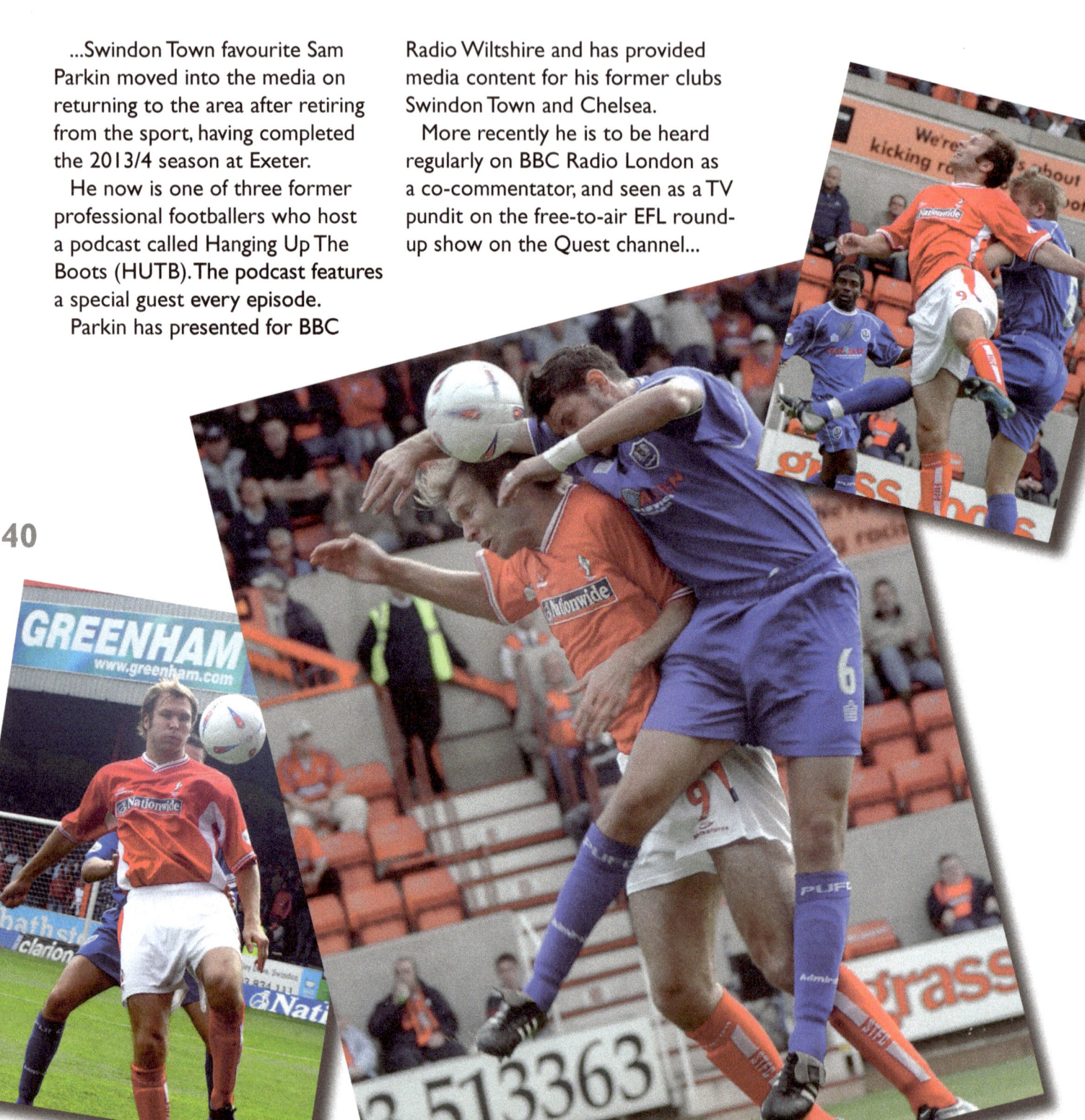

...of course there's also Glen Hoddle, Dennis Wise, Neil "Razor" Ruddock, Osvaldo Ardiles and Lou Macari too...

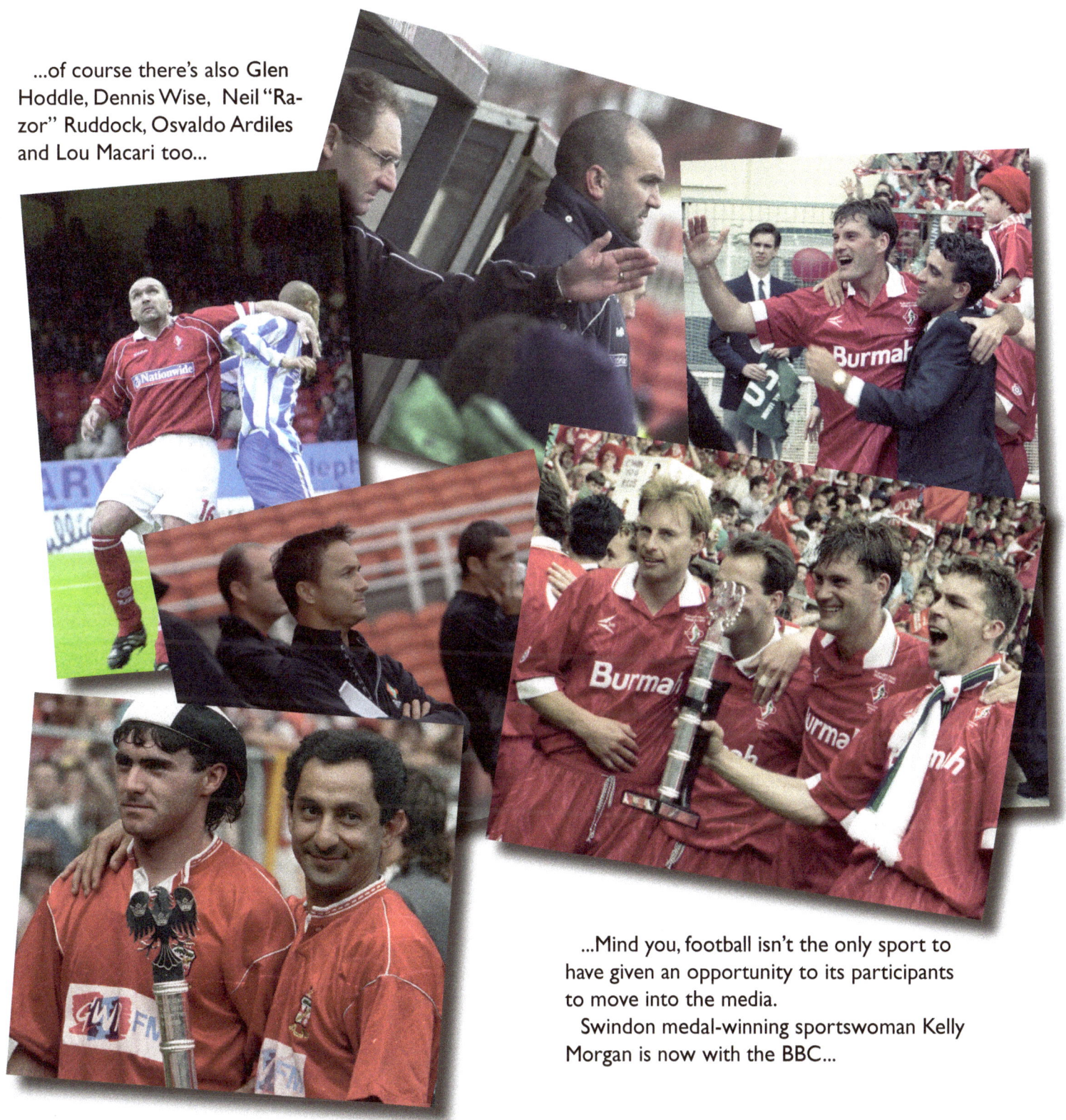

...Mind you, football isn't the only sport to have given an opportunity to its participants to move into the media.

Swindon medal-winning sportswoman Kelly Morgan is now with the BBC...

...Kelly comes from a sporting military family.

She started out in the sport of javelin throwing, and won the English schools junior girls title in 1994; then a year later, at age 15, won the AAA under-20 title.

Called into British junior squad, an injury caused her to miss two seasons, however she retook the AAA under-20 title in 1998, and represented the UK in the World Junior Championships.

With a new model of javelin available she took the UK junior record with a throw of 54.61 m (179.2 ft), going on to win the AAA senior title in 2000, when she also broke two British under-23 records.

Further injuries happened, but she overcame them to represent the United Kingdom in the 2002 European Athletics Championships and England in the 2002 Commonwealth Games, achieving third place.

2002 was by far Morgan's best year for javelin: she broke multiple records, including with her personal best of 64.87 mts, and was at one point ranked second in the world.

Injury led to her missing the 2003 season, and she also missed the 2004 Olympics.

Following in her mother's footsteps playing netball, she represented England in 2001 against Australia for the England Development Team.

But it is boxing that she is best known for in Swindon, claiming the World Boxing Council's silver middleweight belt in 2015.

Kelly was forced to retire from boxing due to a sparring injury and now reports for BBC Wiltshire News...

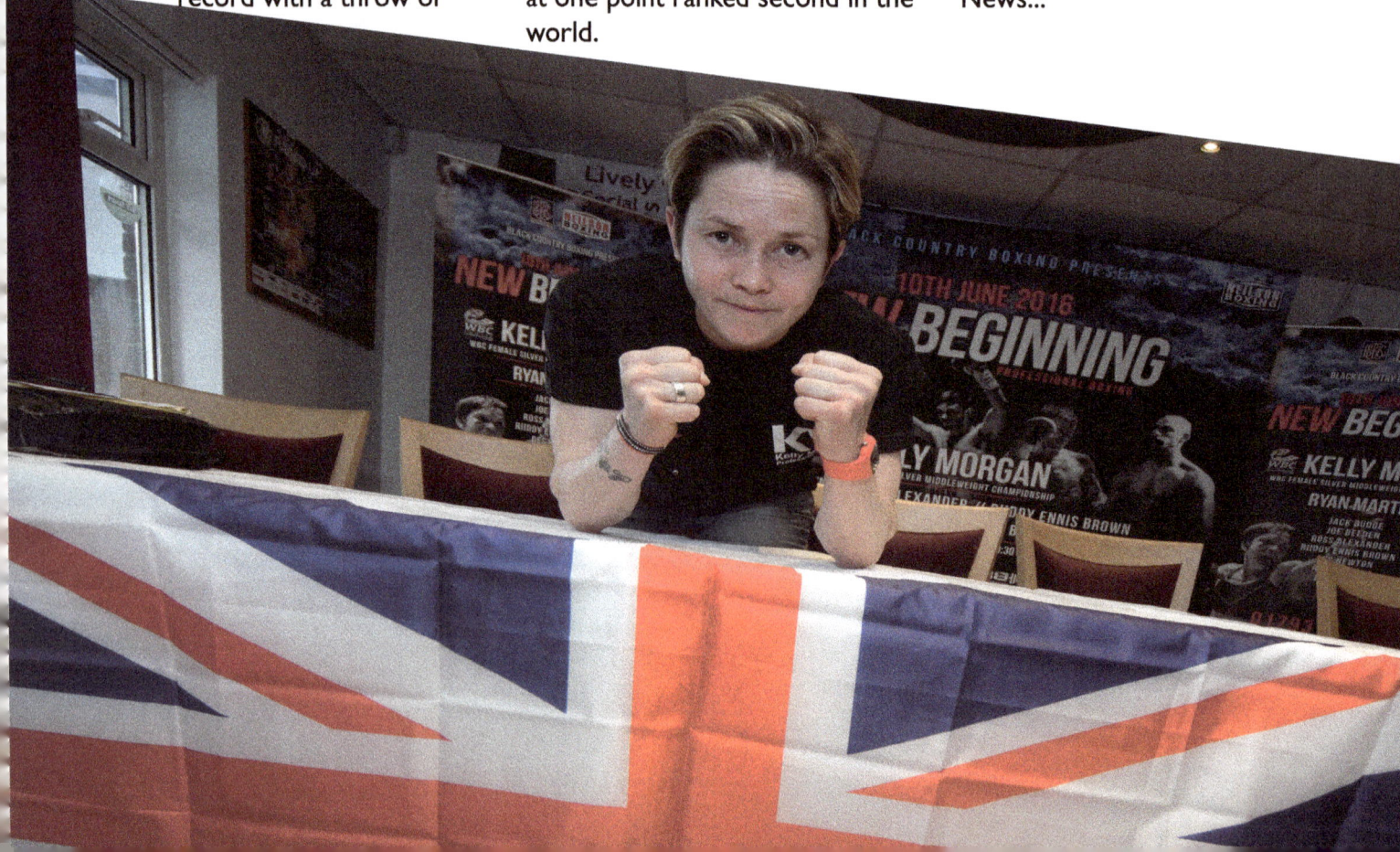

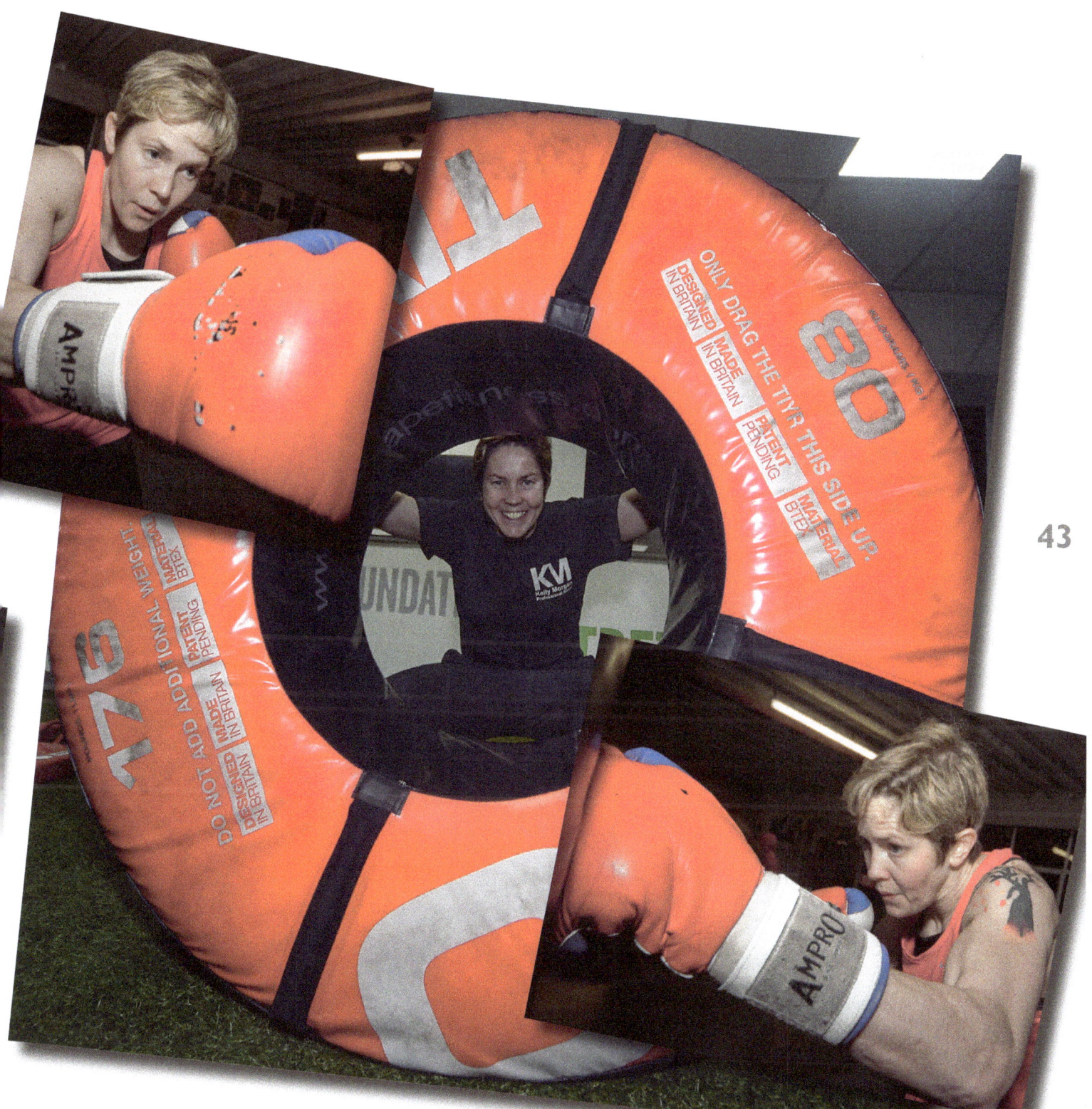

...Swindon's golf hero David Howell has taken turns behind the microphone too.

He also occasionally works for Sky Sports as a commentator and analyst, as well as writing regular golf-related columns.

He started at the Swindon Council-owned Broome Manor course, going on to fame as a member of the winning European Ryder Cup teams in 2004 and 2006.

In 2014, David was one of a five-man selection panel selecting Europe's 2016 Ryder Cup captain Darren Clark, and his work behind the scenes goes on as, in 2017, he succeed Thomas Bjørn as chairman of the European Tour's Tournament Committee.

The first time I photographed David was when he was picked to represent Great Britain and Ireland in the 1995 Walker Cup match at Royal Porthcawl Golf Club in Wales. The event was won by the Great Britain and Ireland team 14 to 10.

The Walker cup, first played in 1922, is the amateur equivalent of the professionals' Rider Cup, and is named after George Herbert Walker who was president of the USGA in 1920 when the match was initiated.

Walker, as it happens, is the grandfather and namesake of George H.W. Bush and great-grandfather of George W. Bush, the 41st and 43rd Presidents of the United States, respectively.

As of 2021, the U.S. lead the Walker Cup series 38 to 9 and David was in the third great Britain and Ireland team to win the cup...

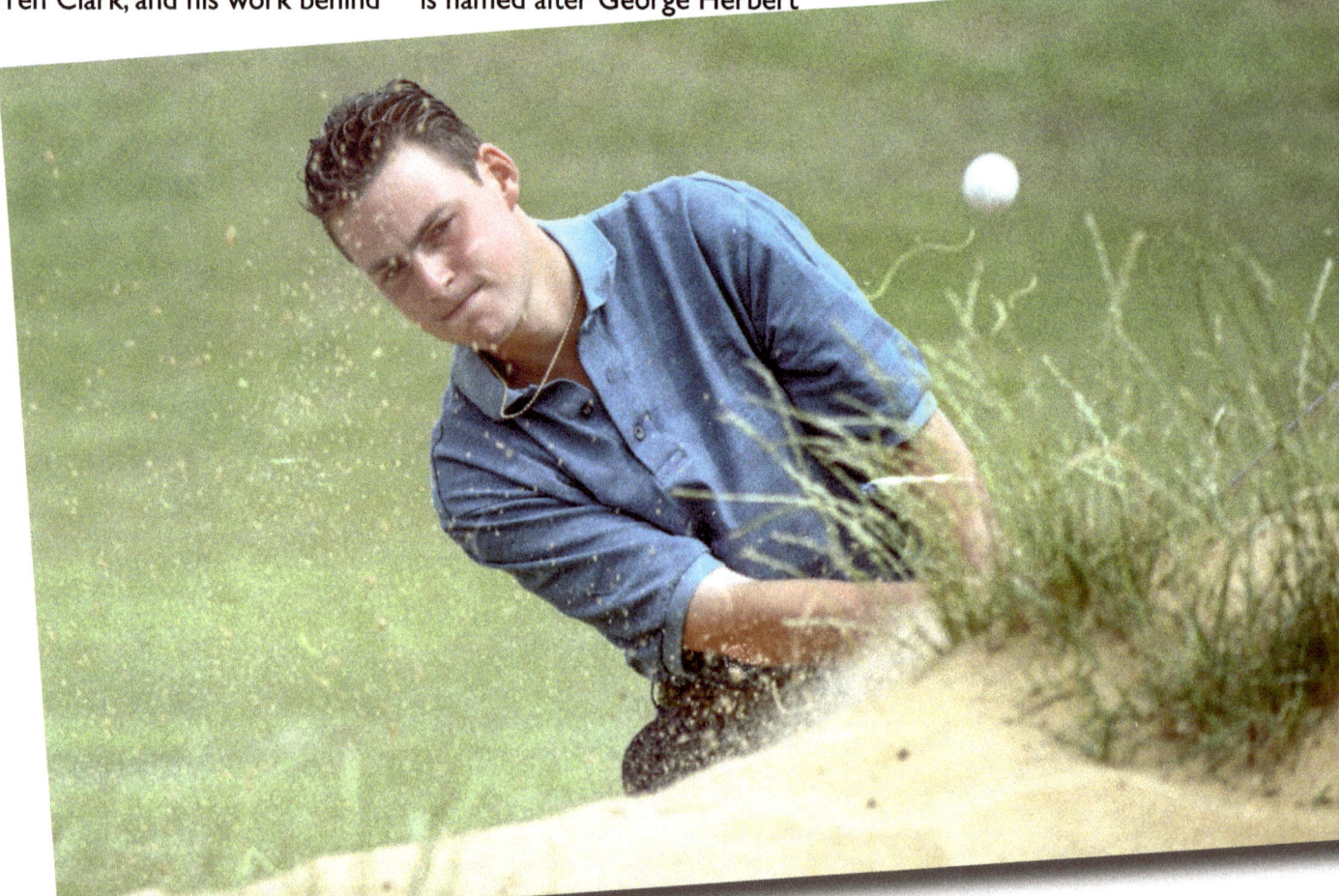

...David was brought up playing golf on the Broome Manor council-owned course, whose new driving range was opened by Welshman Ian Woosenam in 1991.

As a demonstration of the Welshman's hitting power, he hit one drive out of the complex.

To quote BBC reporter and Swindon Town fanatic Vic Morgan, who interviewed Woosnam, on the day "He actually drove the ball longer than the range."...

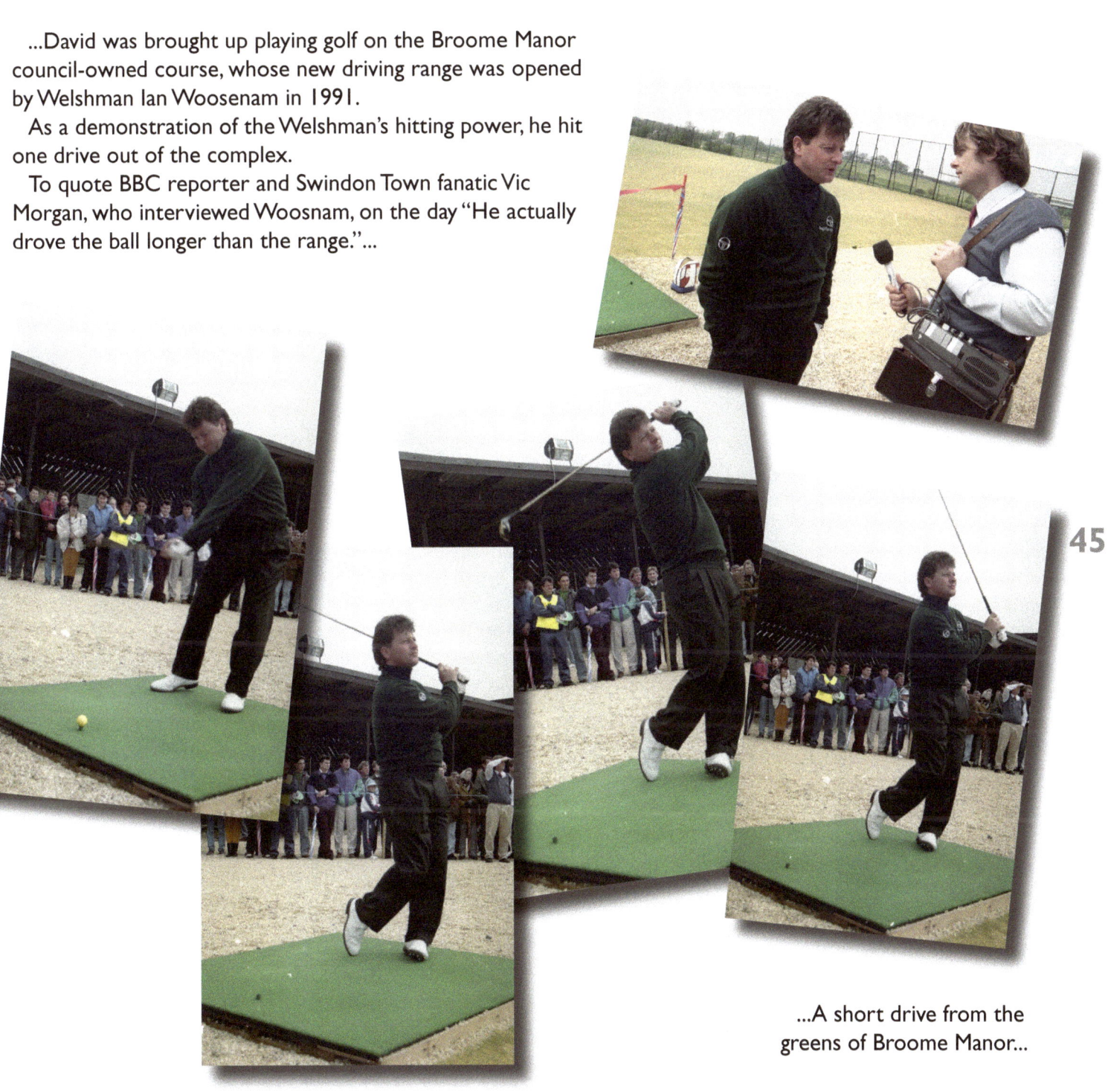

...A short drive from the greens of Broome Manor...

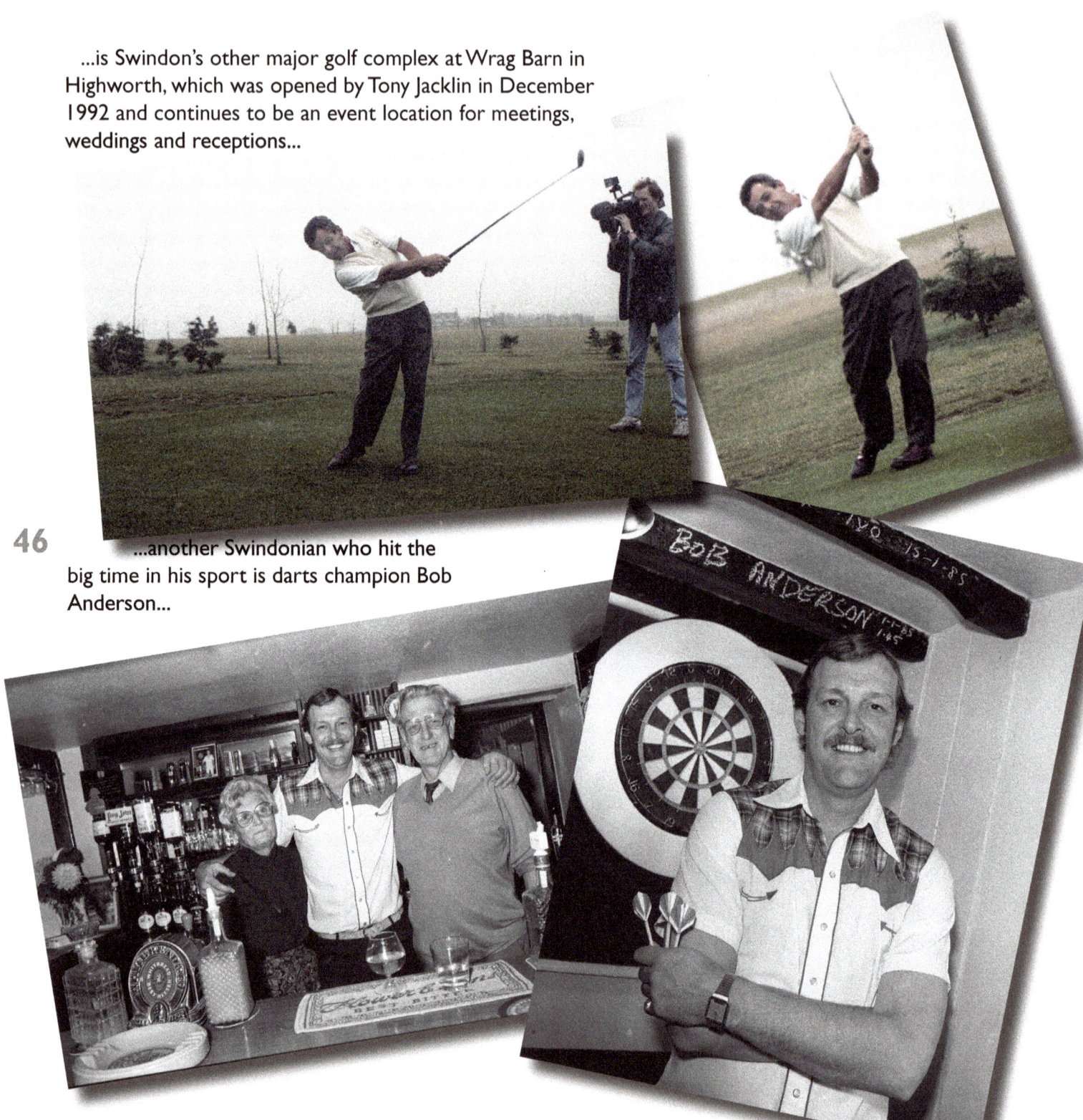

...is Swindon's other major golf complex at Wrag Barn in Highworth, which was opened by Tony Jacklin in December 1992 and continues to be an event location for meetings, weddings and receptions...

...another Swindonian who hit the big time in his sport is darts champion Bob Anderson...

...Swindon Robins manager Alun Rossiter was a successful Speedway rider and was made England Team manager...

...Malcolm Holloway was a successful speedway rider, too...

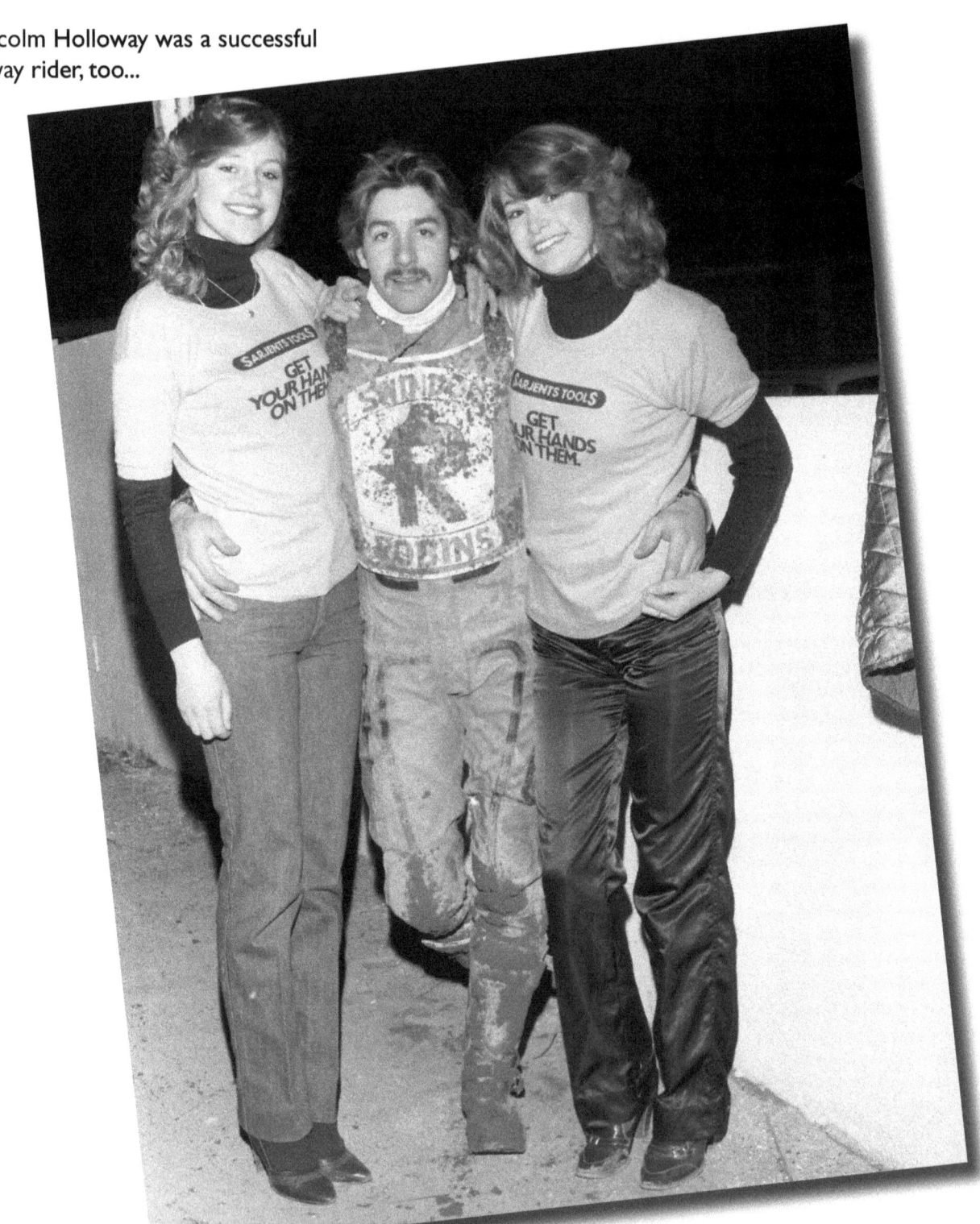

...not all Swindon sports stars are household names; for instance, British Motostar Charlie Nesbitt, who races in the Motocycle Grand Prix series of races...

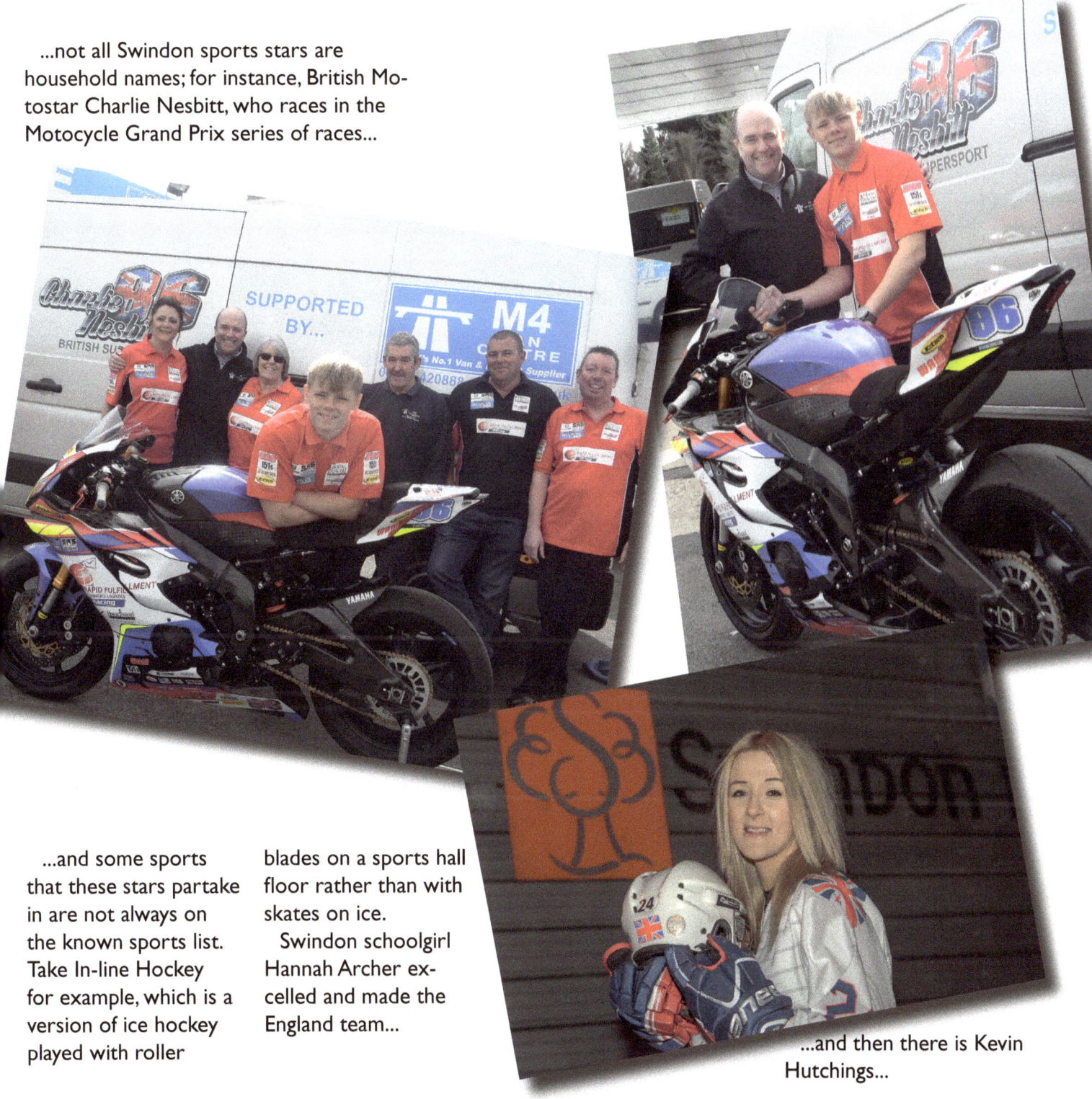

...and some sports that these stars partake in are not always on the known sports list. Take In-line Hockey for example, which is a version of ice hockey played with roller blades on a sports hall floor rather than with skates on ice.

Swindon schoolgirl Hannah Archer excelled and made the England team...

...and then there is Kevin Hutchings...

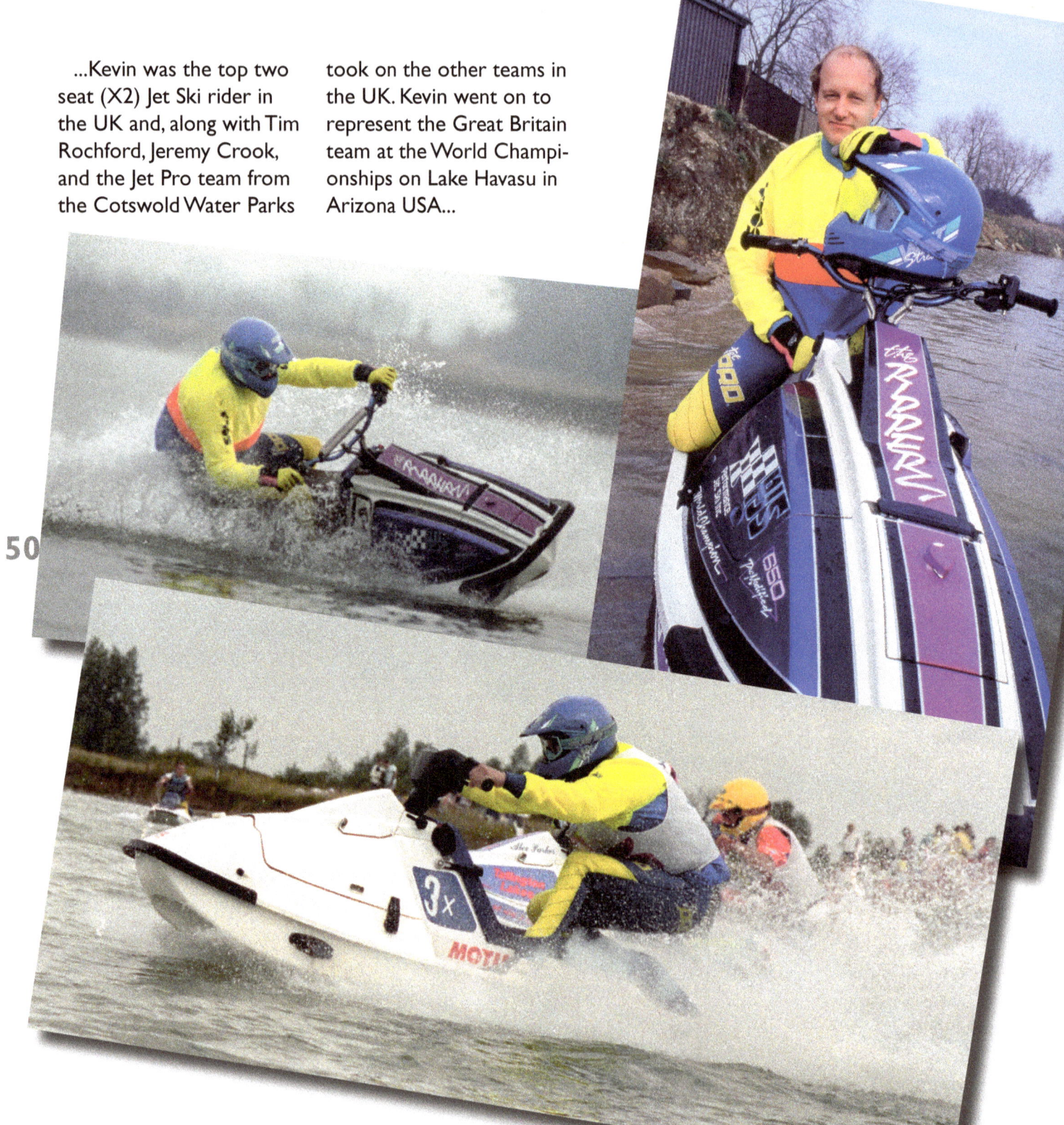

...Kevin was the top two seat (X2) Jet Ski rider in the UK and, along with Tim Rochford, Jeremy Crook, and the Jet Pro team from the Cotswold Water Parks took on the other teams in the UK. Kevin went on to represent the Great Britain team at the World Championships on Lake Havasu in Arizona USA...

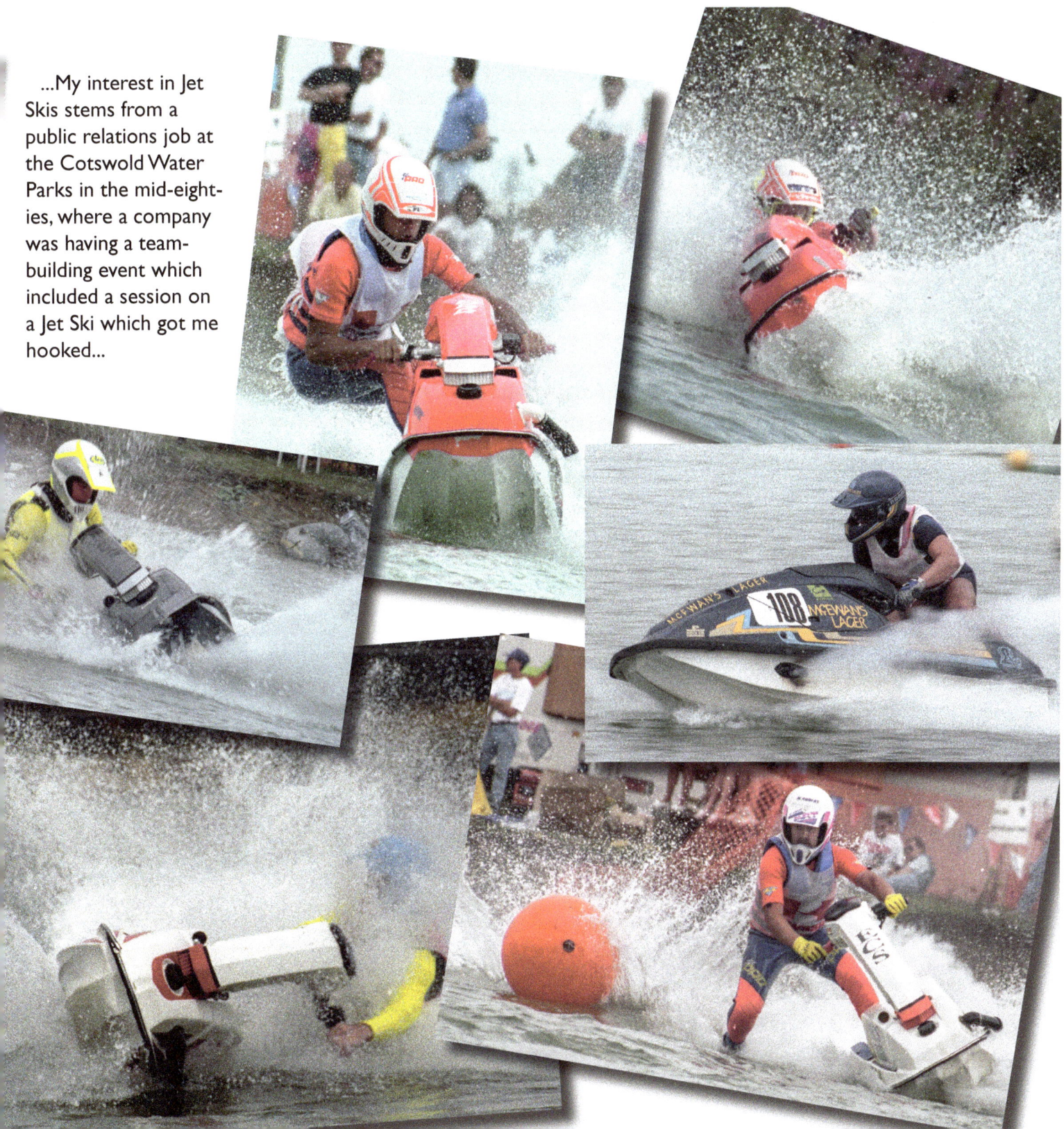

...My interest in Jet Skis stems from a public relations job at the Cotswold Water Parks in the mid-eighties, where a company was having a team-building event which included a session on a Jet Ski which got me hooked...

...Jet Skis were introduced into the UK by entrepreneur Tony Walker after a trip across the pond to America, where it was popular with thrill-seeking recreational riders.

Japanese motorcycle maker Kawasaki introduced the first production stand-up Personal Water Craft (PWC) in October 1972. It was powered by modified 400cc 2-stroke twin cylinder engine.

The design concepts of these original craft included a fully enclosed impeller for safety and self-righting, self-circling features. The self-circling allowed the rider to swim back to the idling craft after falling off. Kawasaki originally called them "Water Jet" and "Power Skis" before they settled on the name "Jet Ski".

Later models had 550 and 750cc engines and a 650cc sit-on version.

Tony set up Jet Ski UK on one of the lakes on the Cotswold Water Parks in the early eighties and it became the centre of the new sport, which attracted thousands of followers in the eighties and nineties.

In America, there was a section of fans who wanted to go faster and faster: so the sport of Jet Ski racing was born and eventually Tony and one of his staff Jeremy Crook made contact with the after-market and spare parts industry in the States and introduced Jet Ski racing to the UK.

The rules sort of followed the land-based sport of motocross, which incidentally held big national events at Fox Hill near Wanborough; but more on this later.

A motocross rider turned jet skier, Alan Pickard broke both his legs, wrists, ankles, collarbones and most of his teeth taking part in the land-based sport until he discovered a jet ski, and he was hooked. 'It is motocross on water except you don't break 'owt when you come off,' he says.

My involvement was that I had two racing skis, just slightly modified, but still capable of about 25mph at zero feet over the lake's surface.

This interest led me to create the art of Jet Ski photography, as no one else was doing pictures of any quality for the racers.

These days, with modern equipment, the way I obtained the spectacular images looks dangerous and I am sure the Health and Safety bods would have a fit, but that's now: then, we had to get in the water close up to the action.

Water and cameras don't go well together, and a Swindon company specialised in underwater cameras, so I obtained one for the film camera I was using at the time.

There were a range of dedicated waterproof cameras such as the Nikonos, which was a development of the famous underwater cameraman Jacques-Yves Cousteau. Although they are very versatile, they have one disadvantage for use in the sort of photography I was pursuing. They only have wide-angle lenses, as underwater work requires you to be close-up.

The type of underwater camera housing I chose had lead weights in it to allow it to sink or have neutral buoyancy, but that's not much good if you're working on the surface; so the housing was depleted of weights, which allowed it to float if needed.

I also modified the front lens unit on the housing to take a long lens, as the further away from the action the safer I felt, and the less hindrance I offered to the racers.

Kitted out in full racing protective gear, which included a dry suit, life jacket, helmet, back impact support, and various odd protectors, I was taken out to the selected spot in the lake and dumped overboard, to float, waiting for the action.

As I said, today's kit of GoPro® cameras would be attached to jumps, to floats anchored around the course and of course to the jet skis themselves, giving high quality 4K video and stills, all controlled from an app on a phone in the tea room; but it's not as much fun!..

...Photographically, a little bit of history was made at the Jet Ski lake in the Water Parks, when I organised a conference for an organisation representing freelance news agencies.

The conference was for the National Association of Press Agencies, and took place at the Blunsdon House Hotel on a Sunday.

As agencies were attending from all over the UK, most arrived on the Saturday; so I arranged a day of Jet Skiing for the delegates on the Saturday.

The event was quite expensive, and Canon Cameras were persuaded to sponsor the event to show off their new analogue electronic cameras.

These cameras were the precursors of today's electronic offerings but were not digital. They were analogue, producing a still TV picture you could just about use.

The images were on a micro floppy disc, a computer medium some may remember, and were read in a small reader with a modem attached. This modem could be coupled to the "brick-type" mobile phones through an acoustic coupler and sent via the analogue mobile signal to a base computer, which was set up in the conference room at the Blunsdon House,

So the delegates skied and had their pictures taken in the wet suits and on the crafts. They then transmitted them to the hotel, where Canon had a printer set up so the participants could take away the evidence of the new technology.

We used the camera for the Swindon Town v Gillingham match at Crystal Palace, and it was a disaster; fortunately, we had a film back-up and just about made the sports pages locally.

Needless to say the cameras never really took off, as more portable negative scanners and then digital technology came in....

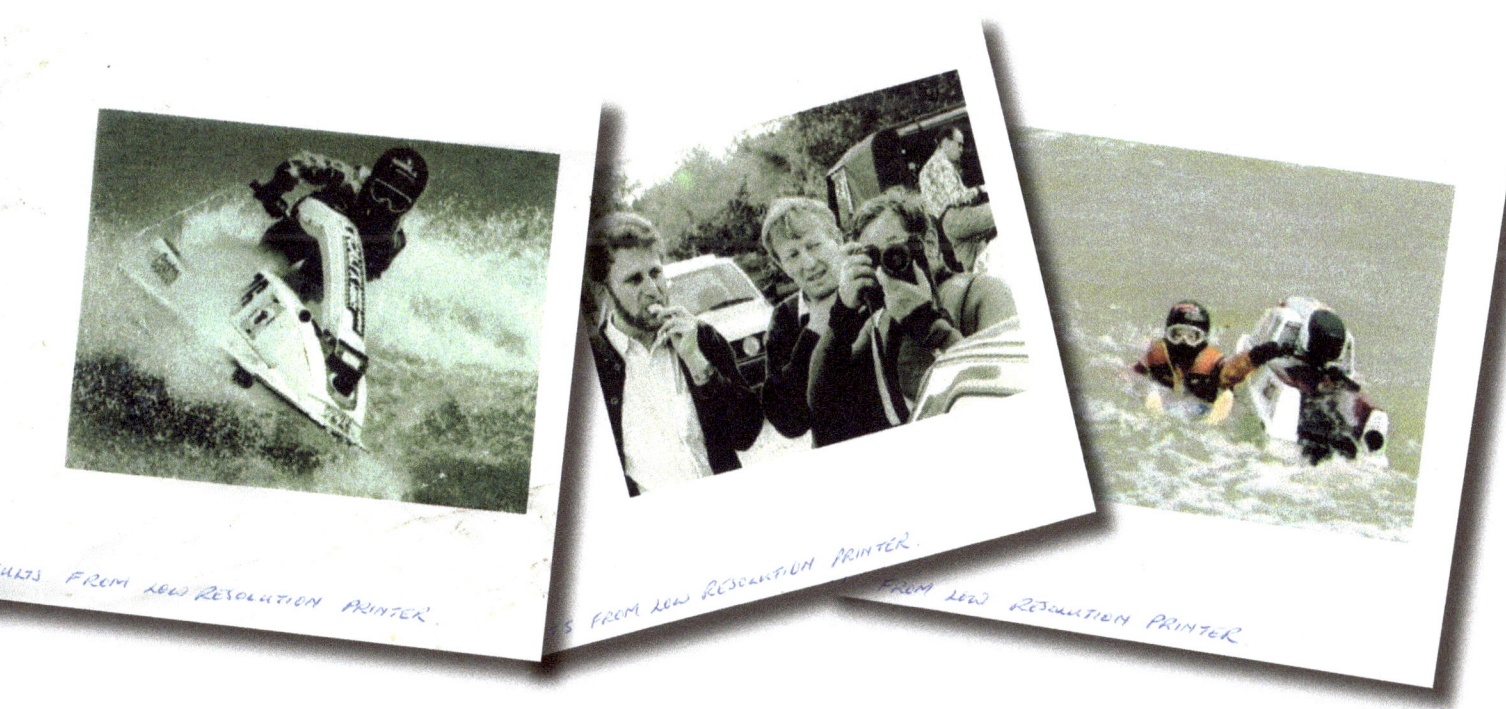

...One of the more interesting venues that we raced at was in the docks at Glasgow during the city's Garden Festival.

As a racer, there were many problems as the walls reflected the wash from the skis giving the riders a very rough surface to traverse. The high walls meant that we had to clamber up and down for each race. Even the Jet Skis had to be craned in and out of the water.

It did, however, give a different perspective to photographing the action; from above, as well as from the water level which the waves made very difficult..

During the racing we were watched by the Glasgow actor Mark McManus, better known as the detective Taggart, while he was filming some footage about the Garden Festival.

In true Taggart style, one of the marshals revealed that only the night before we raced they'd pulled a body out of the dock!..

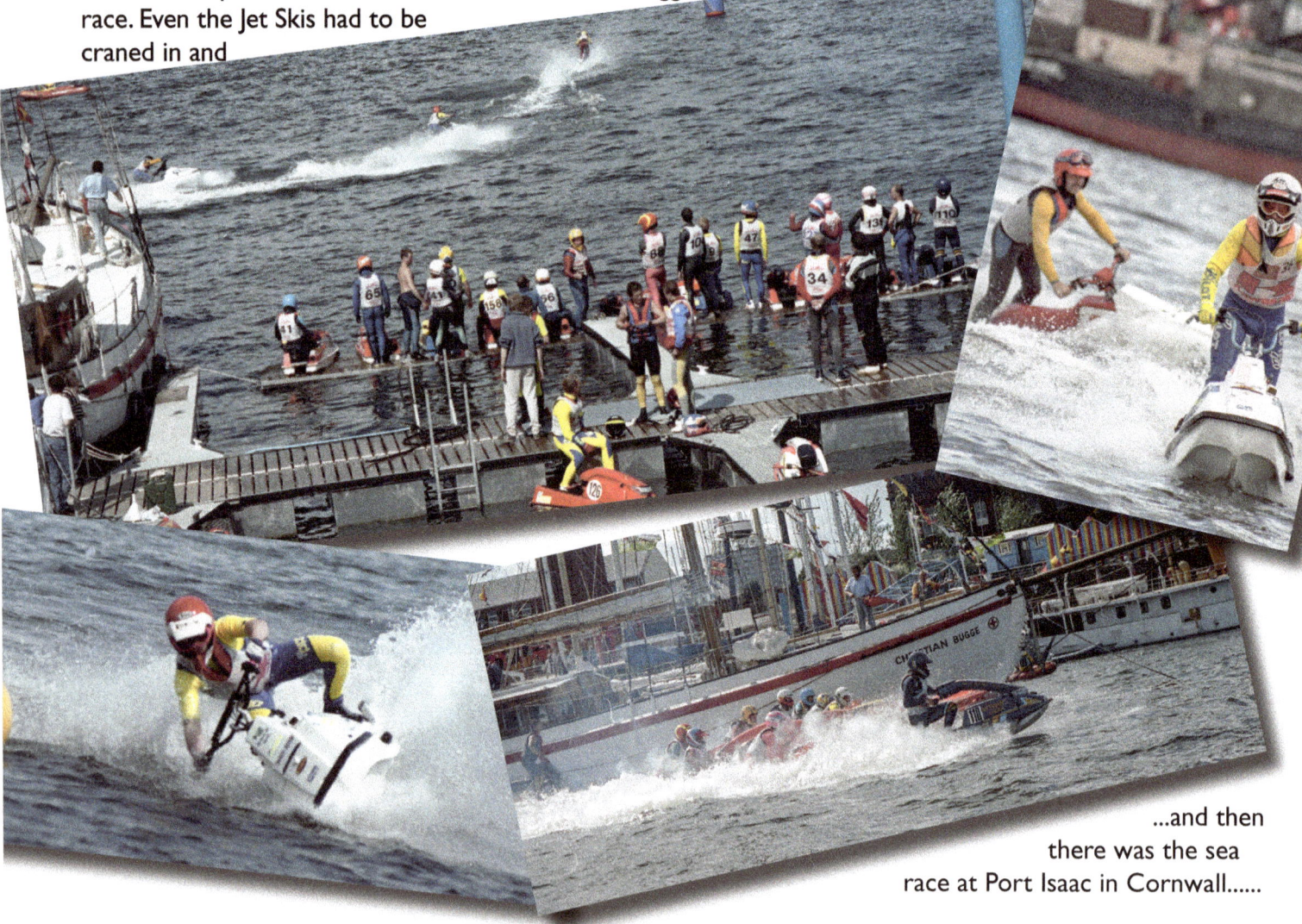

...and then there was the sea race at Port Isaac in Cornwall......

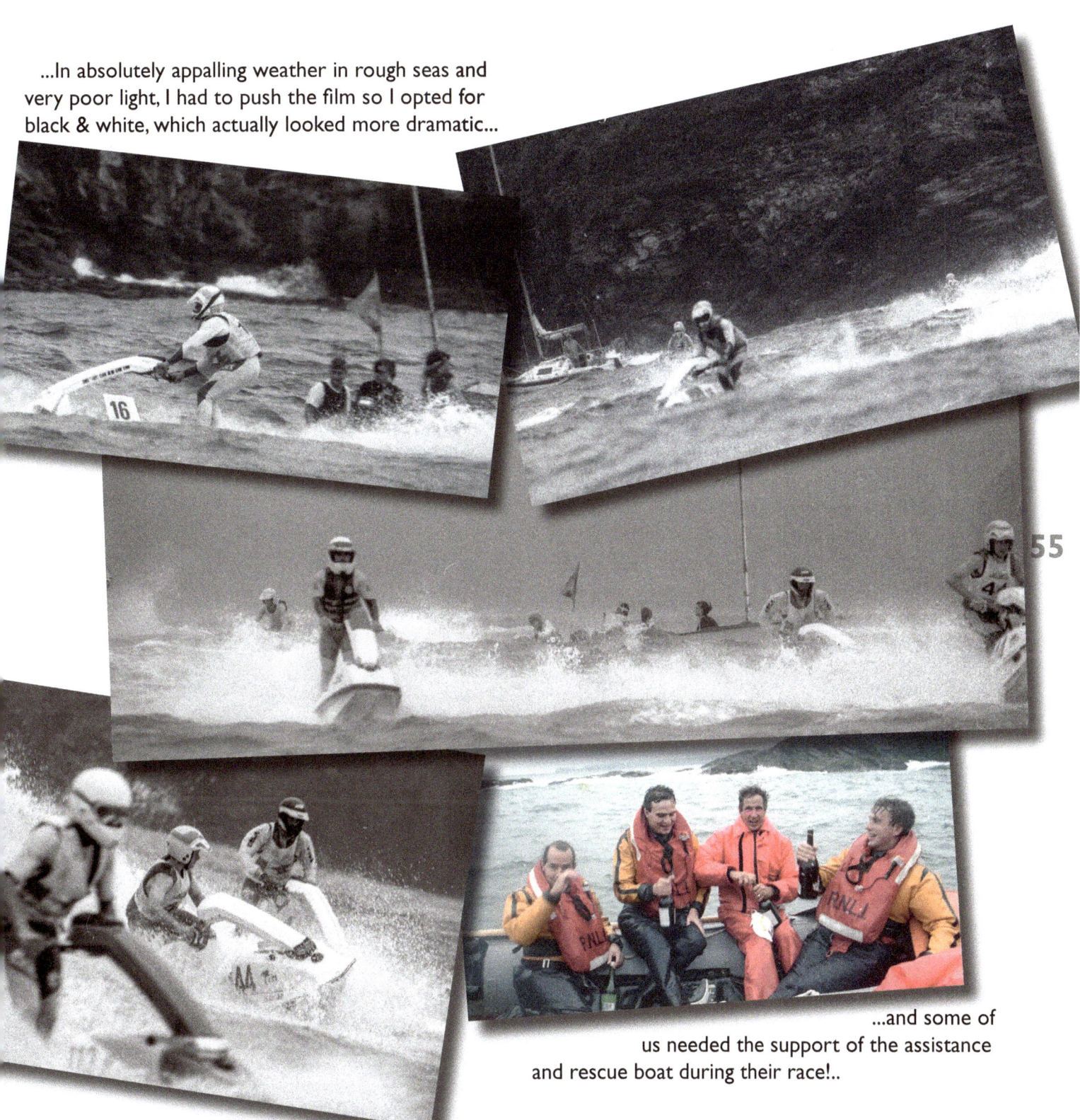

...In absolutely appalling weather in rough seas and very poor light, I had to push the film so I opted for black & white, which actually looked more dramatic...

...and some of us needed the support of the assistance and rescue boat during their race!..

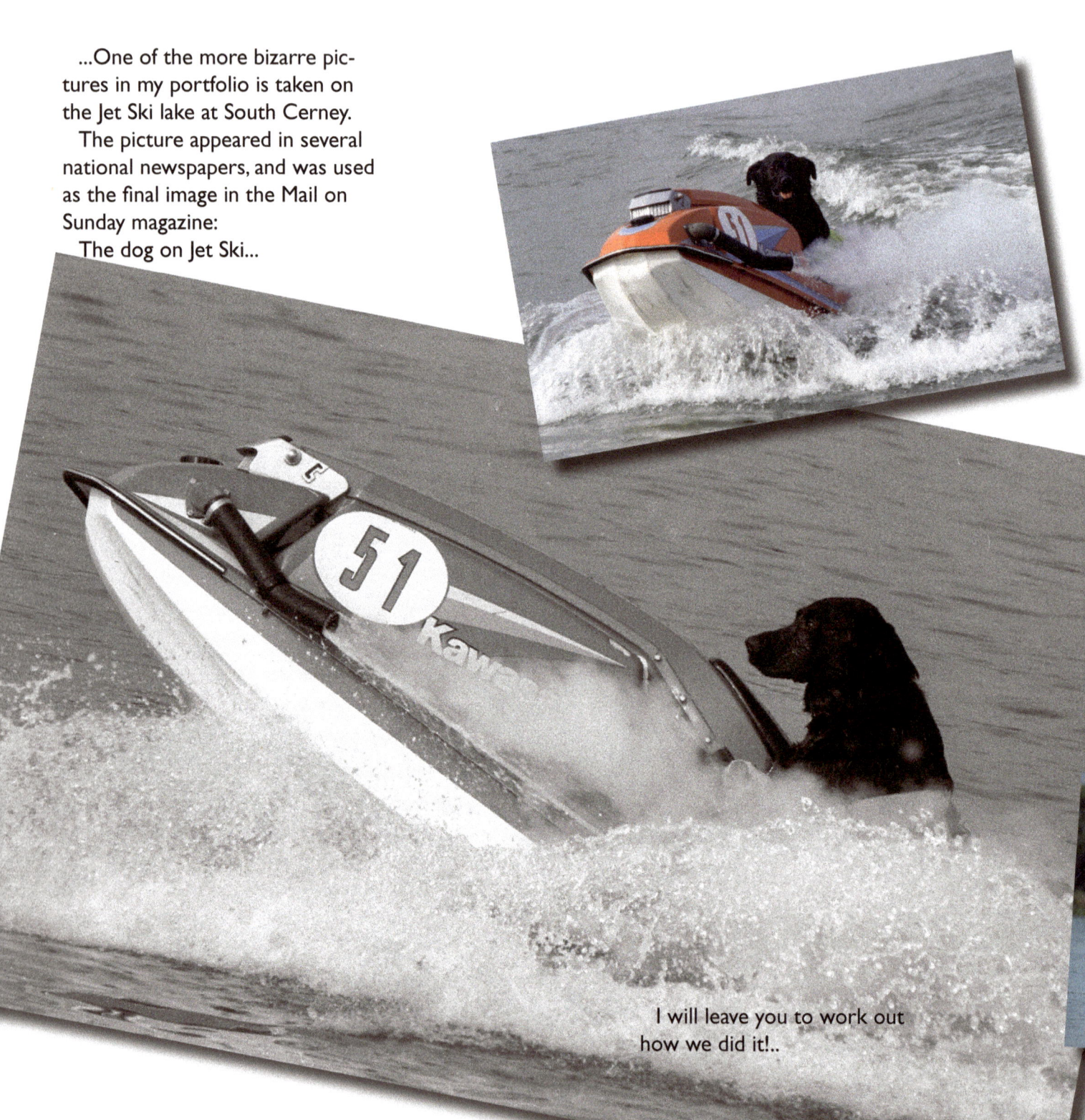

...One of the more bizarre pictures in my portfolio is taken on the Jet Ski lake at South Cerney.

The picture appeared in several national newspapers, and was used as the final image in the Mail on Sunday magazine:

The dog on Jet Ski...

I will leave you to work out how we did it!...

...The imagery created around the world of personal water craft lends itself to glamorous photoshoots, even in the UK - we do get sunshine occasionally - so my contacts within the sport led to some interesting requests from picture desks, but not of the racing.

Fashion shoots presentations, Page 3 models, and one that made international journals.

Andy Kyle was the picture editor of the *Mail on Sunday* magazine, and he knew I was connected with the Jet Ski world as I had submitted several racing images to him, but with no success.

He phoned me one Tuesday morning with an idea. Sunday paper picture desks start the week's work on a Tuesday, as they work until very late on a Saturday in case there is a breaking story that can go in the last edition of the paper.

The *YOU* magazine in those days had a centre page "Big Picture" two page colour spread of quirky images that would not fit anywhere else in the paper, but deserved a decent showing.

As a result of the conversation with Andy I contacted the people at Jet Ski UK on the Cotswold Water Parks and started to sort out a quirky picture that would make the spread.

The idea originally was a flying jet ski jumping over some object, like a boat, but the scenario developed as the days went by into a rather spectacular image and a rather risky shoot

I approached a local model to do the shot I had suggested, and then went to the guys at the lake and they agreed to set it up.

With a bit of planning, especially around the weather, Tim Rochfort from the company came up with the final plan.

The boat would be anchored firmly, quite a way into the lake. The bikini clad model, Melissa, would sit on the stern of the craft and Tim would jump over the front.

After three or four practice runs without Melissa in the boat, which enabled Tim to get the line of the jump sorted out, she was taken to her position in the boat by one of the two-seater Jet Skis.

Here is where the fun started, as Tim's first jump of the boat was to much to the centre, and soaked Melissa.

I was shooting on a very long lens from the bank and using a Fuji Film called Reala which, although very slow, has very little grain; so makes it the ideal medium to use to get the size of image required from the shoot, hence the need for a sunny day...

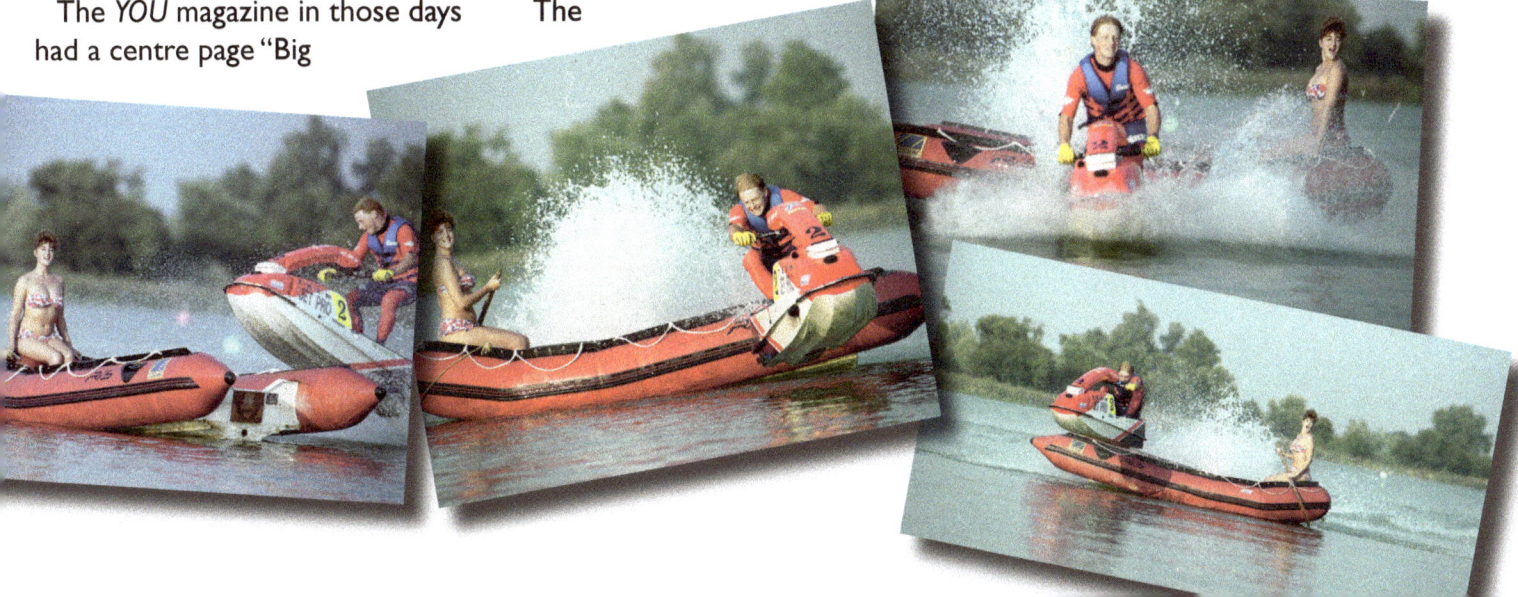

...After several more attempts, I thought we had the picture and decided to call it a day. We then took to the watercraft for a bit of fun.

In those days you had to develop and print the image to see what you had; so, with bated breath, I developed the film and selected some of the images to print. The final run had just the image we wanted, and it made the Big Picture spread....

As I said earlier, I am sure that with the Health and Safety executive breathing down your neck you couldn't do that picture now!..

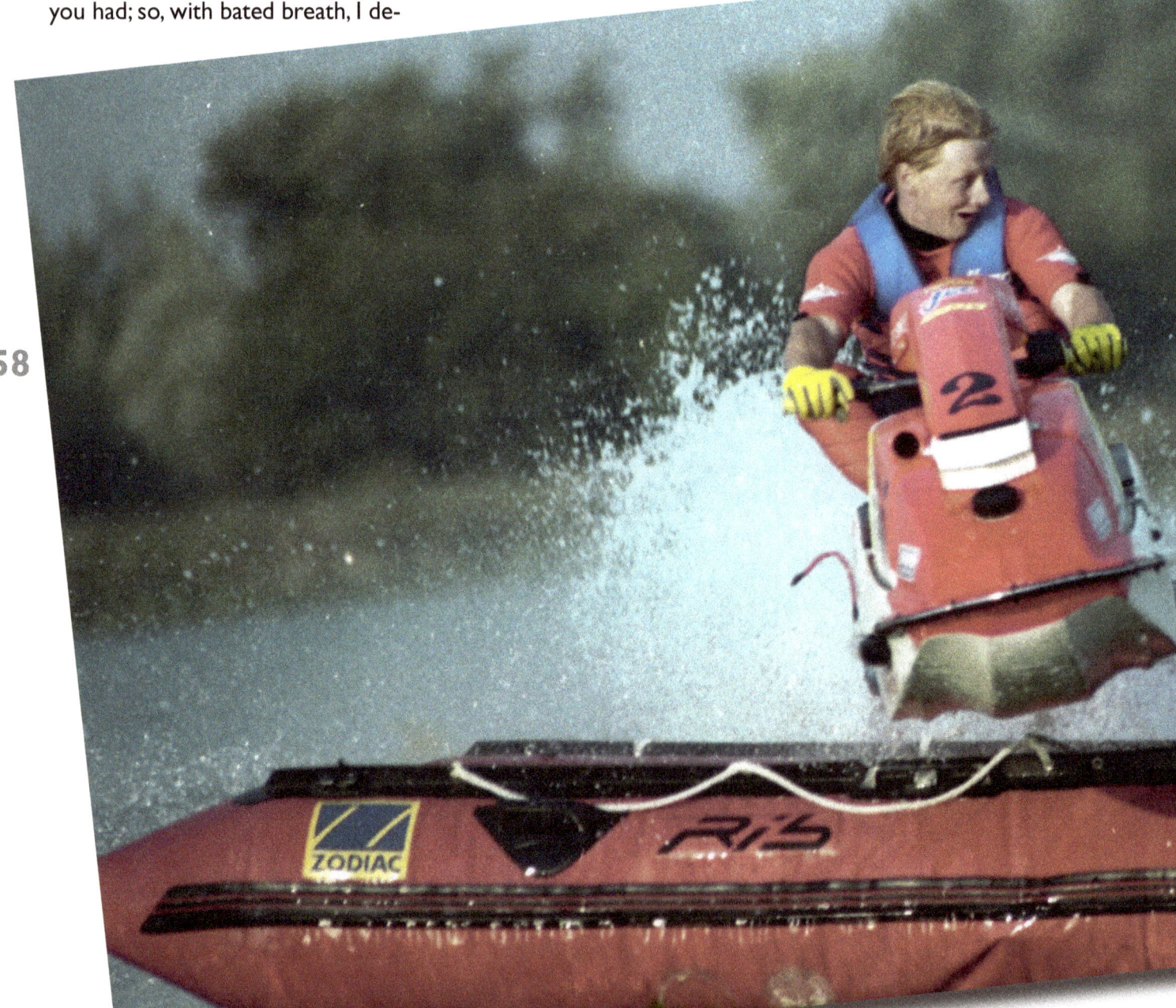

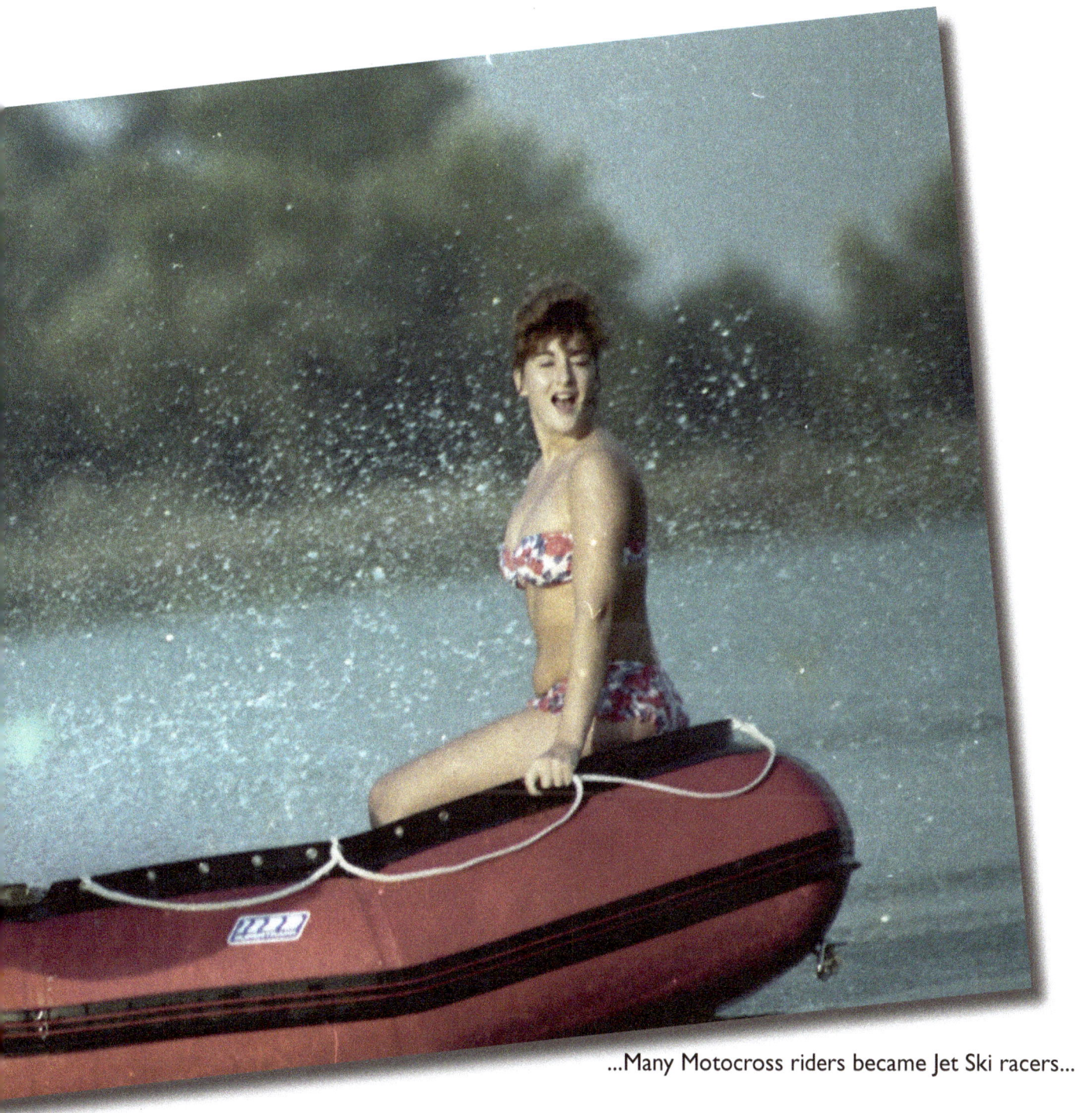

...Many Motocross riders became Jet Ski racers...

...Buried in a valley just outside Swindon near Foxhill is what was rated one of the UK's best Motocross circuits; the Foxhill circuit. In fact, it was so highly rated that, in 1995, it was given the privilege of hosting the first ever 125cc and 250cc Grand Prix as a double header, with both classes being held on one day.

Even bigger accolades were bestowed on the circuit when, in 1998, the Grand Prix was held there. It hosted Motocross des Nations in September, and the 125cc, 250cc, and 500cc triple header in 2000...

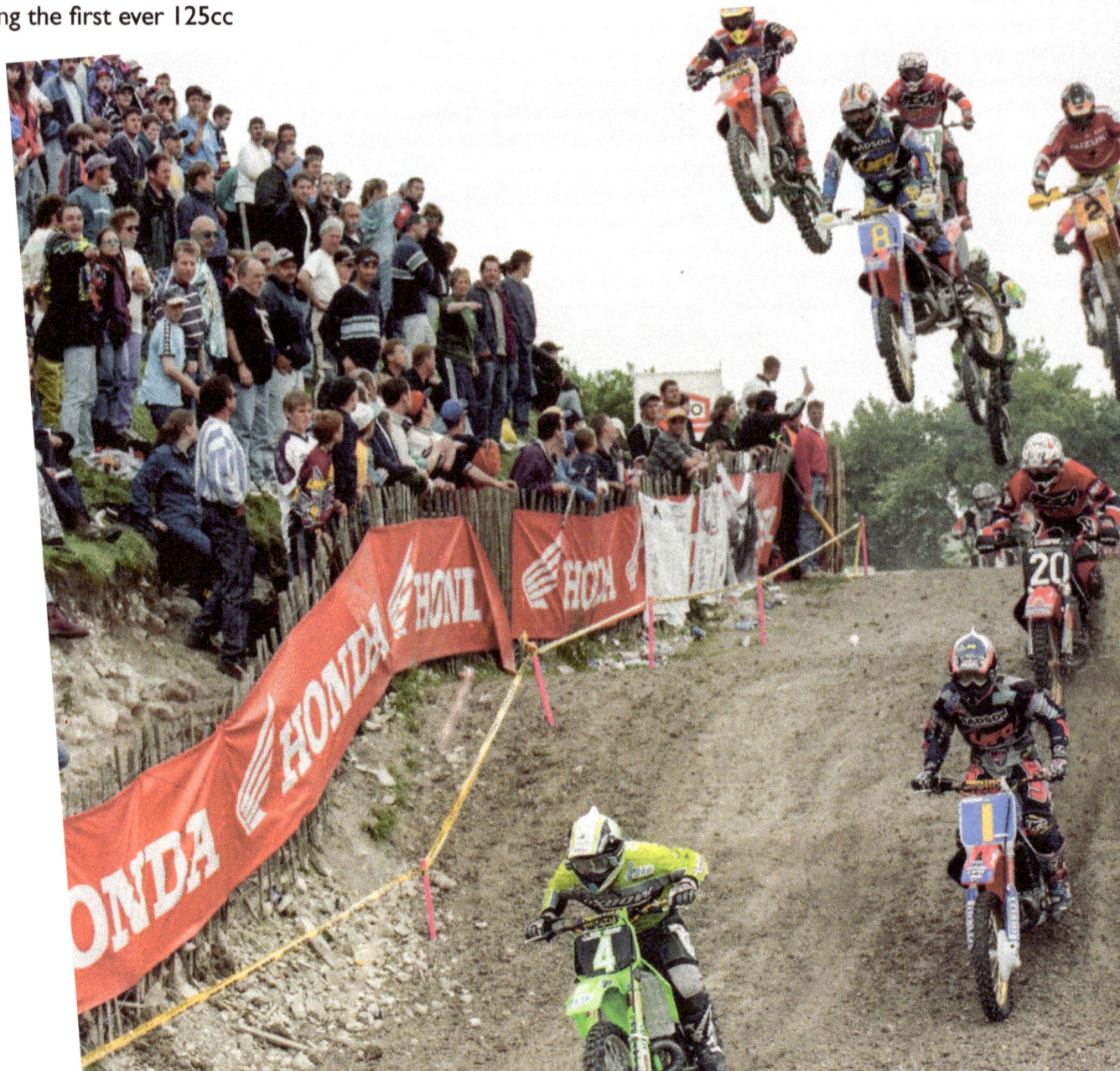

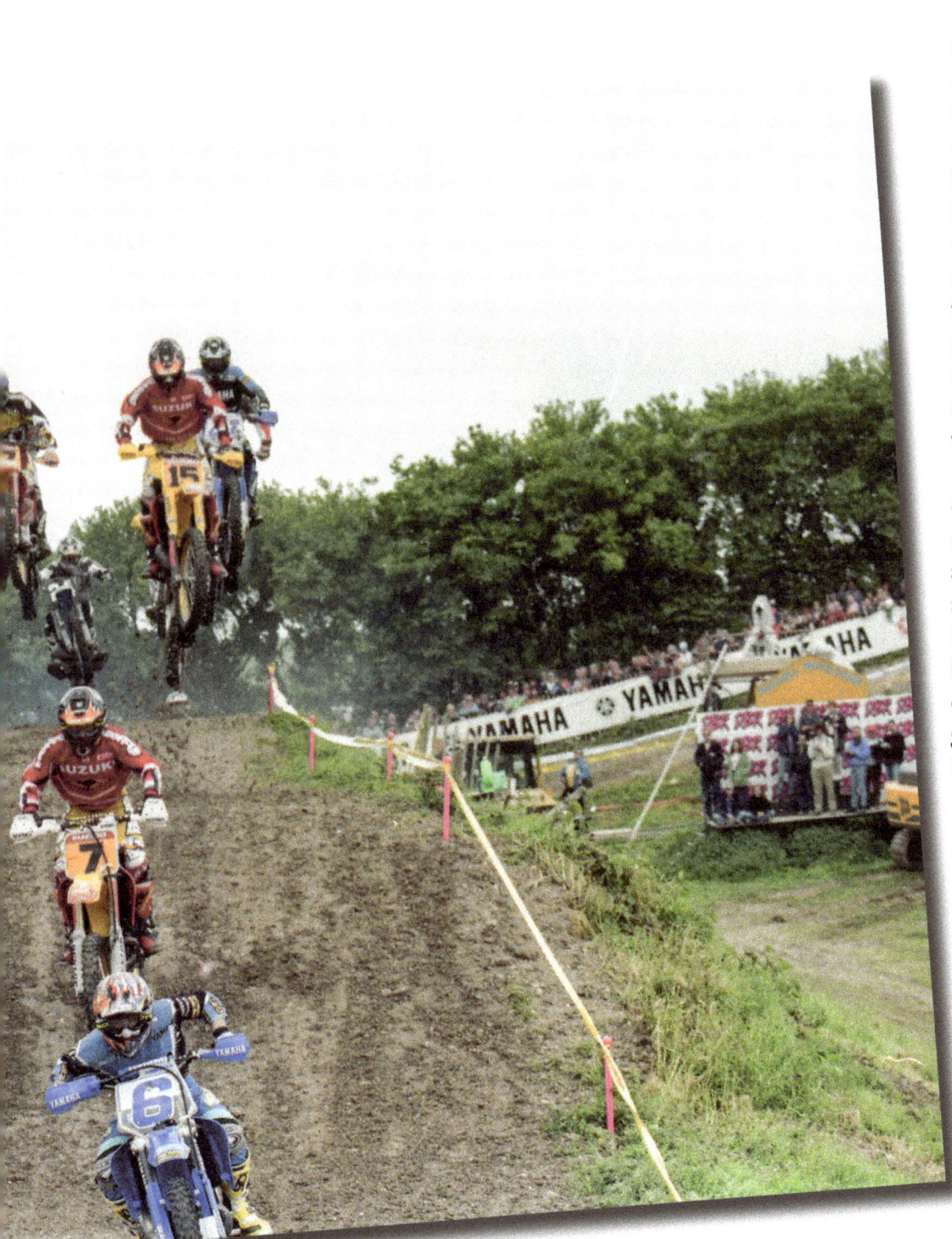

...Unfortunately, the British weather helped in the demise of the circuit with a postponement then cancellation of the racing on the Sunday of the triple header. That and subsequent planning decisions meant that the circuit fell into decline as a professional circuit, but in recent years it has become a popular amateur venue.

Photographing Motocross has similarities to photographing Jet Skis, as the movement and speed of the machines is alike; only you don't have to have special cameras. Also you don't get wet, unless of course it rains!..

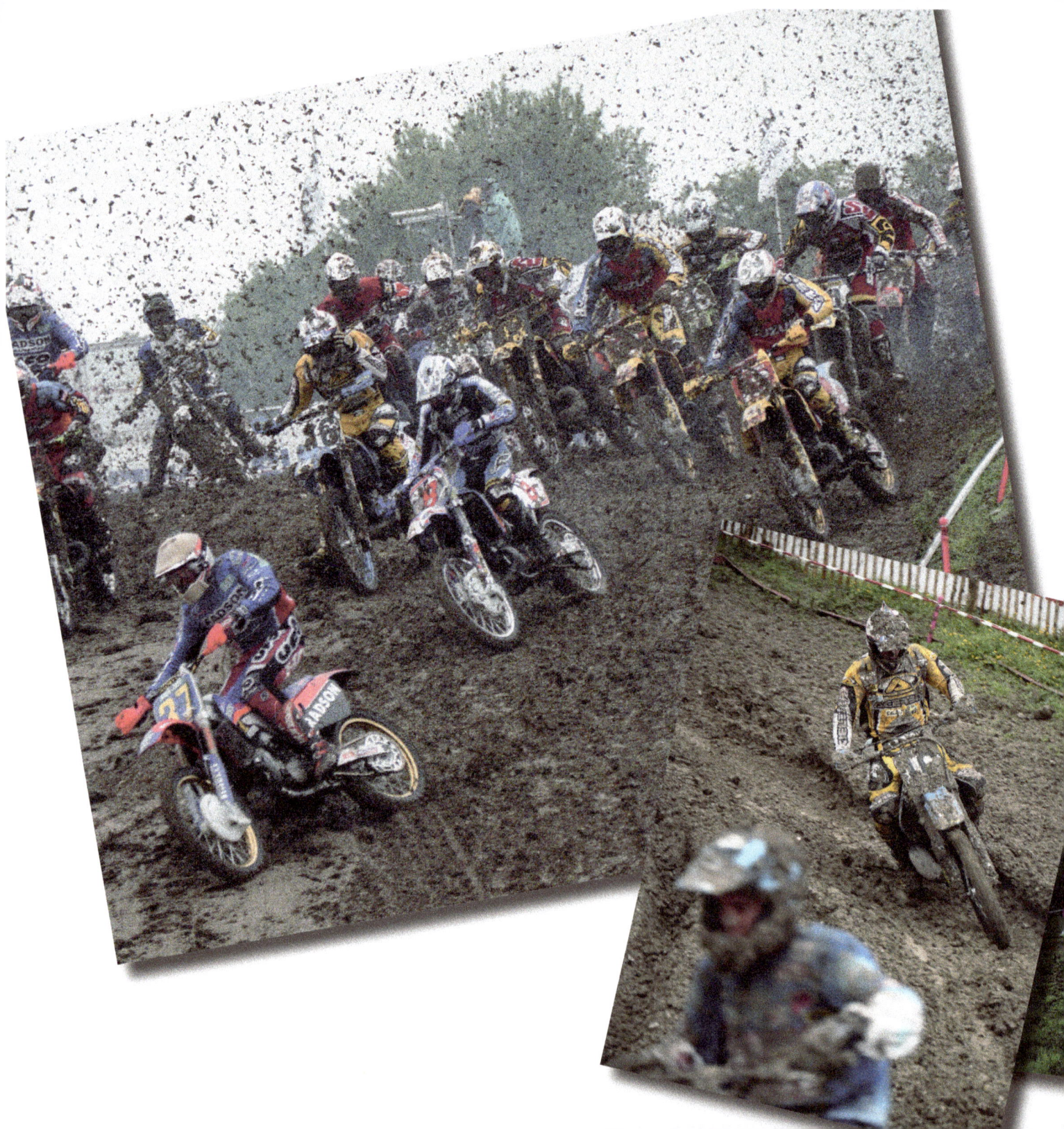

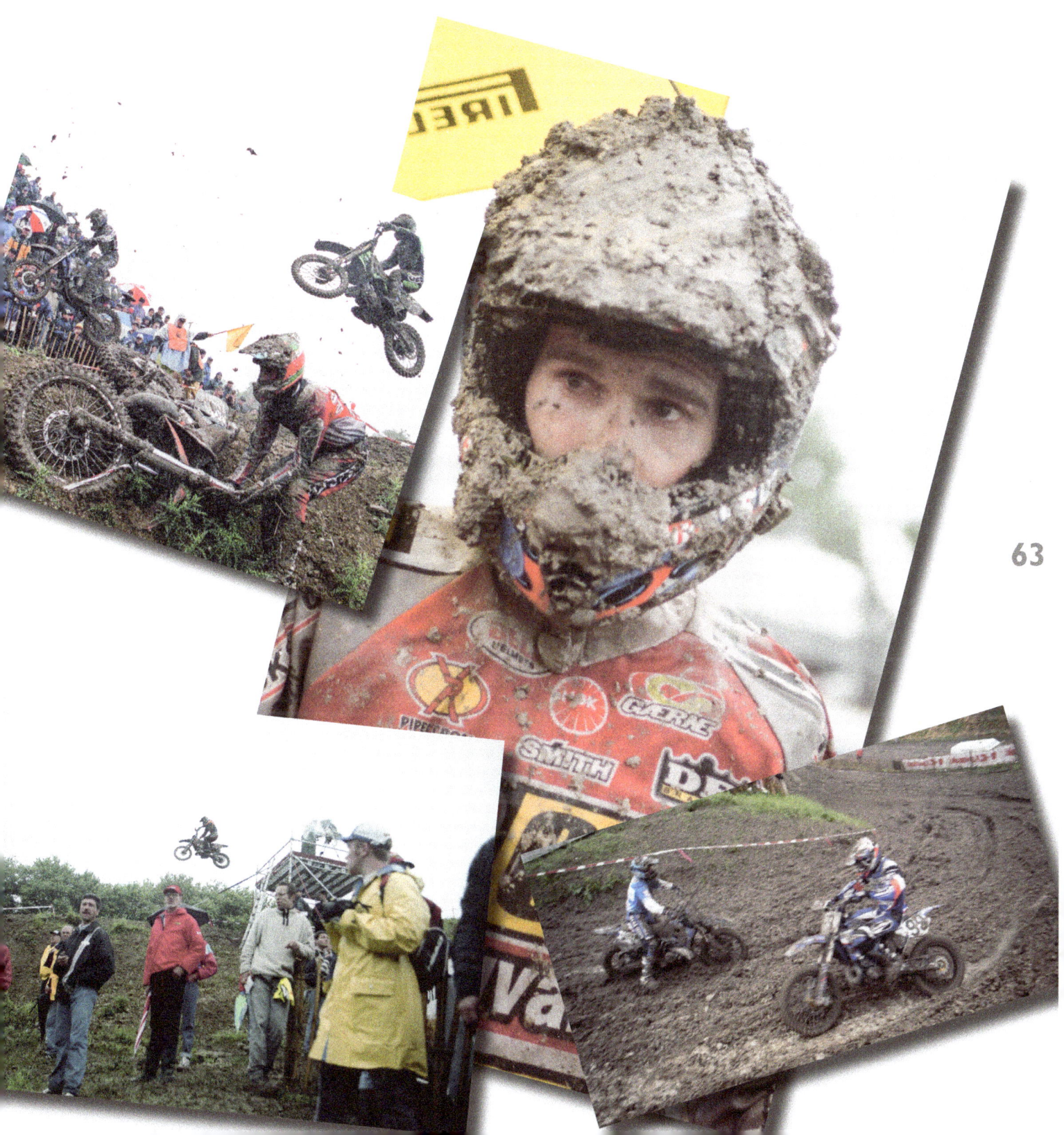

...Jet Ski racing started in America, and Swindon seems blessed with American sports.

As I said earlier in the book, we have a successful Ice Hockey Team, we also have an American Football team; The Swindon Storm...

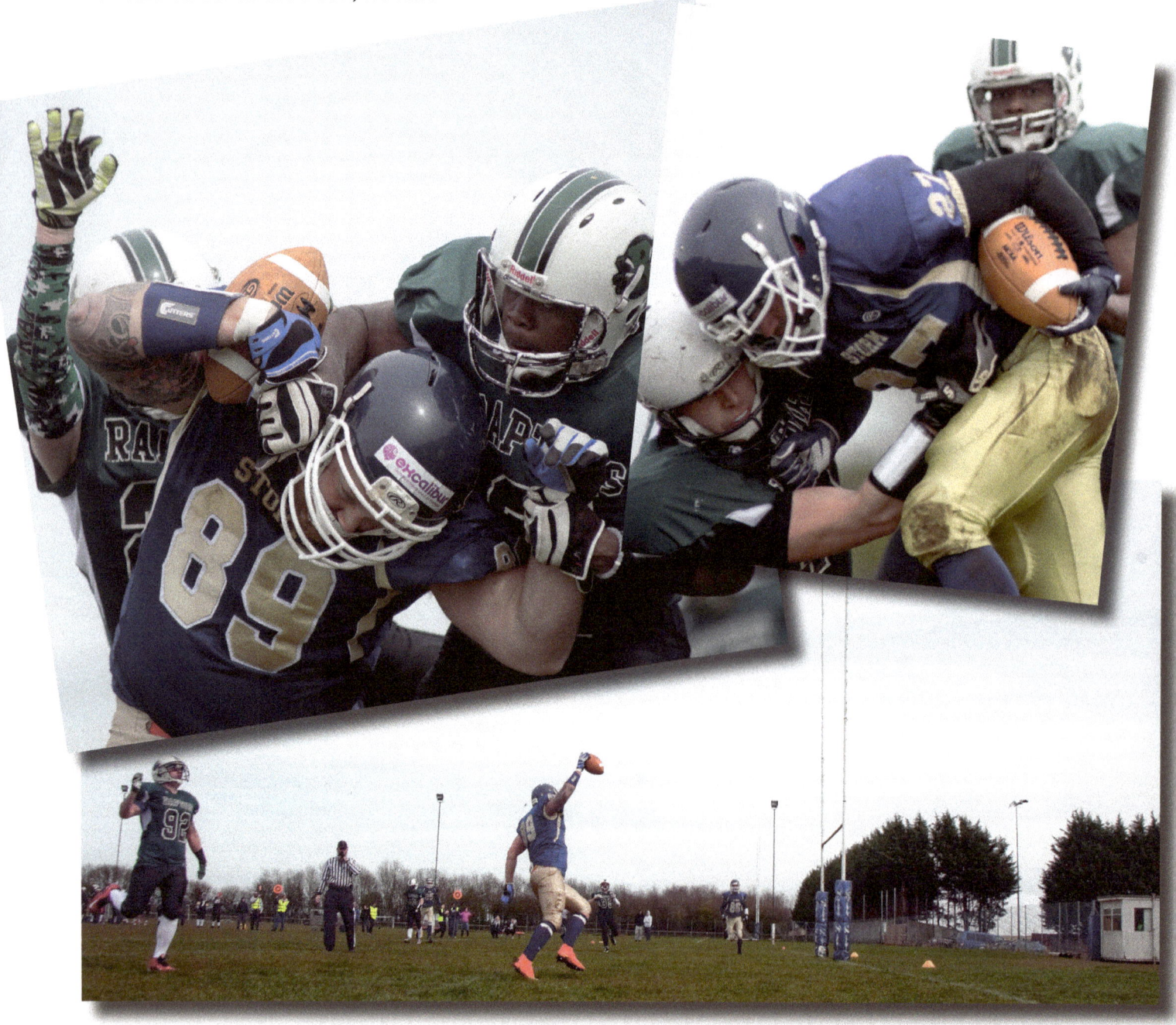

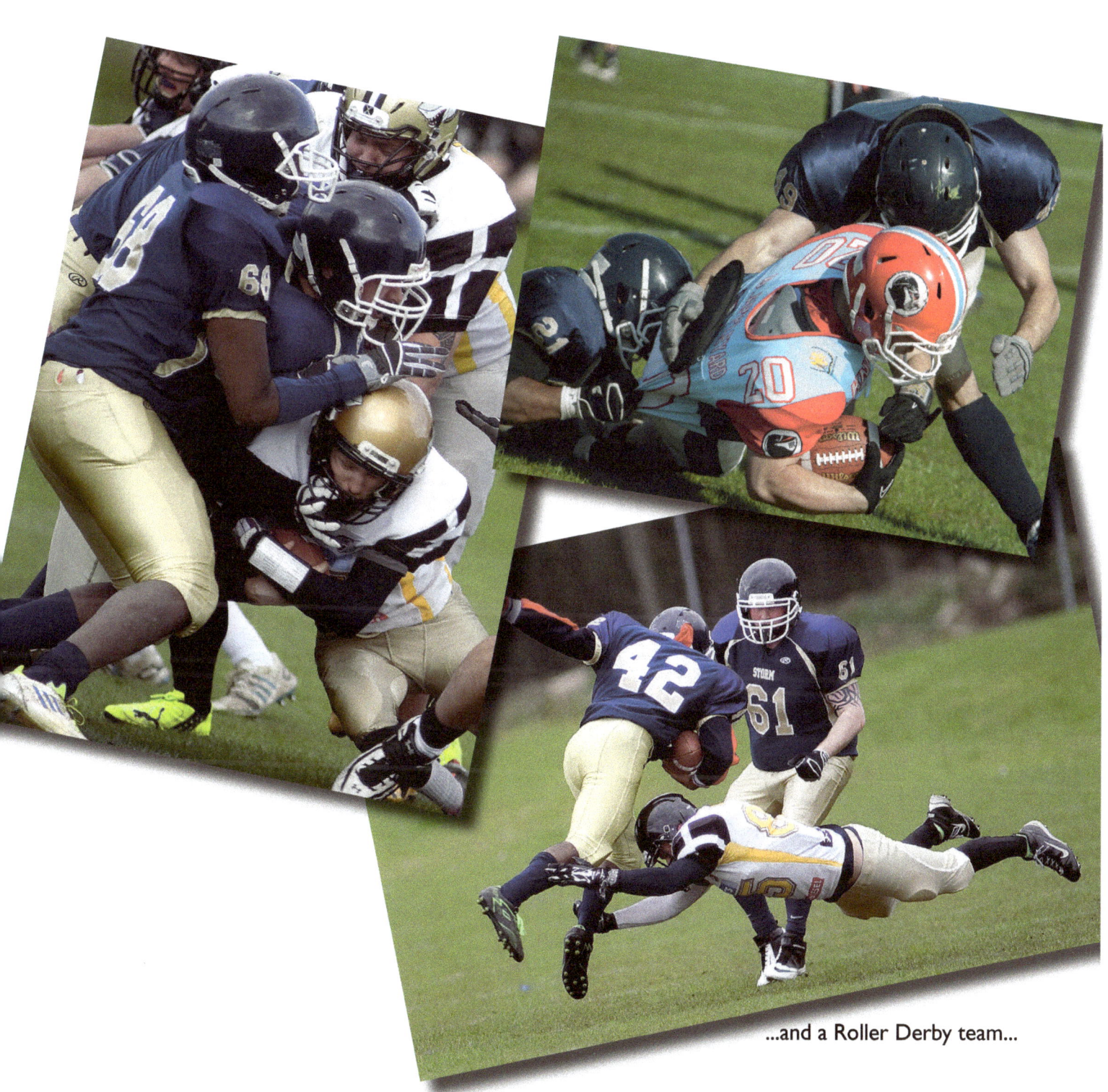

...and a Roller Derby team...

...Roller derby is a contact sport, played by two teams of five members roller skating in the same direction around a track.

Photographing in the Oasis sports hall or the Futsal indoor arena with its poor lighting is a difficult task at the best of times. Add in some high-speed action needing a long lens and it means you have to be very aware of what the camera can produce for you.

No matter how good the photo editing software is, if the image isn't there you can't do much with it.

So what is roller derby?

Game play consists of a series of short matchups ("jams") in which both teams designate a scoring player (the "jammer") who scores points by lapping members of the opposing team. The teams attempt to assist their own jammer while hindering the opposing jammer — in effect, playing both offence and defence simultaneously. Basically a legalised brawl!

Roller derby is hugely popular and is played by more than 1,200 amateur leagues throughout the world.

While the sport has its origins in the banked-track roller skating marathons of the 1930s, Leo Seltzer and Damon Runyon are credited with the basic evolution of the sport to its initial competitive form.

Professional roller derby quickly became popular; in 1940, more than 5 million spectators watched in about 50 US cities.

In the ensuing decades, however, it predominantly became a form of sports entertainment where the theatrical elements overshadowed the athleticism. This gratuitous showmanship largely ended with the sport's contemporary grassroots revival in the first decade of the 21st century. Although some sports entertainment qualities such as player pseudonyms and colourful uniforms were retained, scripted bouts with predetermined winners were abandoned.

Modern roller derby is an international sport dominated by all-female amateur teams, in addition to a growing number of male, co-ed, and junior roller derby teams, and is as a roller sport under consideration for the future Olympics...

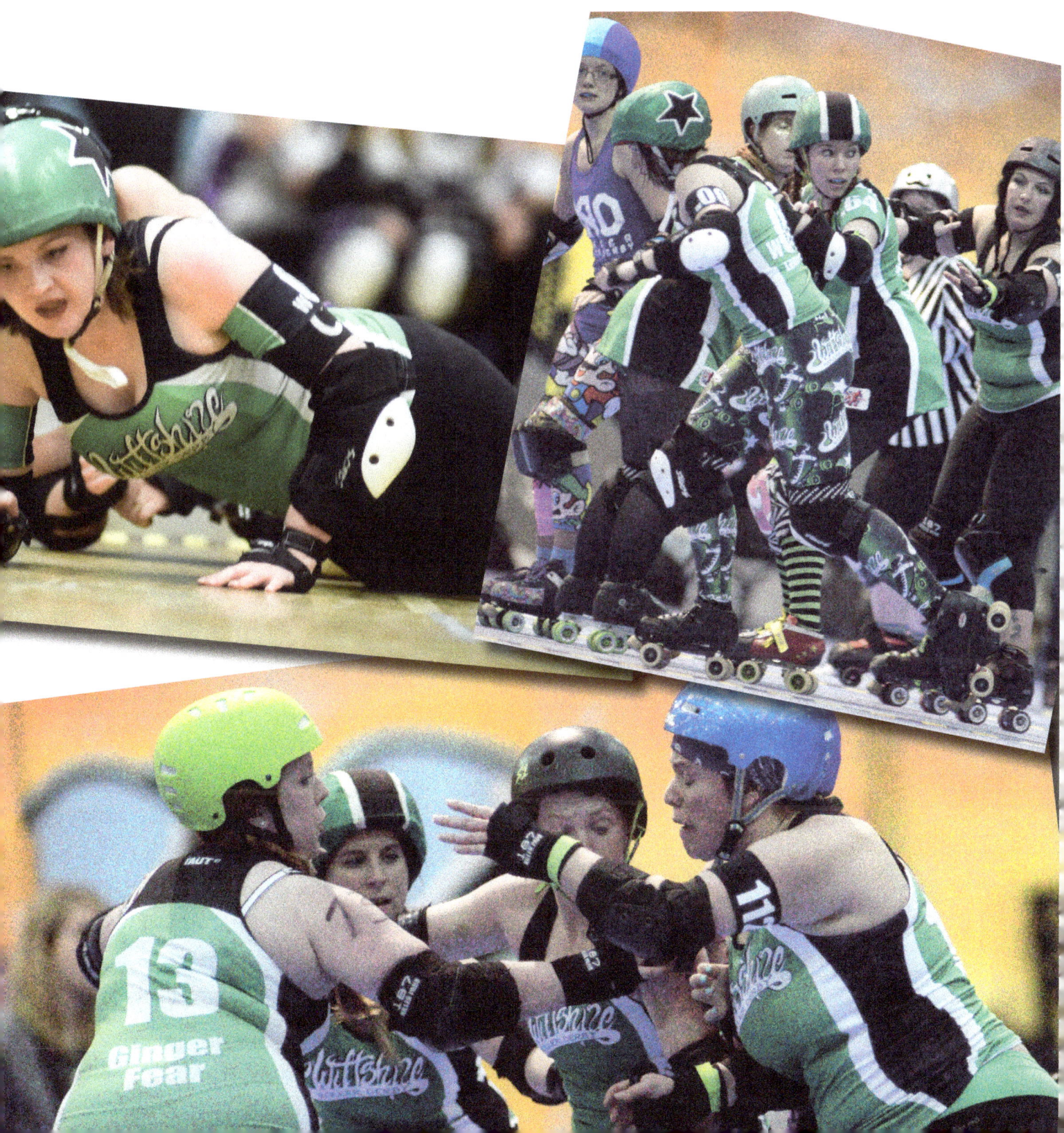

...A sport that originated on the American continent, in fact Canada, is also played in Swindon.

That sport was known over the pond as Murderball before it was changed to Quad Rugby, over here it's Wheelchair Rugby, a wheelchair edition of Rugby League...

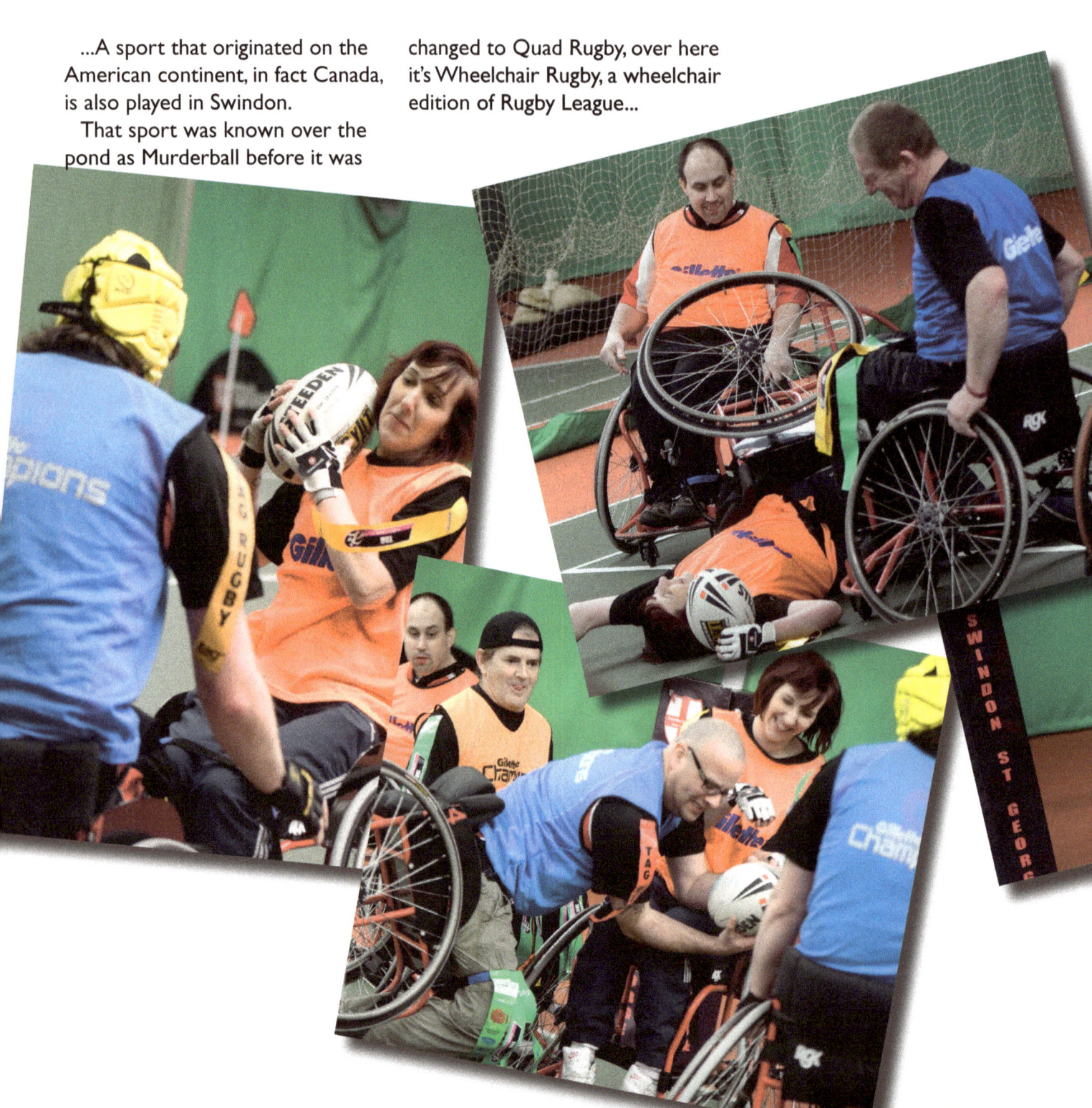

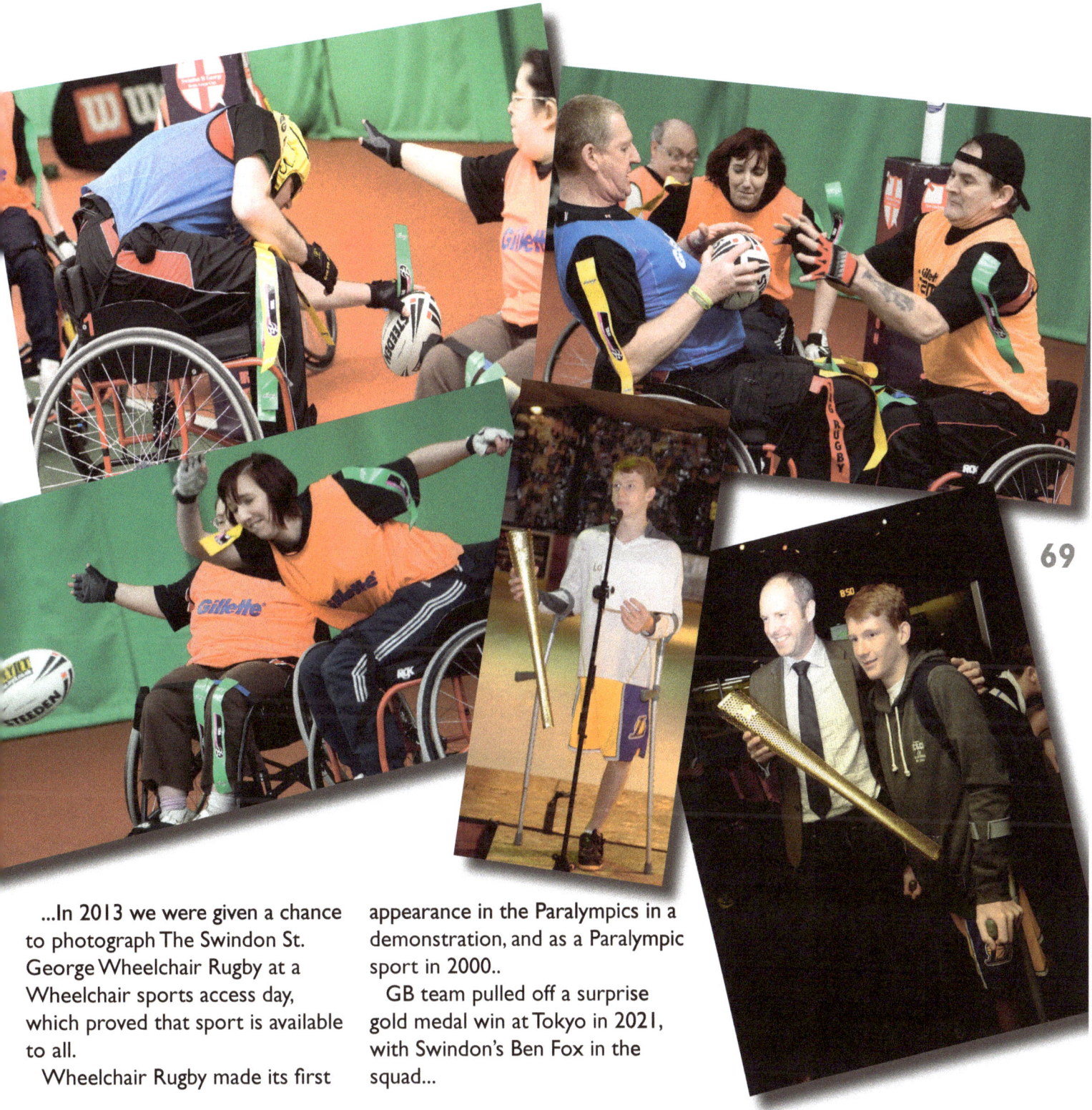

...In 2013 we were given a chance to photograph The Swindon St. George Wheelchair Rugby at a Wheelchair sports access day, which proved that sport is available to all.

Wheelchair Rugby made its first appearance in the Paralympics in a demonstration, and as a Paralympic sport in 2000..

GB team pulled off a surprise gold medal win at Tokyo in 2021, with Swindon's Ben Fox in the squad...

...The Tokyo 2020 games, held in 2021, produced bronze medals for Great Britain in some new sports, one of which was Skateboarding; where Sky Brown became the youngest medallist ever at the tender age of just 13.

Skateboarding produces one of the most surreal set of pictures of the sporting year when the historic Malmesbury Abbey is converted into a skate park for a few days each year.

Skaters flying through the air with a backdrop of the stained glass windows and the vaulted celling gives the photographer an interesting challenge and a slightly dangerous one too.

To get the best images you have to tuck yourself in on the ground beside the ramps looking up at the roof and wait for the skaters to fly past, praying the board goes with them and not fall in your direction.

The things we do for a picture!..

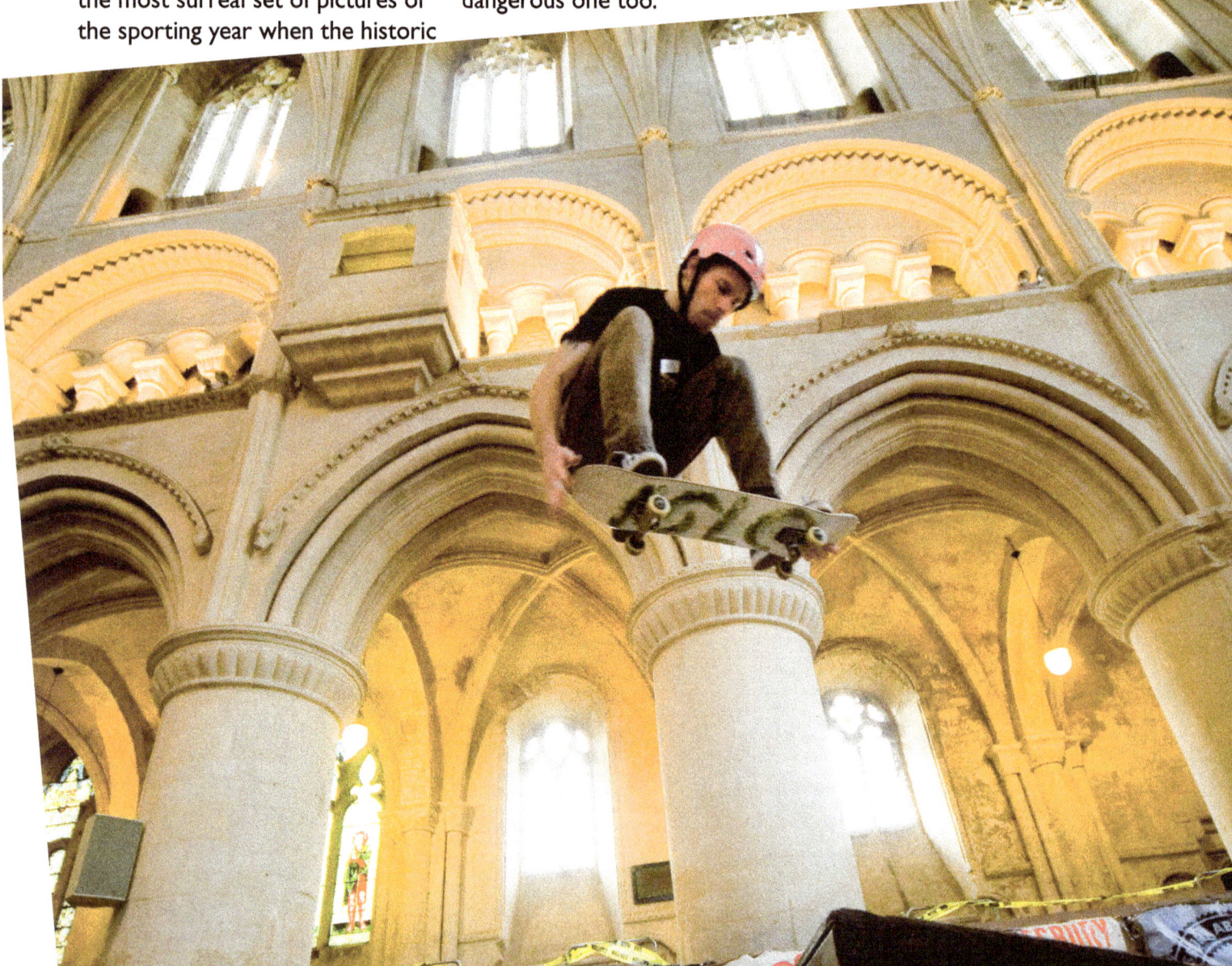

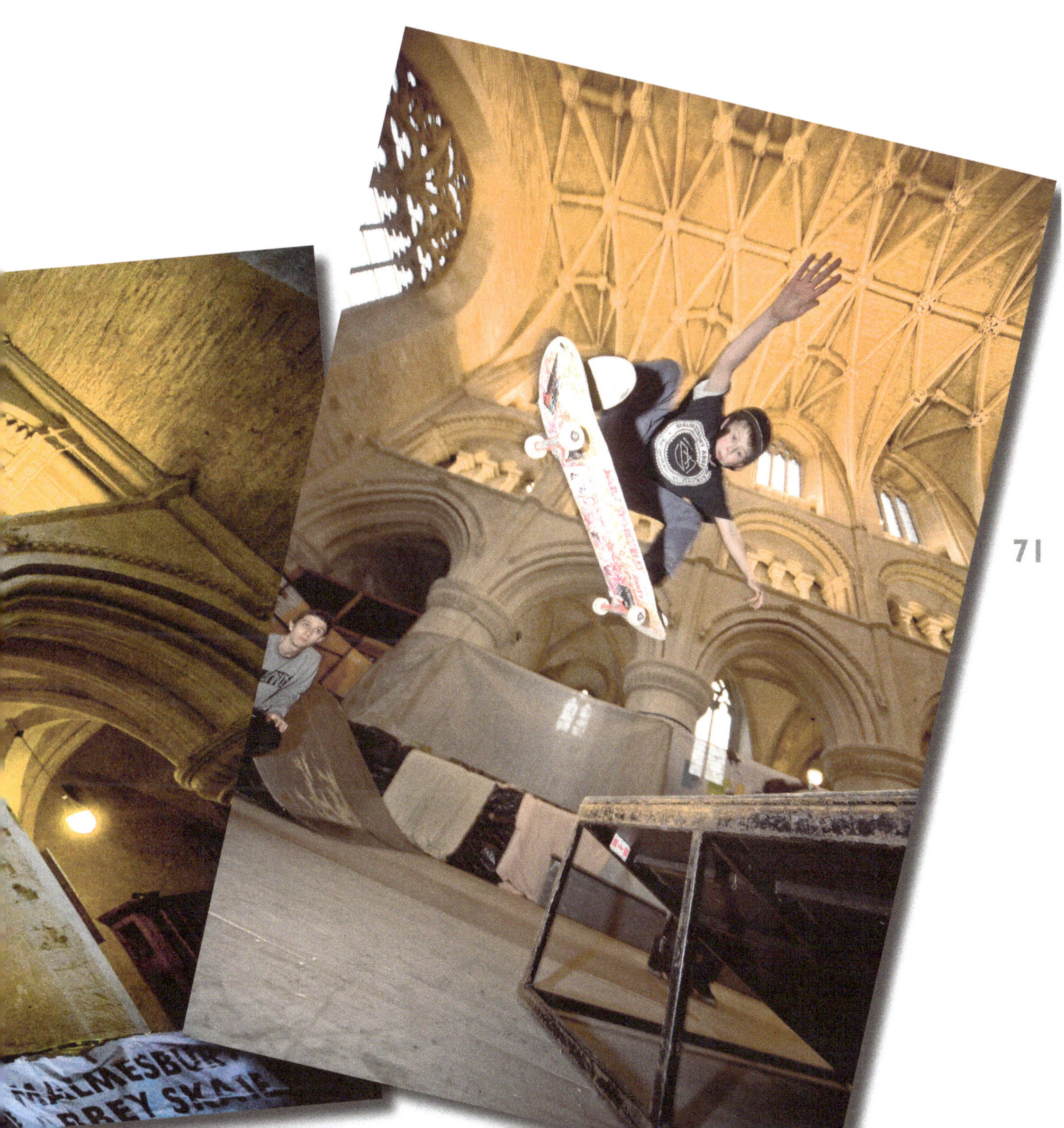

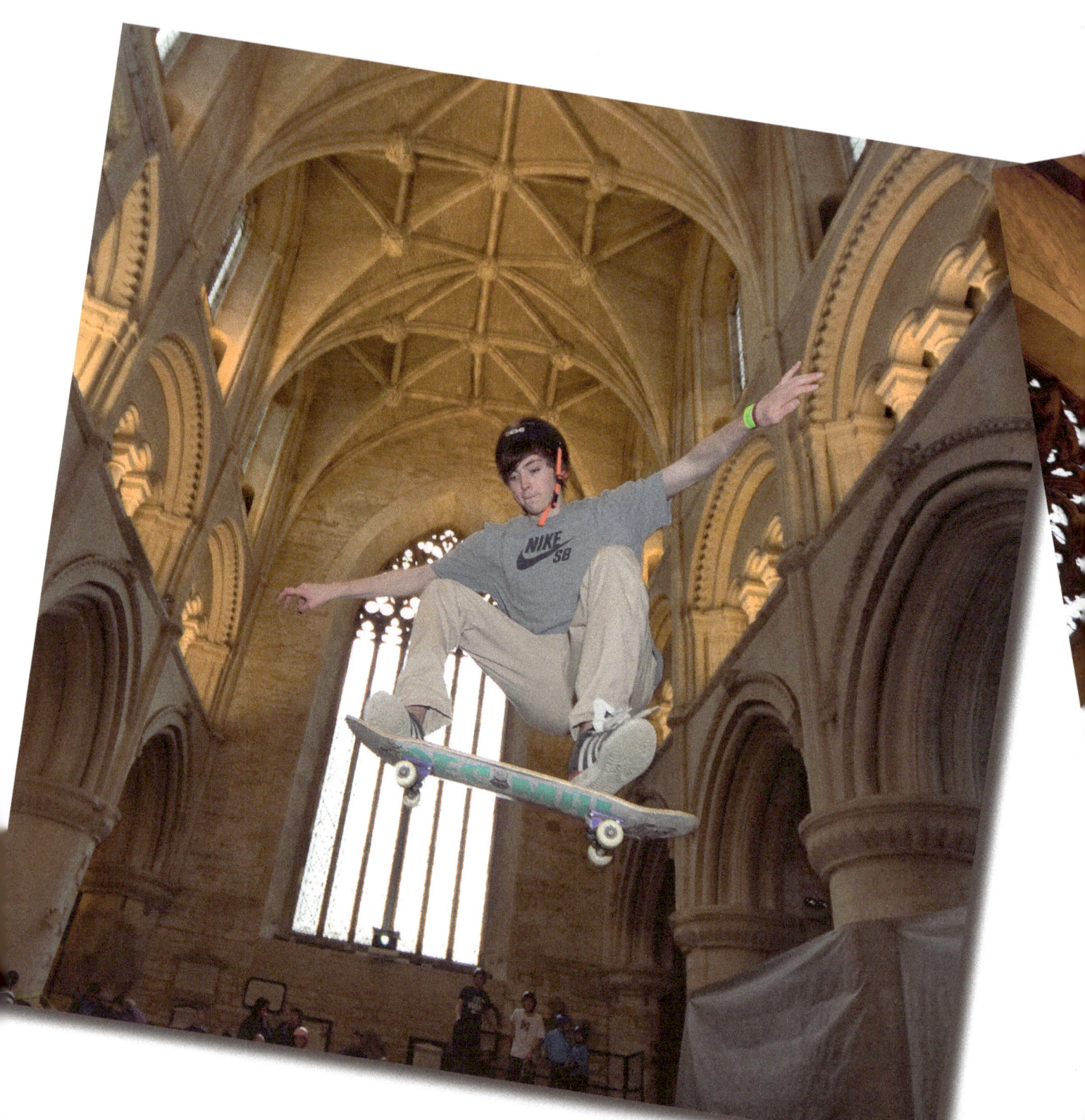

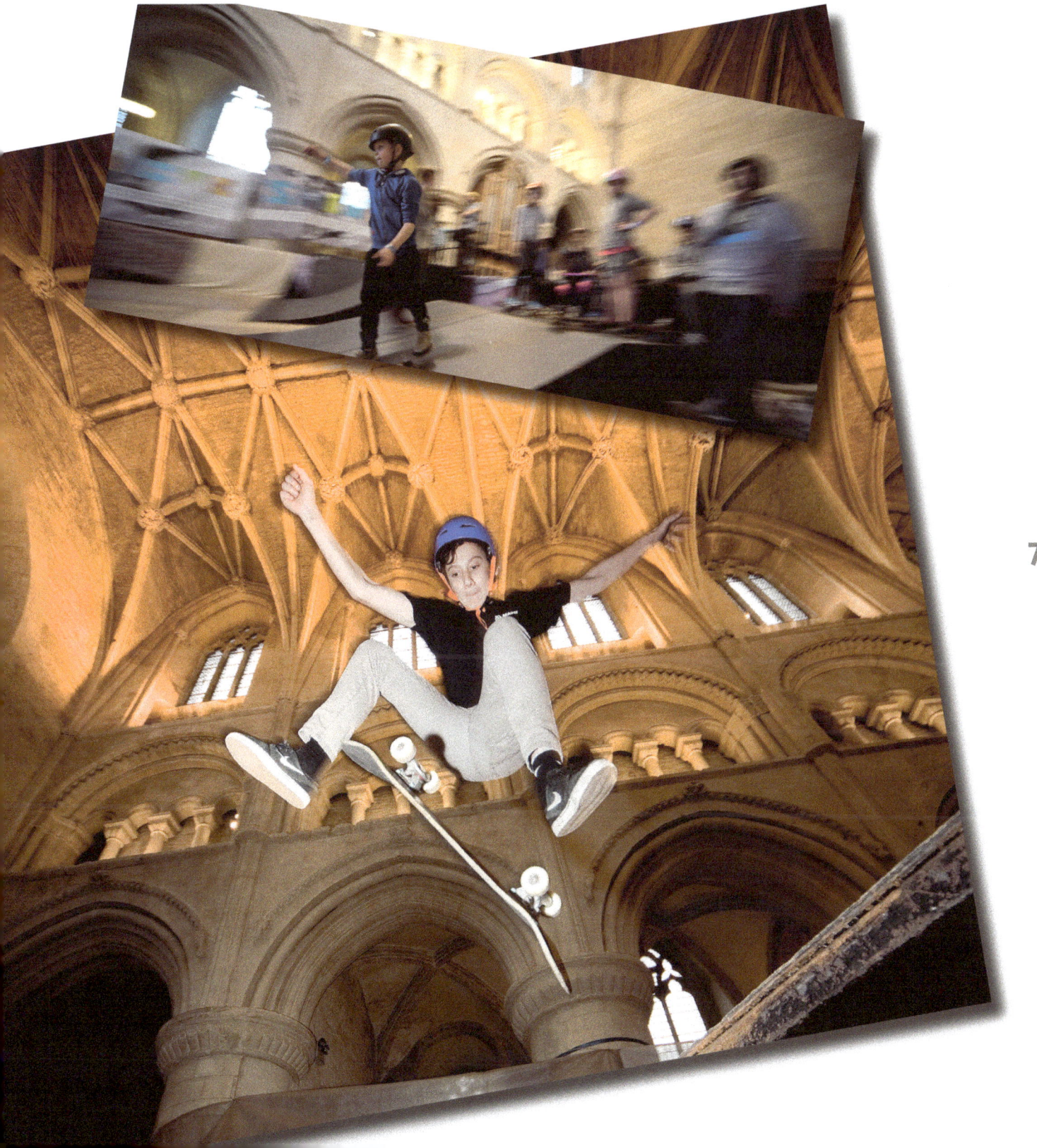

73

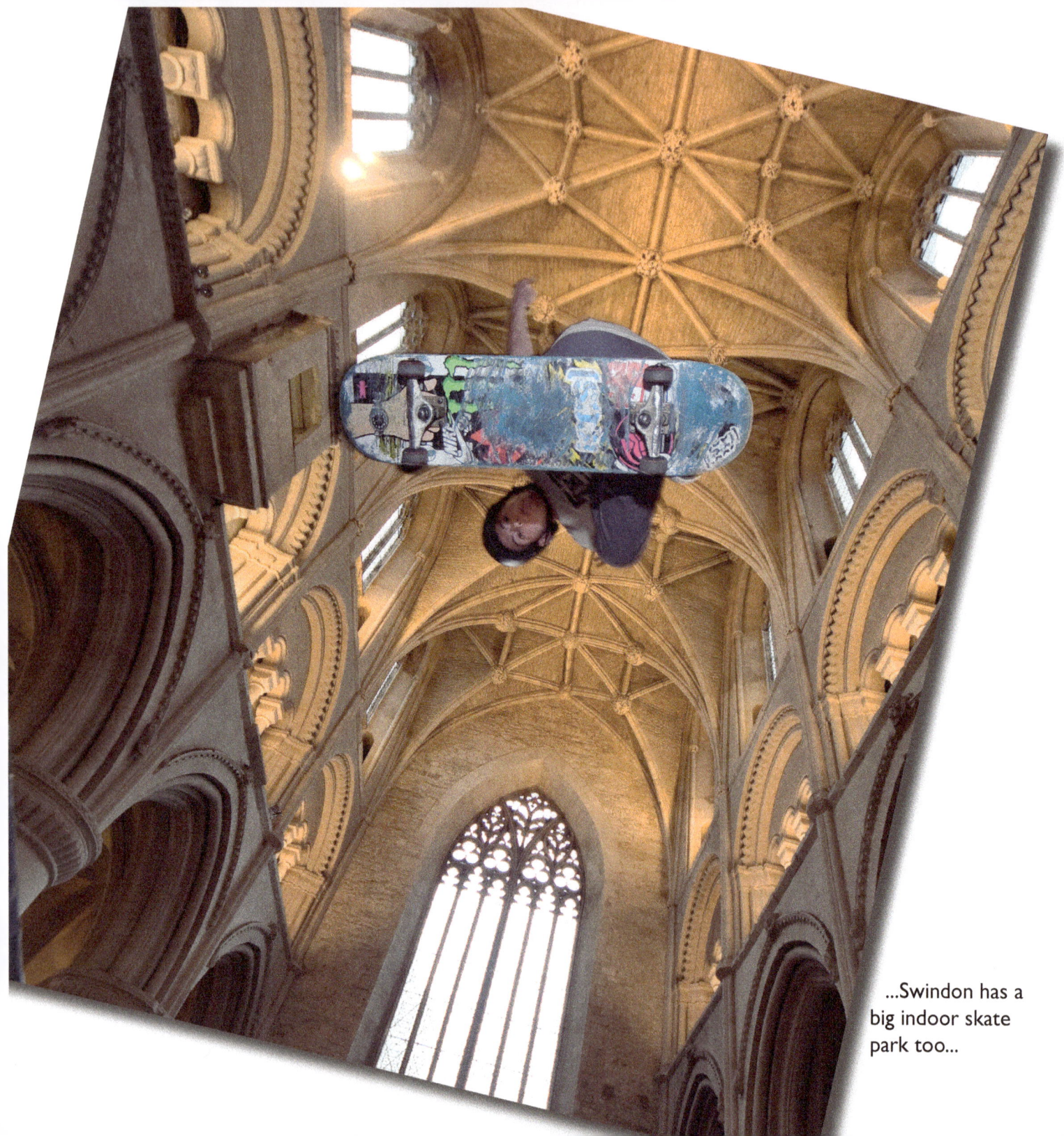

...Swindon has a big indoor skate park too...

...In the shadow of the Oasis on Hawksworth Industrial Estate exists a unit which houses a skate park, and is the magnet that draws skaters from far and wide to compete ...

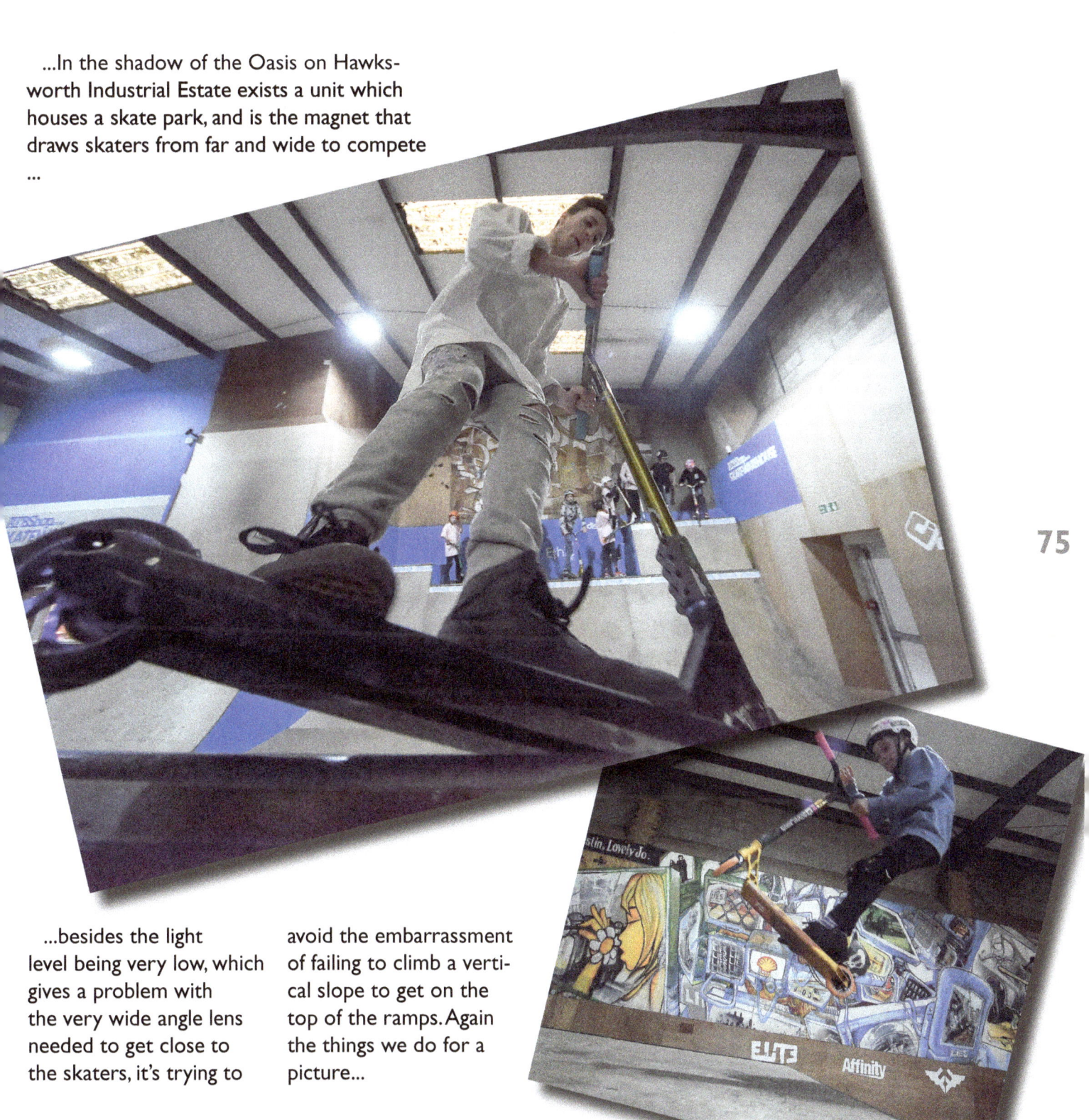

...besides the light level being very low, which gives a problem with the very wide angle lens needed to get close to the skaters, it's trying to avoid the embarrassment of failing to climb a vertical slope to get on the top of the ramps. Again the things we do for a picture...

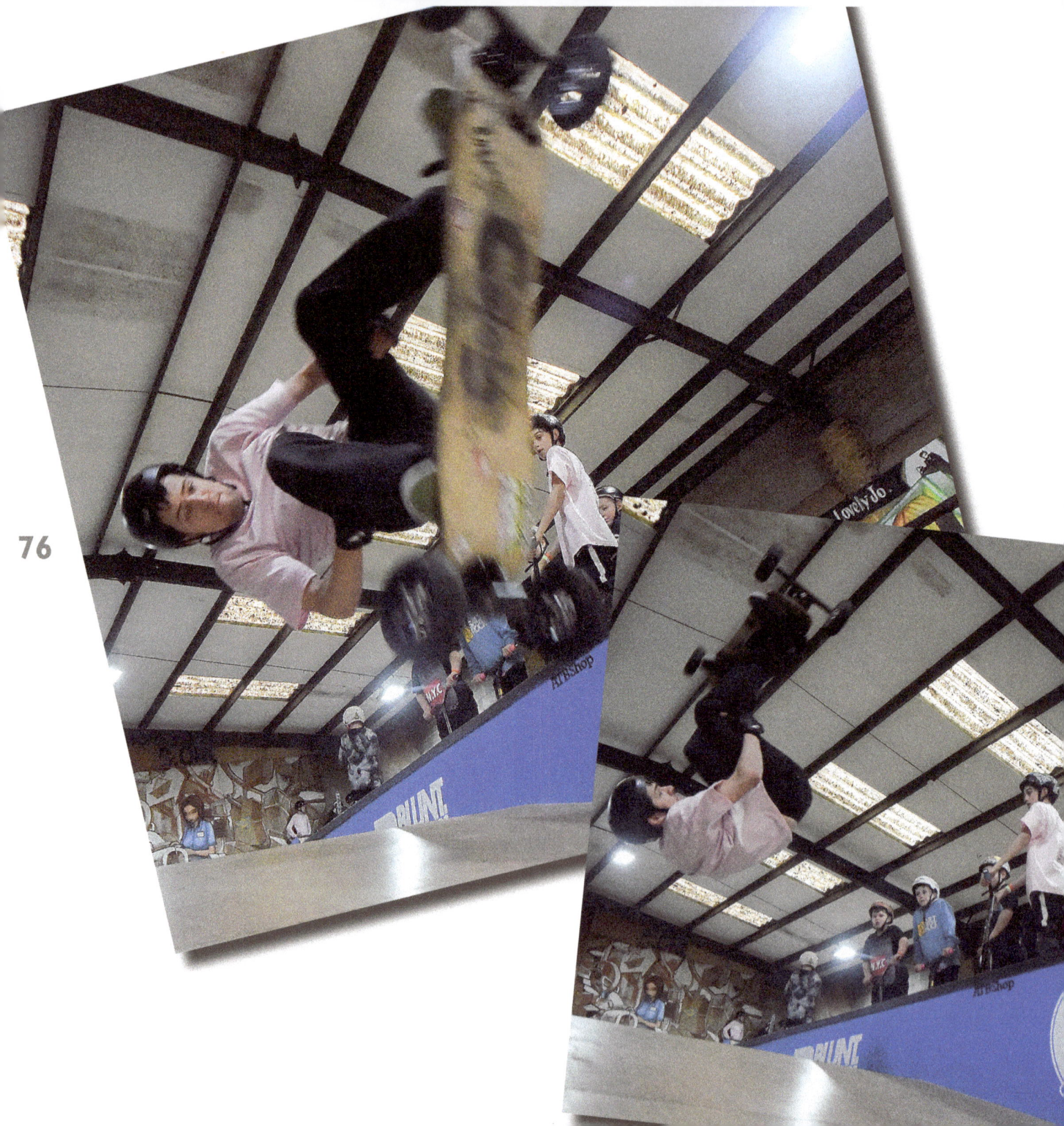

...Skateboarding has made the Olympics, and another off-beat sport Cheerleading will make an appearance at the 2028 games, but don't mention pom-poms to Swindon Lightning Cheerleaders, as cheerleading is a form of team gymnastics.

Competitive Cheerleading is a very athletic sport that does not involve pom-poms, unlike the American College sideline Cheer.

Cheerleading involves completing a high-energy, two and a half minute routine at competitions, and the Swindon Cheerleaders are good at it.

I first came across Swindon Cheerleaders at a community party in Faringdon Park in 2012, which was a modern-day re-creation of the annual Children's Fete of the Great Western Railway workers. It was originally held in the park during July, and the highlight was that every child gets a cake.

One of the displays was the Lightning Cheerleders who were flinging bodies in the air catching them, and then building pyramids. Clearing the taking of pictures with head coach Millie, I took a set of images of them in action...

...Cheerleading is a team-based sport that involves stunting, pyramids, baskets, tumbling, jumps and dance. It was initially started in the USA, and now it's the fastest growing sport in the UK. Why? Because it's fun!

"It's a mixture of stunts, tumbling from gymnastics, strength and conditioning, and flexibility; it's just a huge amalgam of Olympic sports," says the Head Coach Millie.

One has to be very careful photographing young children, and you have to make sure they are all cleared for photography before any pictures are taken. These days, release forms would have to be signed which makes press coverage very tricky as time is of the essence; and quite often we only have minutes to get pictures and move on...

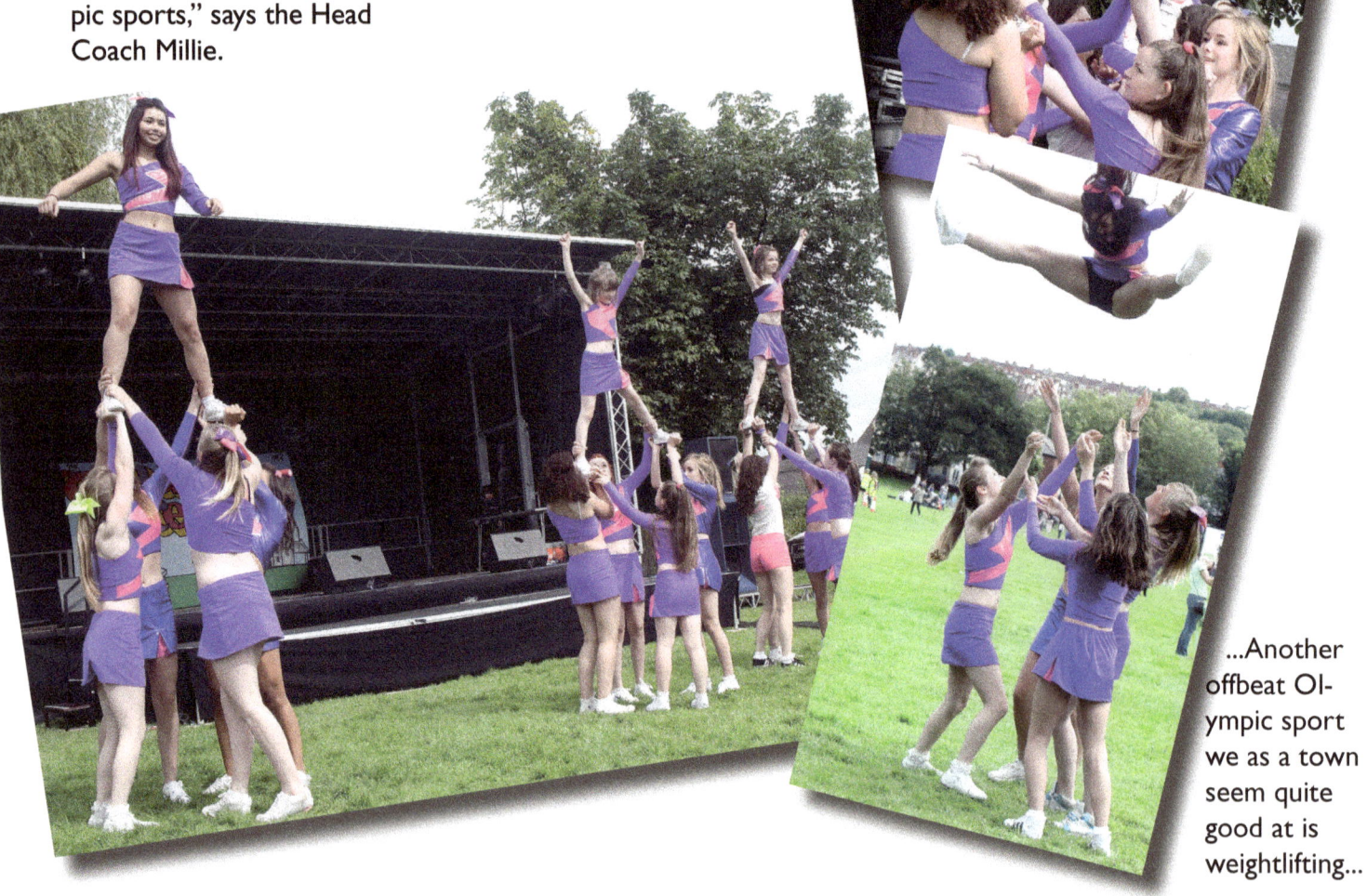

...Another offbeat Olympic sport we as a town seem quite good at is weightlifting...

...Swindon's Charlie Shotton-Gale is in the top echelons of the sport, with a number of championship wins behind her; but, as far back as the start of my career, weightlifting was popular in the town, with some top weight lifters based here...

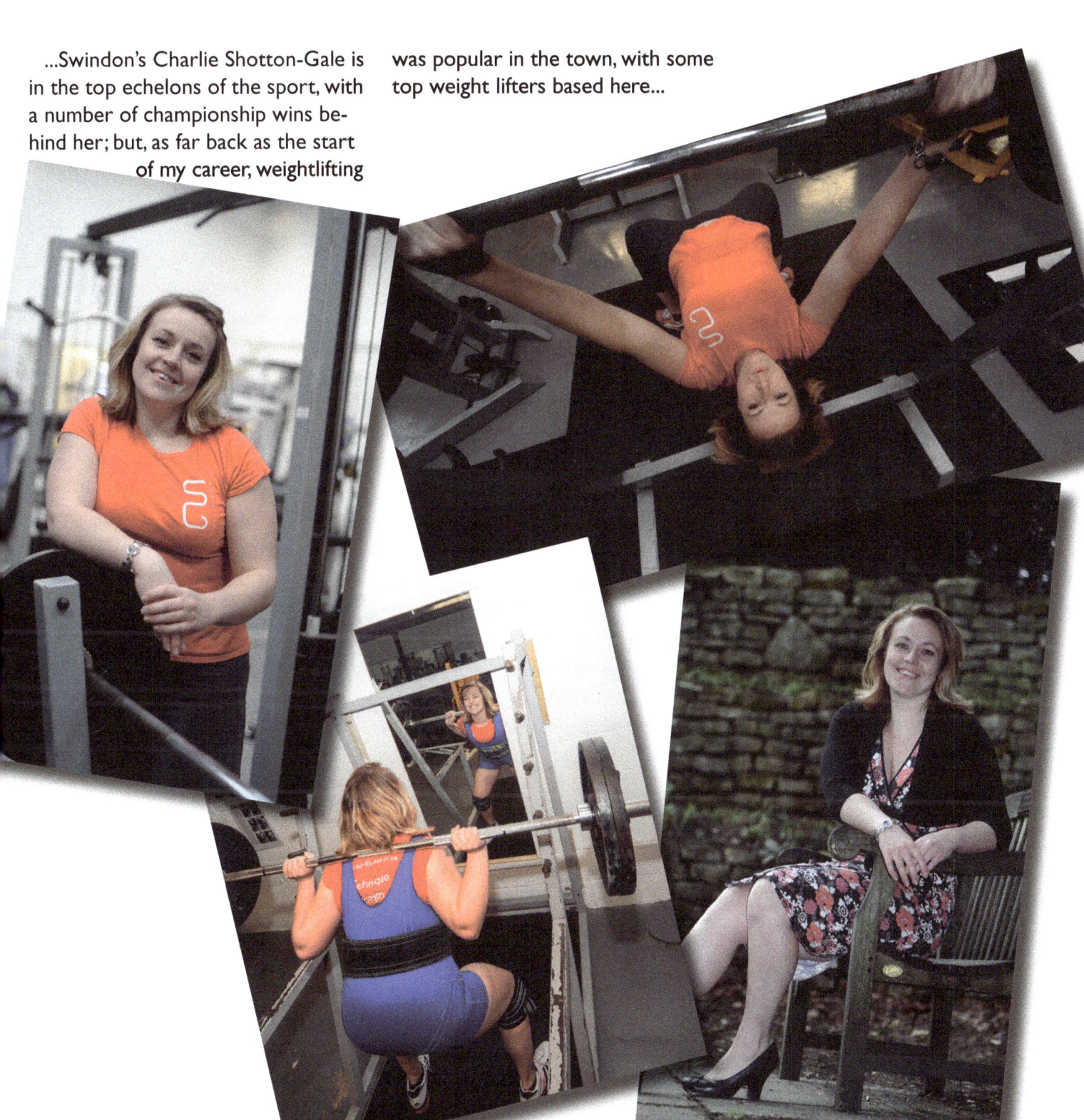

...The Brunel Gym, which was housed above what became Iceland food store in Havelock Square, was the centre of the weightlifting world in the early 1980ies, when Carol Bennett and Mark Barnes were champions in the Powerlifting world....

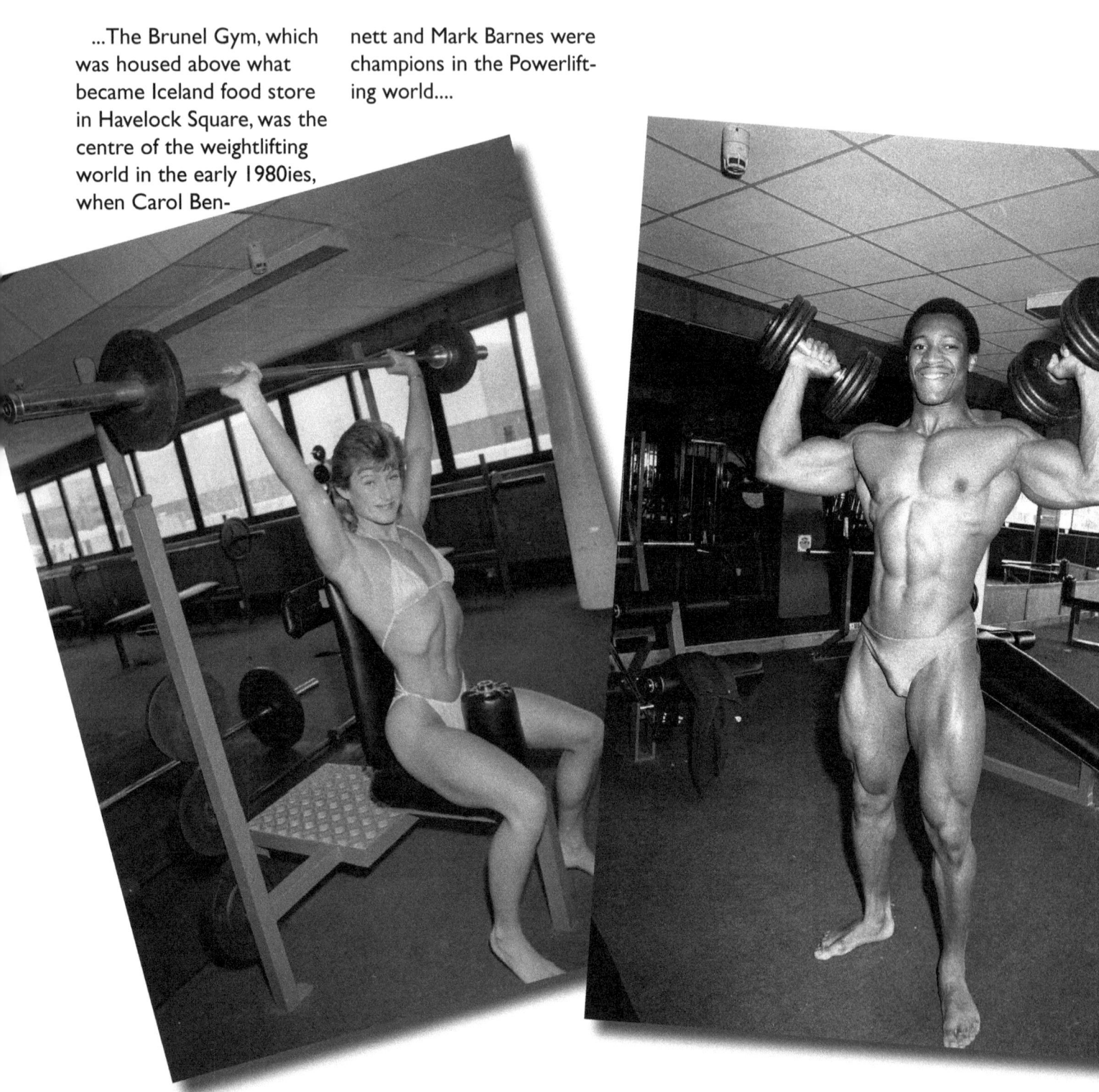

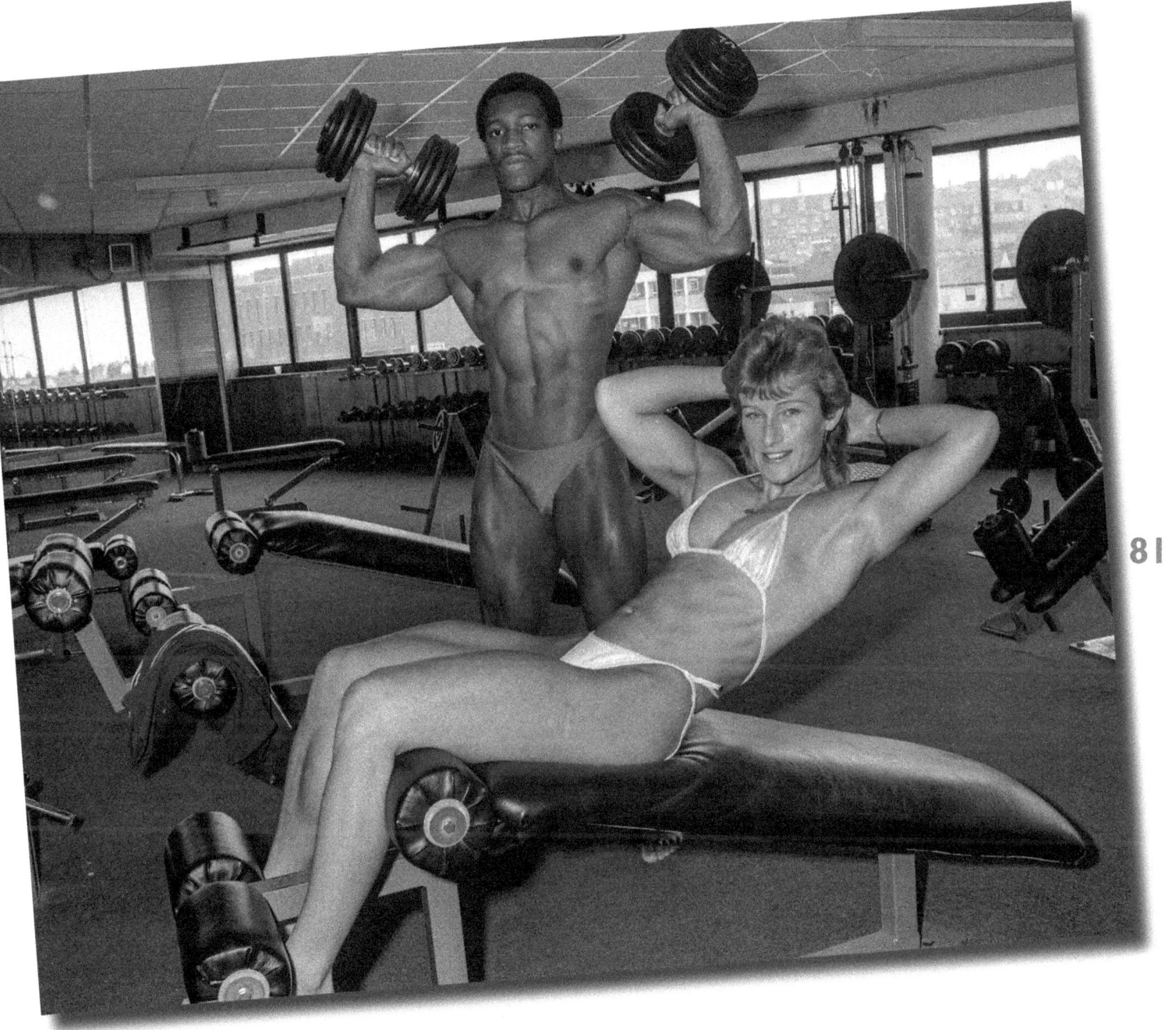

...Weightlifting and body building are synonymous with the world of boxing...

…Boxing to most is a violent sport, and photographing boxing is tricky, as the lighting could be described as violent too.

The square 20 foot ring, with three thick ropes that ring the square, is a problem as it's over three feet off the ground; but, to make things worse, the main source of light in most competitions is from above.

So, in photographic terms, what is the problem?

Because the ring surface is three feet off the deck, you have to shoot upward through the ropes which are about three feet in from the edge of the staging. You can't use a ladder as it obscures the view of the punters, and is dangerous if the boxers fall out of the ring where you are situated. Also, ladders are in a fixed point, at least temporarily, so moving is almost impossible.

These factors mean that your images are in silhouette and, if the lighting is uneven, the problem is even greater. To overcome back lighting there are two alternatives: flash and exposure compensation.

Flash is the obvious way out of the problem, but most events won't allow it as it distracts from the action, and anyway, I feel it kills the picture by taking away the ambience of the background and the surroundings.

Therefore, exposure compensation it is. This technique is where you fool the exposure metering on the camera into thinking the camera is set up differently from what it actually is; for example you tell it that you are on F11 when you are actually using F5.6…

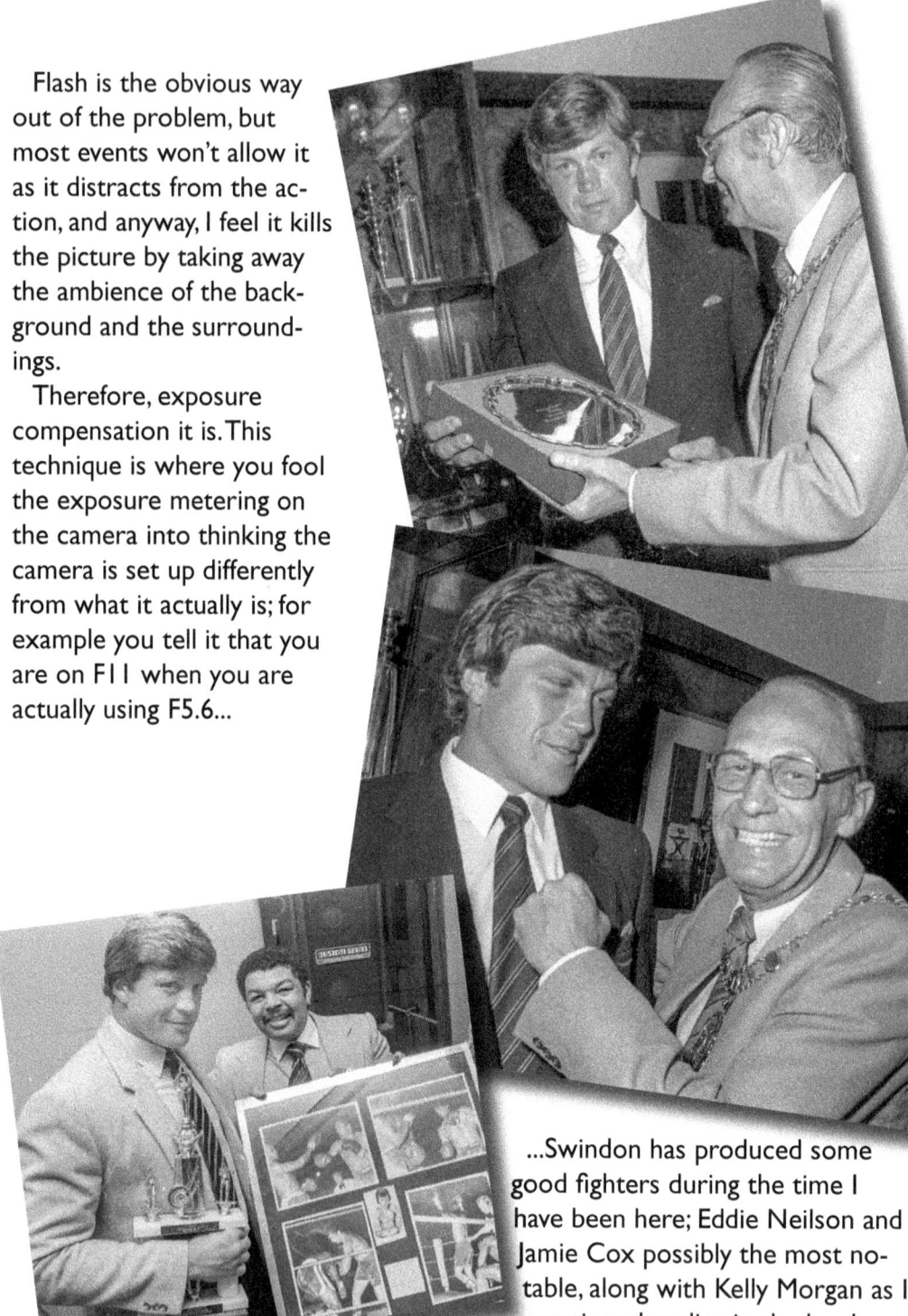

…Swindon has produced some good fighters during the time I have been here; Eddie Neilson and Jamie Cox possibly the most notable, along with Kelly Morgan as I mentioned earlier in the book…

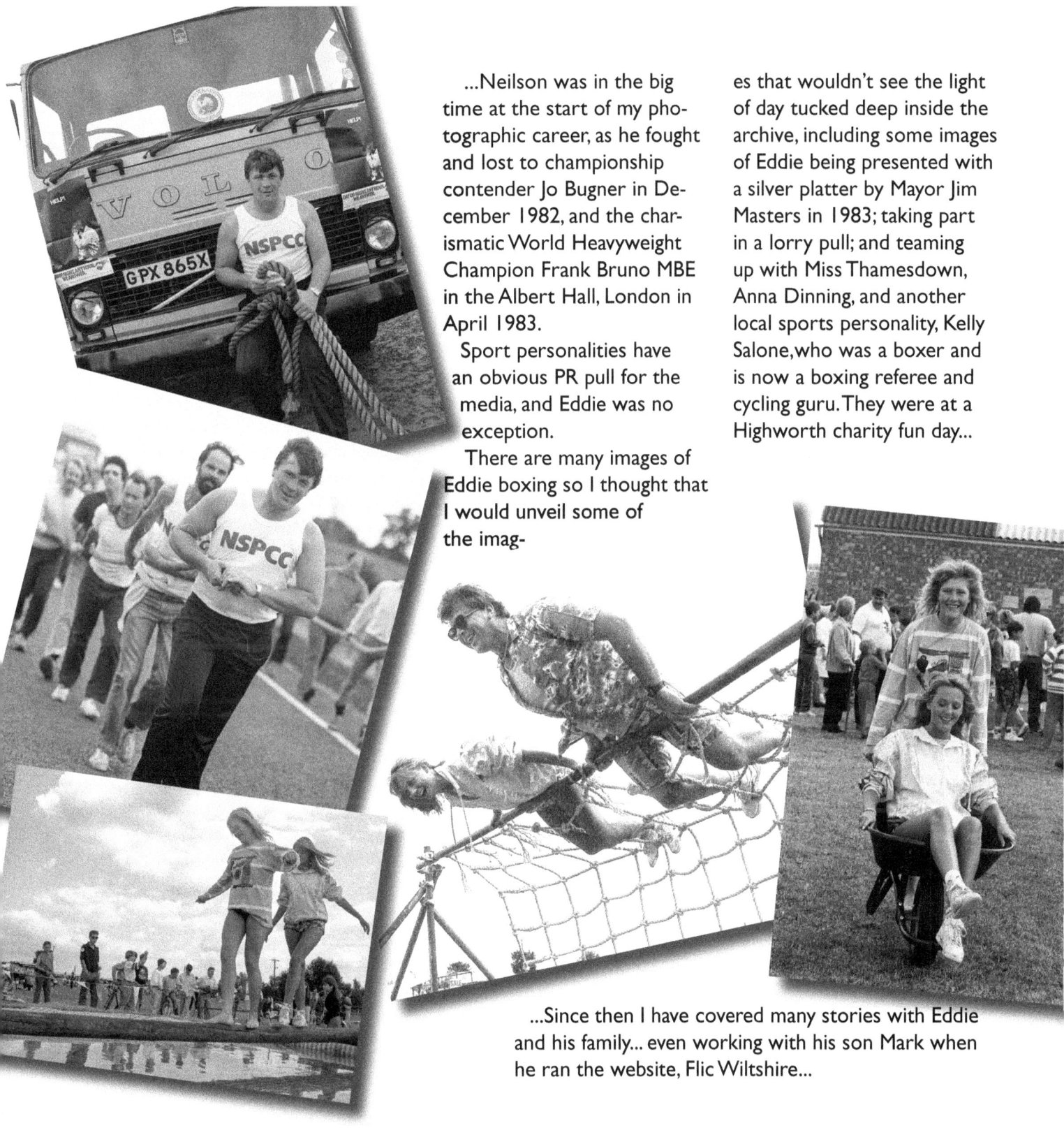

...Neilson was in the big time at the start of my photographic career, as he fought and lost to championship contender Jo Bugner in December 1982, and the charismatic World Heavyweight Champion Frank Bruno MBE in the Albert Hall, London in April 1983.

Sport personalities have an obvious PR pull for the media, and Eddie was no exception.

There are many images of Eddie boxing so I thought that I would unveil some of the images that wouldn't see the light of day tucked deep inside the archive, including some images of Eddie being presented with a silver platter by Mayor Jim Masters in 1983; taking part in a lorry pull; and teaming up with Miss Thamesdown, Anna Dinning, and another local sports personality, Kelly Salone, who was a boxer and is now a boxing referee and cycling guru. They were at a Highworth charity fun day...

...Since then I have covered many stories with Eddie and his family... even working with his son Mark when he ran the website, Flic Wiltshire...

...Another gym across in West Swindon is Scrappers Gym, who provide fitness for all.

As the name suggests, boxing is the main activity,

Their sessions include children's, young adults, and women-only boxing sessions; along with agility and fitness for all sessions, which are aimed at people with disabilities.

Scrappers also run monthly Women's Boxing Academy (WBA) sessions, and have recently set up a Scrappers Amateur Boxing Club (ABC)...

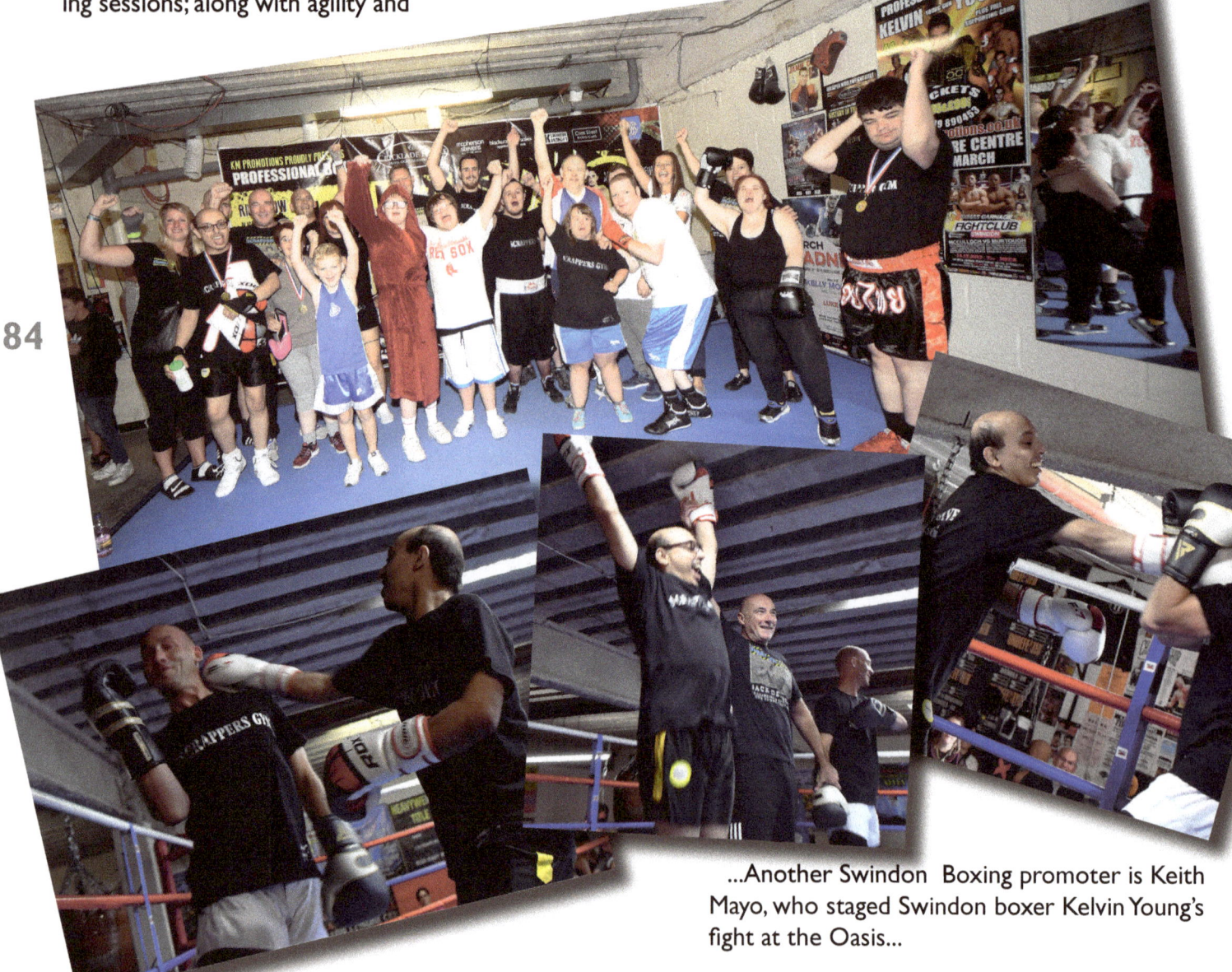

...Another Swindon Boxing promoter is Keith Mayo, who staged Swindon boxer Kelvin Young's fight at the Oasis...

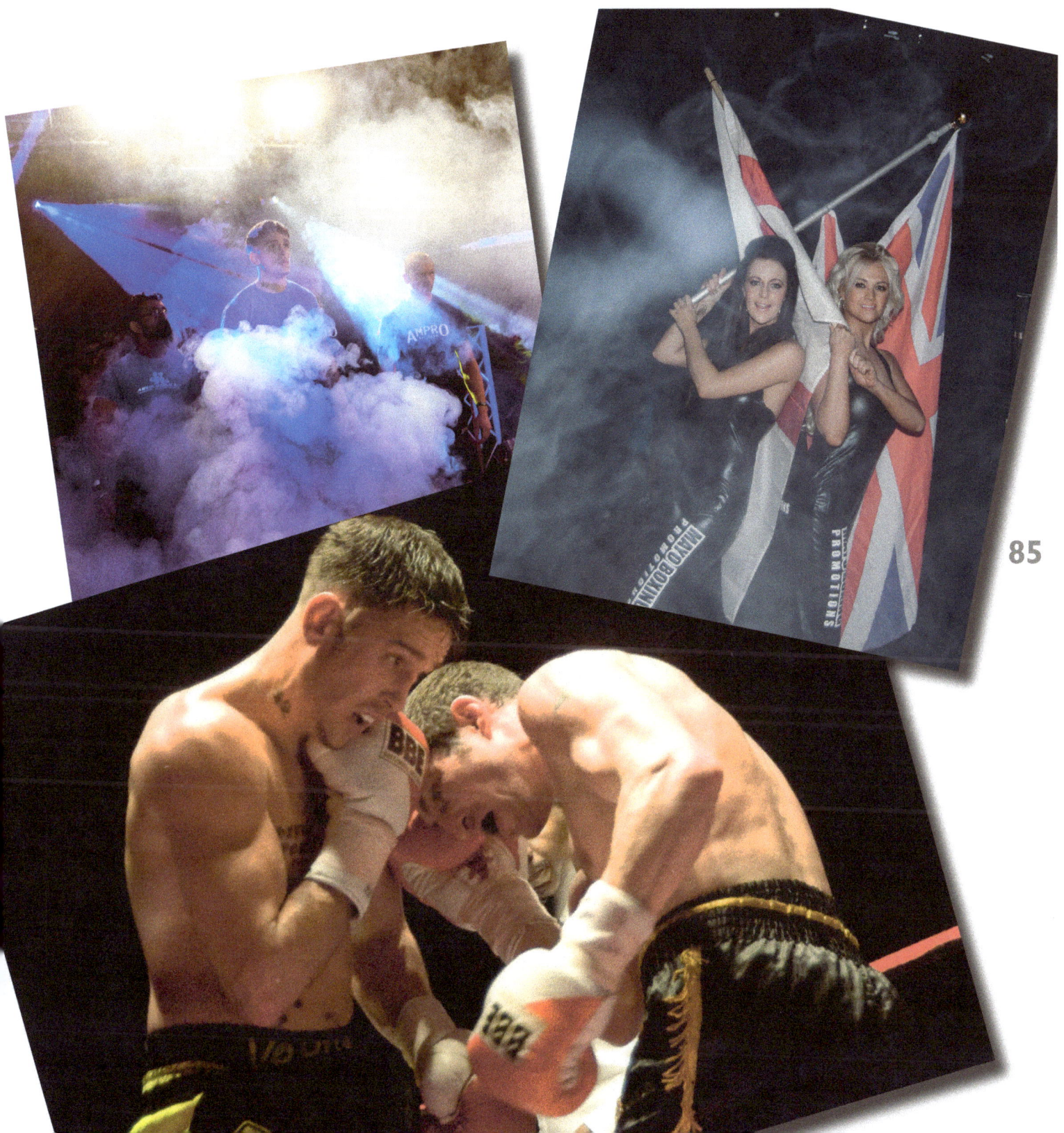

85

...Jamie Cox boxed for the Walcot ABA club in Swindon at Light Welterweight, winning the 2005 ABA championships, and he won gold for England in the 2006 Commonwealth Games in Melbourne. His walkover victory came when his opponent Moses Kopo of Lesotho pulled out of the final.

He returned to Swindon to fight at the Oasis in June 2013, where a full house saw him score a points victory over Frenchman Matiouze Royer...

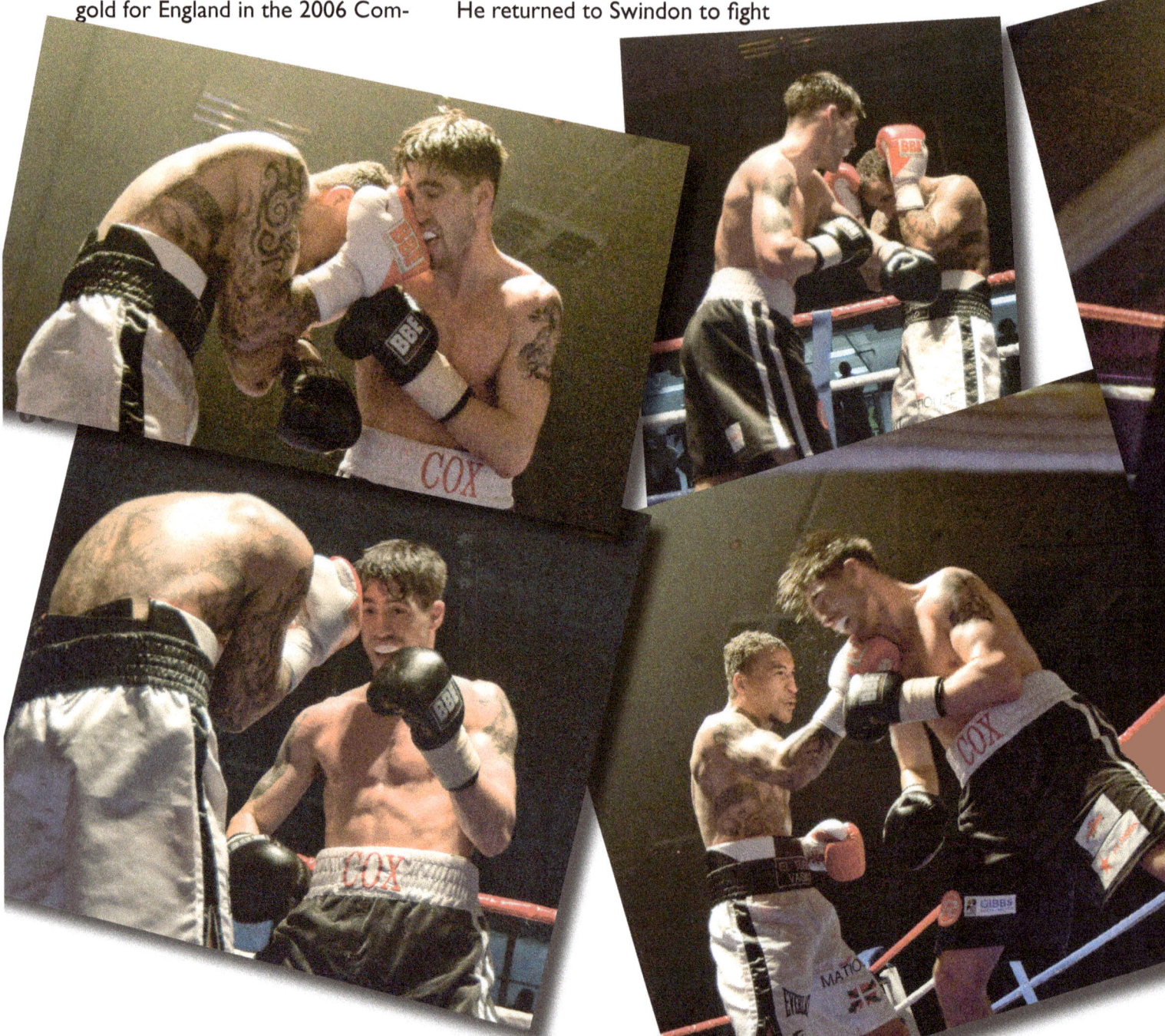

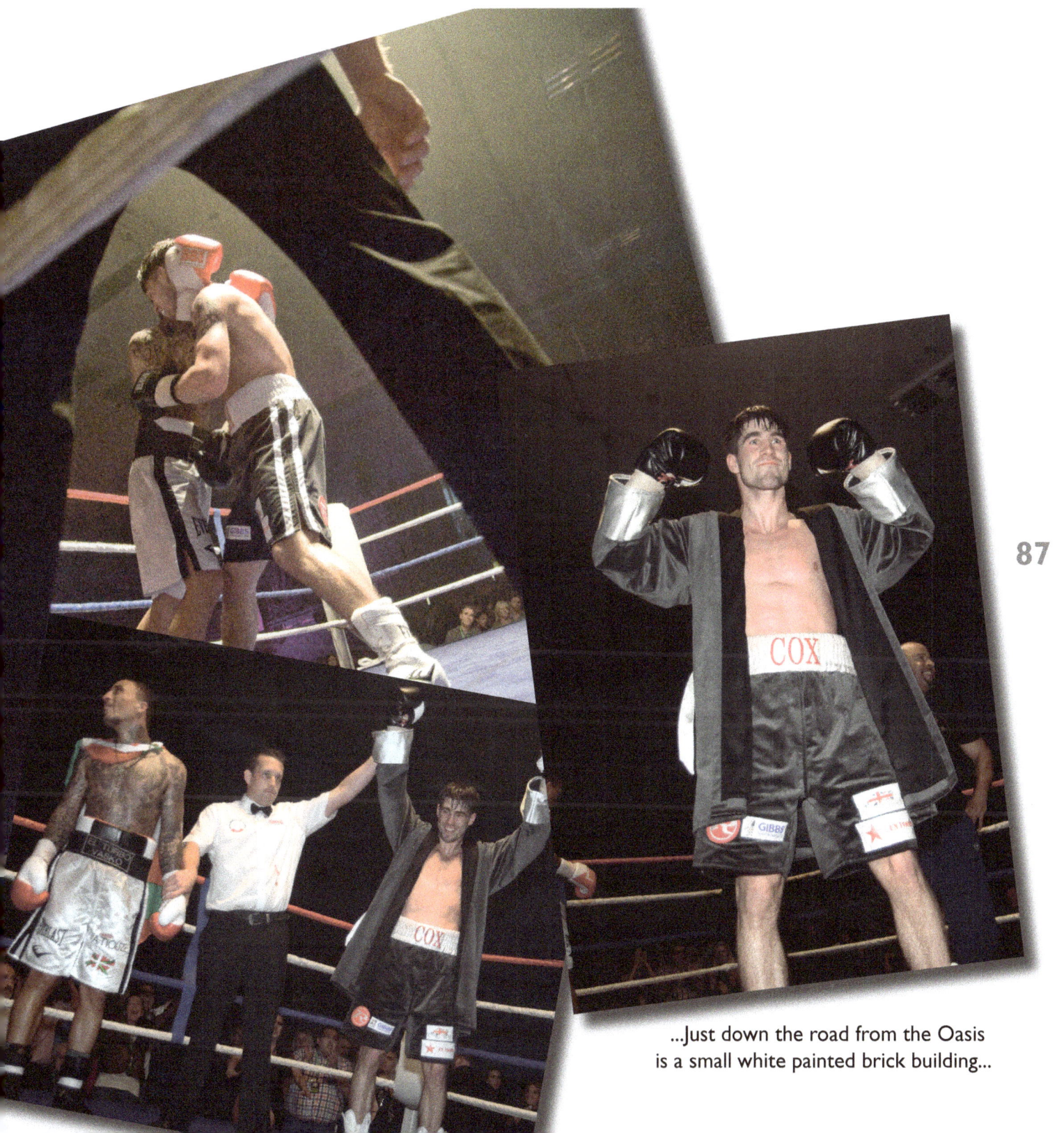

...Just down the road from the Oasis is a small white painted brick building...

...The road side frontage is marked up as Paddy Fitzpatrick's Boxing Gym.

The building is Tardis-like, as it stretches back from Ferndale Road, encompassing a boxing gymnasium complex.

Paddy trained Jamie Cox, but is better known for his association with World Super Middleweight title holder George Groves, who he brought to Swindon's Sun Inn at Coate Water in the build-up to his fight with Carl Froch at Wembley.

In 2017, Groves knocked out Jamie Cox in the fourth round at Wembley Arena.

Paddy's autobiography *Hats, Handwraps and Headaches: A Life on the Inside of Boxing*, took centre stage during the 2015 Swindon Festival of Literature at the Arts Centre on Devizes Road, where he was interviewed by Anna Whitwham and Festival Director Matt Holland...

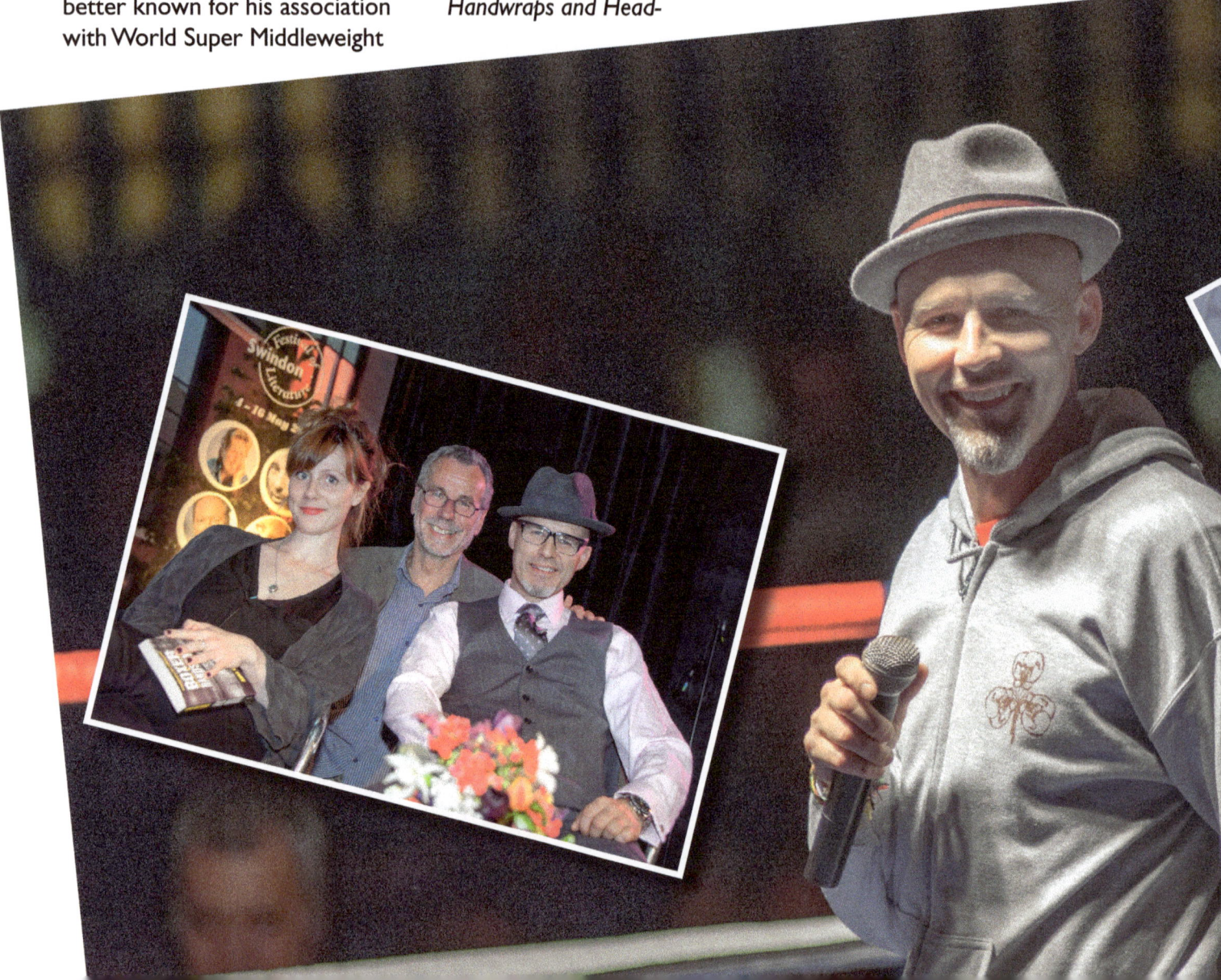

...The Festival Chronicle is the blog about the Festival of Literature, and it records that Paddy didn't talk about strength or force. He talked about Composure - a lot - and The Art. And repetition – not practice – doing the same thing over and over. Study your opponent, think during training, so when the boxer steps into the ring he (or she) reacts, adjusts and reacts. Think in the ring and the fight is lost. Don't think before the fight and you have lost. The winner is the one who distracts his opponent.

"You still feel pain. You still feel nervous. You learn to act differently," Paddy explains, in answer to a question from the floor.

Paddy has mixed with the kings of the sport and, during a spell training boxers in Las Vegas, he entered the court of the Greatest, Muhammad Ali.

"Ali was cool to know because he was just good fun and never made you feel like he was important.

"With Laila there would be one time of the day when she'd look exactly like him; she'd put on her headgear, stretch her mouth open ready for the gumshield just as you're putting it on and you'd see: Ali!" he said in an interview with the *Sportsman*.

"As a fighter, she's really, really stubborn, really, really driven and gives 100% and you always knew on fight night she would show up - and you can't say that about everybody"....

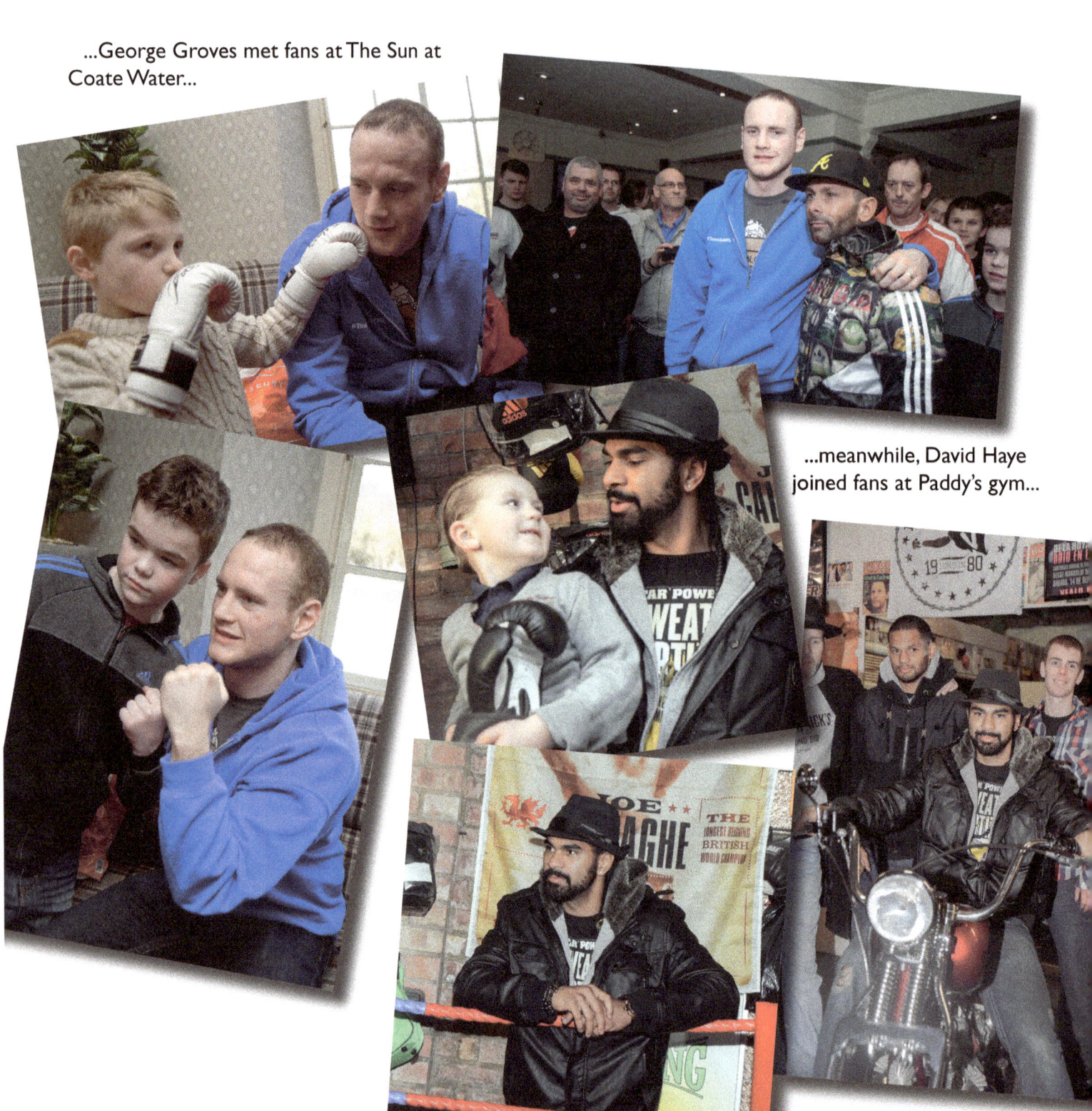

...George Groves met fans at The Sun at Coate Water...

...meanwhile, David Haye joined fans at Paddy's gym...

...Superstars of the boxing ring, David Haye and George Groves, were special guests at Paddy Fitzpatrick's new amateur show, and made a special appearance at the 16-fight card at Swindon's Oasis Leisure Centre in 2012; where spectators saw some of the finest fighters from Swindon...

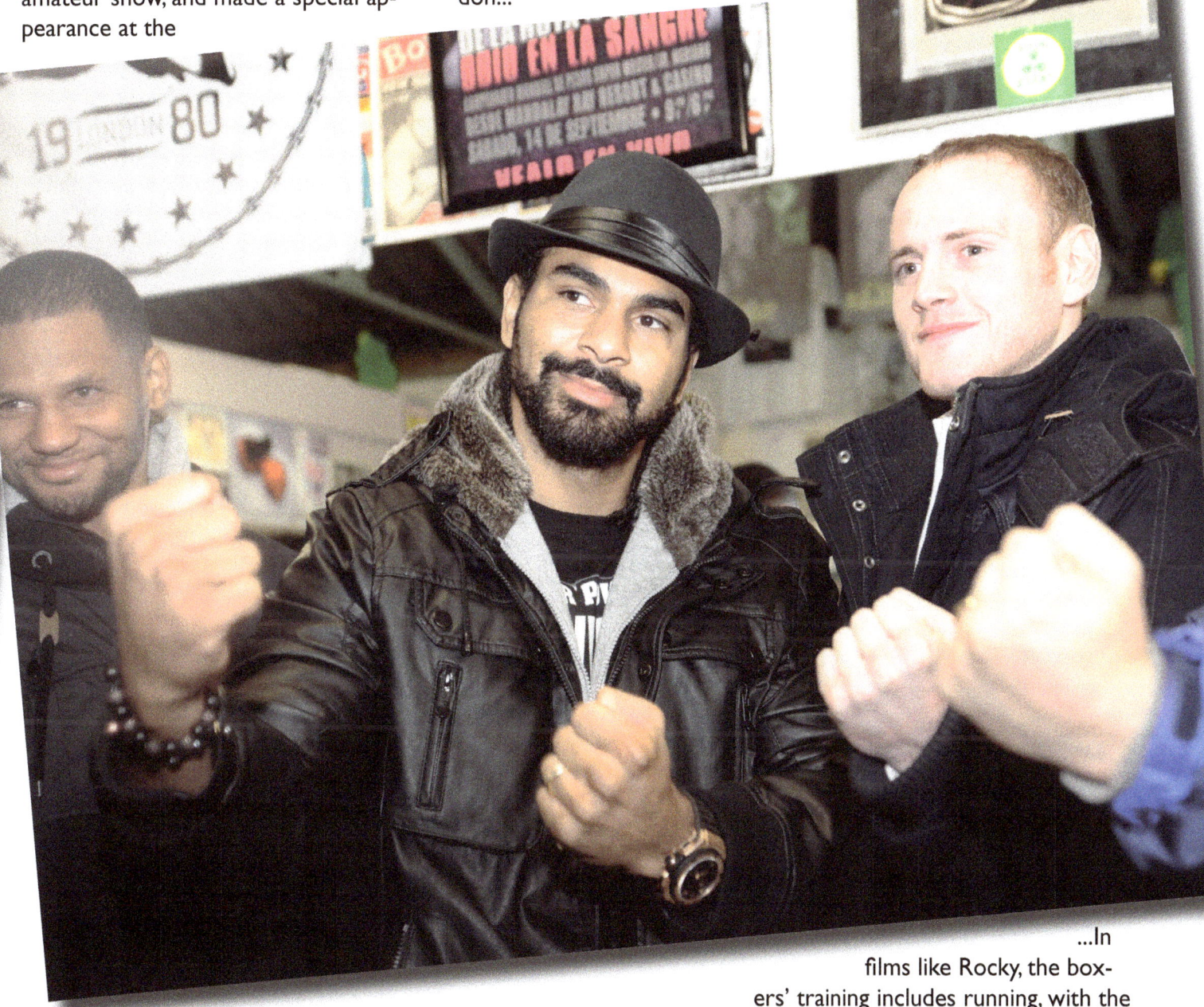

...In films like Rocky, the boxers' training includes running, with the coach on a bike alongside the star...

...Which brings me on to another major event in the Swindon sporting calendar; the Swindon Half Marathon...

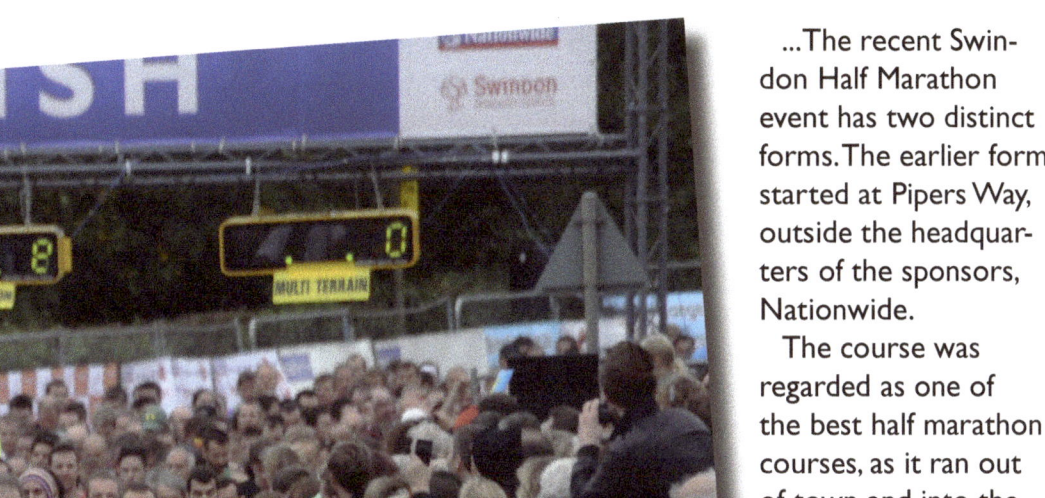

...The recent Swindon Half Marathon event has two distinct forms. The earlier form started at Pipers Way, outside the headquarters of the sponsors, Nationwide.

The course was regarded as one of the best half marathon courses, as it ran out of town and into the rolling Marlborough Downs, finishing with an uphill section, before a steep descent to the finish back in Pipers Way.

That course proved to be too expensive to organise, as many roads had to be shut.

The second incarnation starts at the County Ground car park and takes in many of the town's roads as well as using cycle ways and footpaths, finishing in Commercial Road and Wharf Green.

Swindon, being hilly, gives the runners a good challenge without having the expense of shutting down a chunk of North Wiltshire in the process...

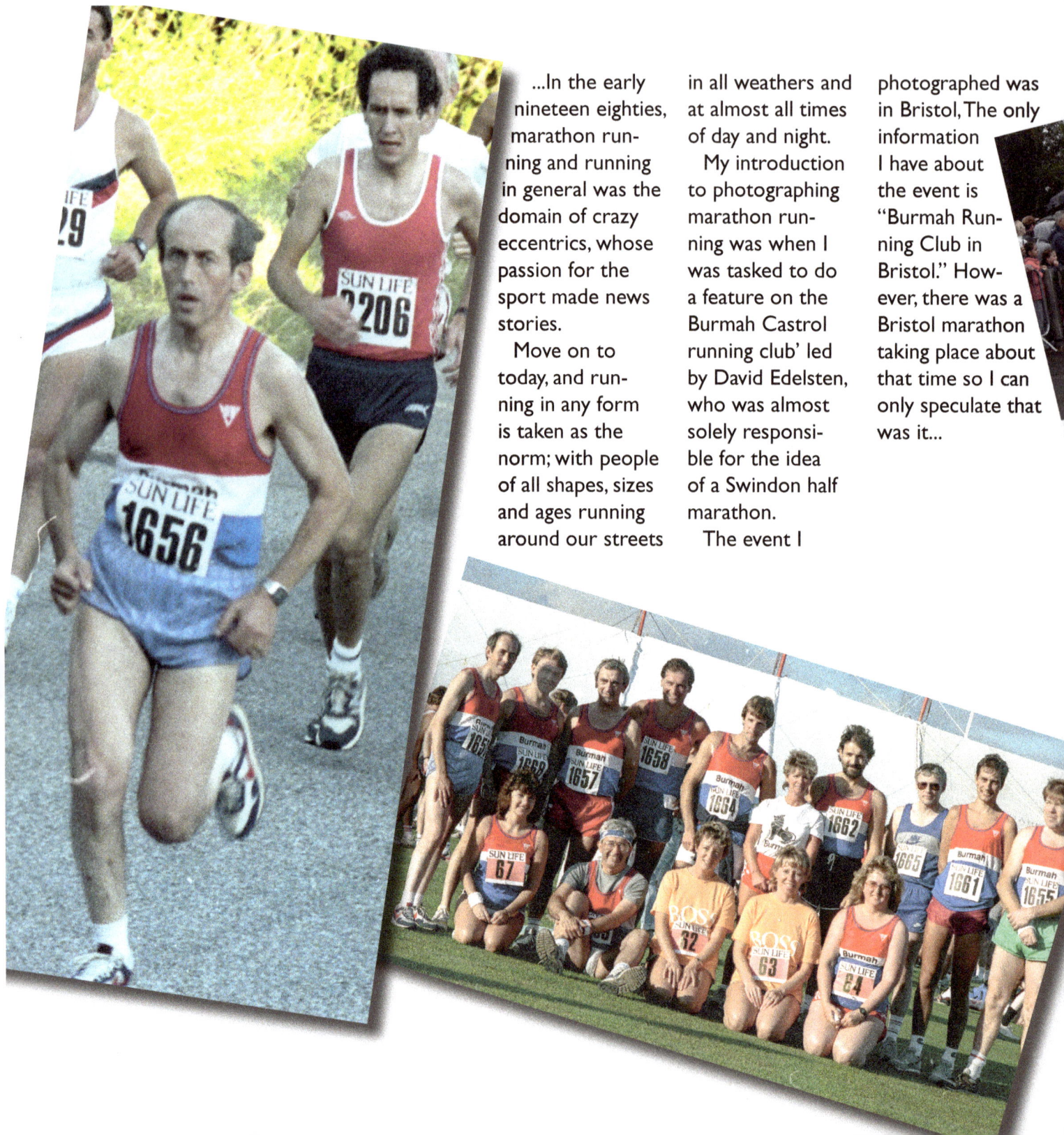

...In the early nineteen eighties, marathon running and running in general was the domain of crazy eccentrics, whose passion for the sport made news stories.

Move on to today, and running in any form is taken as the norm; with people of all shapes, sizes and ages running around our streets in all weathers and at almost all times of day and night.

My introduction to photographing marathon running was when I was tasked to do a feature on the Burmah Castrol running club' led by David Edelsten, who was almost solely responsible for the idea of a Swindon half marathon.

The event I photographed was in Bristol, The only information I have about the event is "Burmah Running Club in Bristol." However, there was a Bristol marathon taking place about that time so I can only speculate that was it...

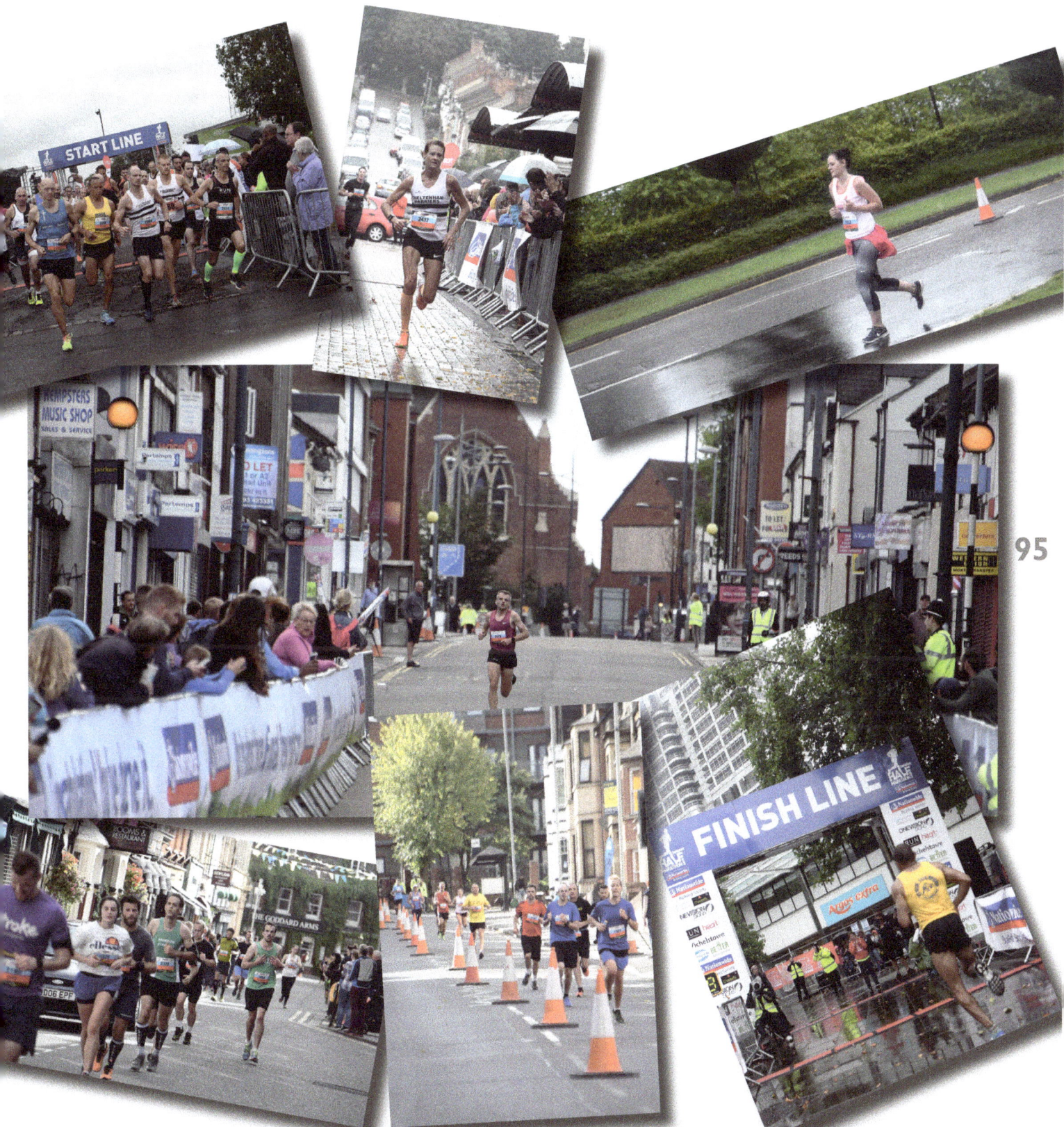

...One event in the running calendar happens every week, as thousands across the country, in fact all over the world, wake up early at the weekend to take part in hundreds of Parkruns.

In the UK alone there are (at the time of writing this book) 1080 events in over 700 locations...

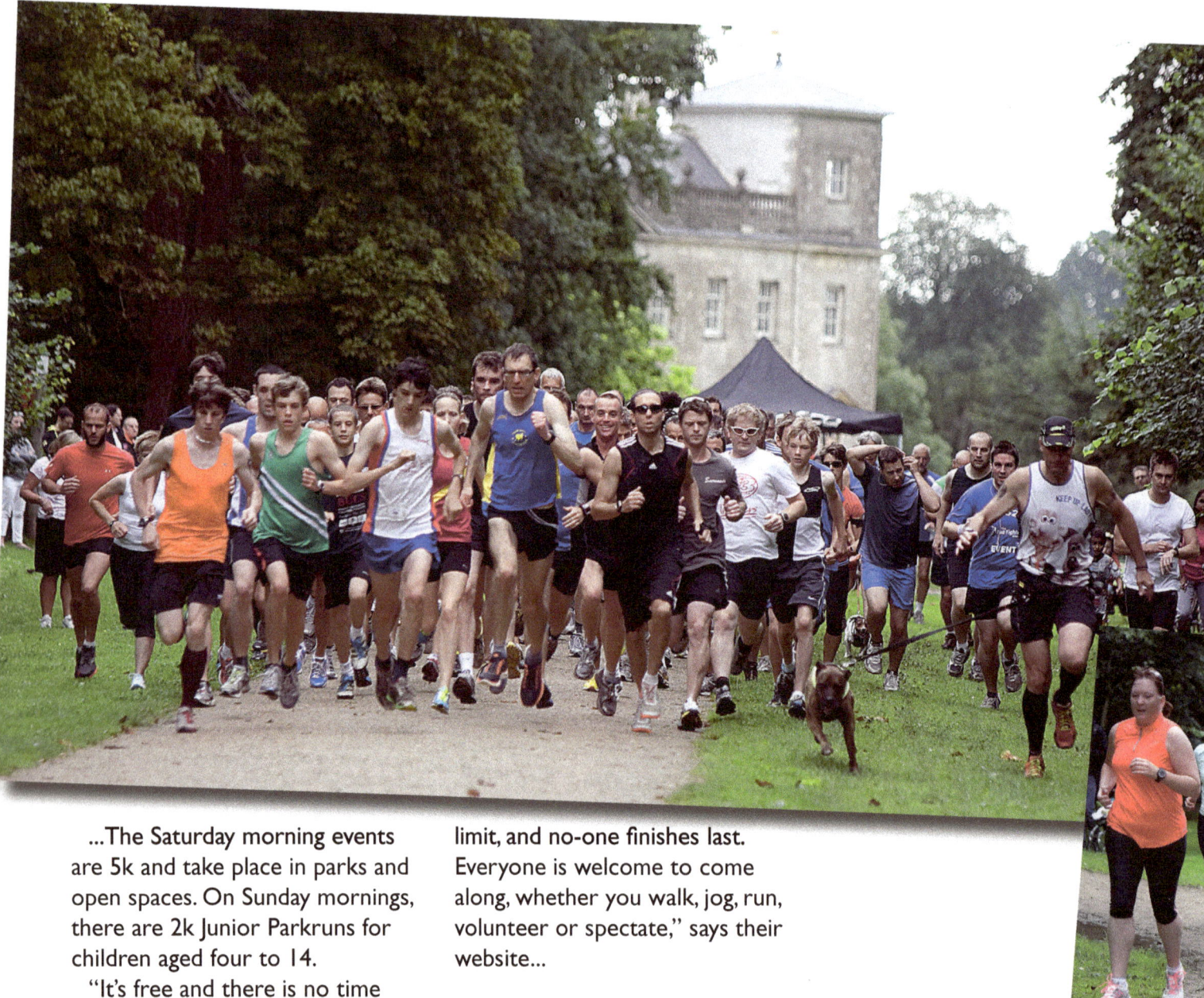

...The Saturday morning events are 5k and take place in parks and open spaces. On Sunday mornings, there are 2k Junior Parkruns for children aged four to 14.

"It's free and there is no time limit, and no-one finishes last. Everyone is welcome to come along, whether you walk, jog, run, volunteer or spectate," says their website...

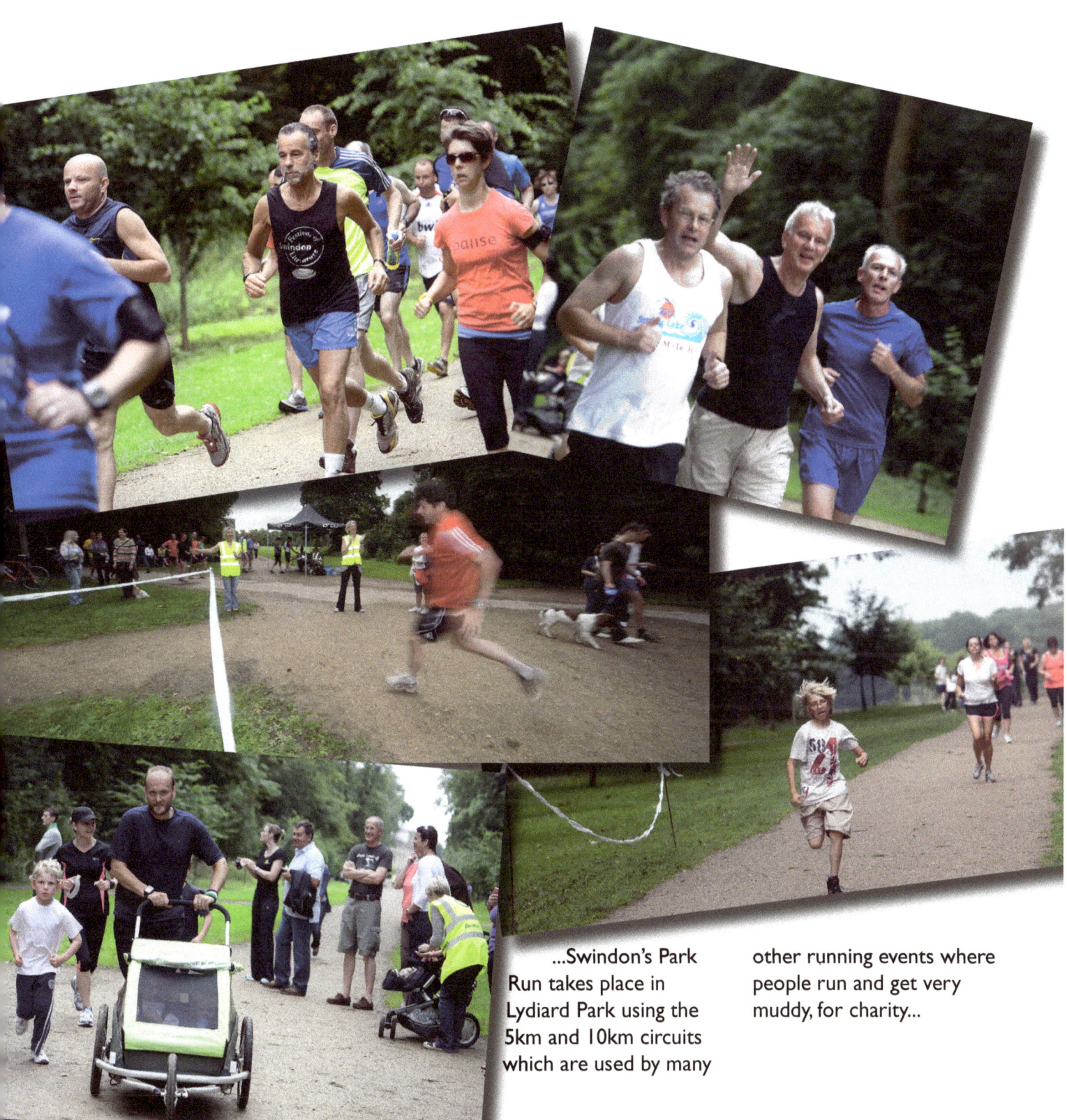

...Swindon's Park Run takes place in Lydiard Park using the 5km and 10km circuits which are used by many other running events where people run and get very muddy, for charity...

...and dress up in funny costumes...

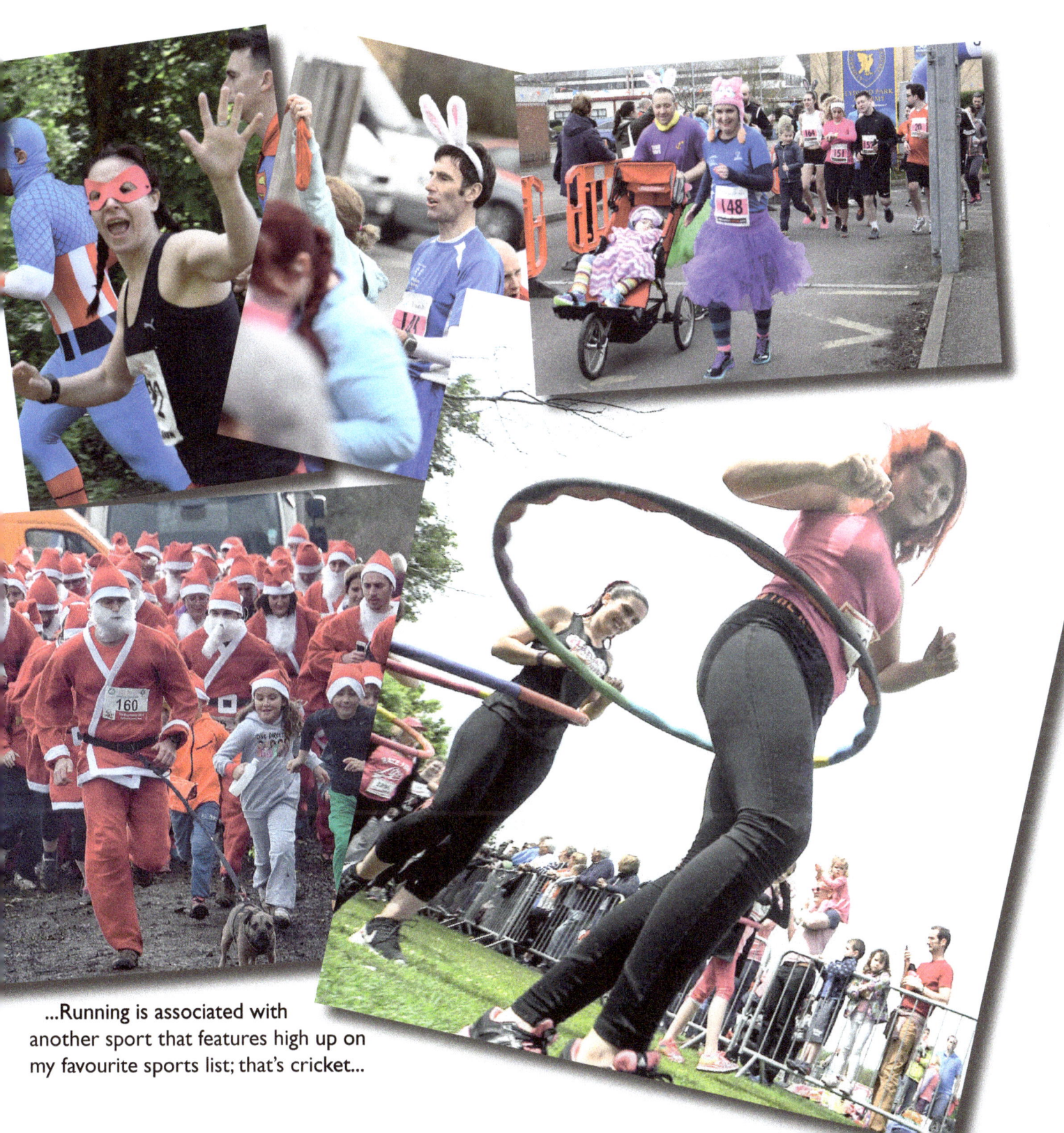

...Running is associated with another sport that features high up on my favourite sports list; that's cricket...

...Buried deep in the archive, while I was looking for sports for this tome, I came across a set of negatives in the 1983 file: Wiltshire v. Northamptonshire in the Nat West Trophy at the County Ground. That's the Cricket County Ground, just over the fence from the football stadium.

I don't remember the match, so I had to research the game using that infamous search engine. The Northamptonshire squad came up first and in it was a name synonymous with the best in the sport; the legendary Indian bowler batsman; Kapil Dev.

As the display of scanned pictures came up, there was Kapil Dev walking back to the pavilion. I tracked the black and white grainy images back a few frames and discovered one of him at the crease, as if he is being stumped.

Another reference on the search engine produced the scorecard which showed:

Kapil Dev bowled Barnes 18, so not a stumping then.

Who was Terry Barnes?

Lincolnshire born Barnes was a left-handed batsman who bowled left-arm medium pace. He started his career in the Minor Counties with Lincolnshire, and played for several other counties before joining Wiltshire in 1983.

It is recorded in the online encyclopedia that he played a total of nine List A matches for four different teams. In those nine matches, he scored 14 runs at a batting average of 4.66 and a high score of 13. With the ball he took 8 wickets at a bowling average of 50.00, with best figures of 2/95. One of those wickets was the great Kapil Dev....

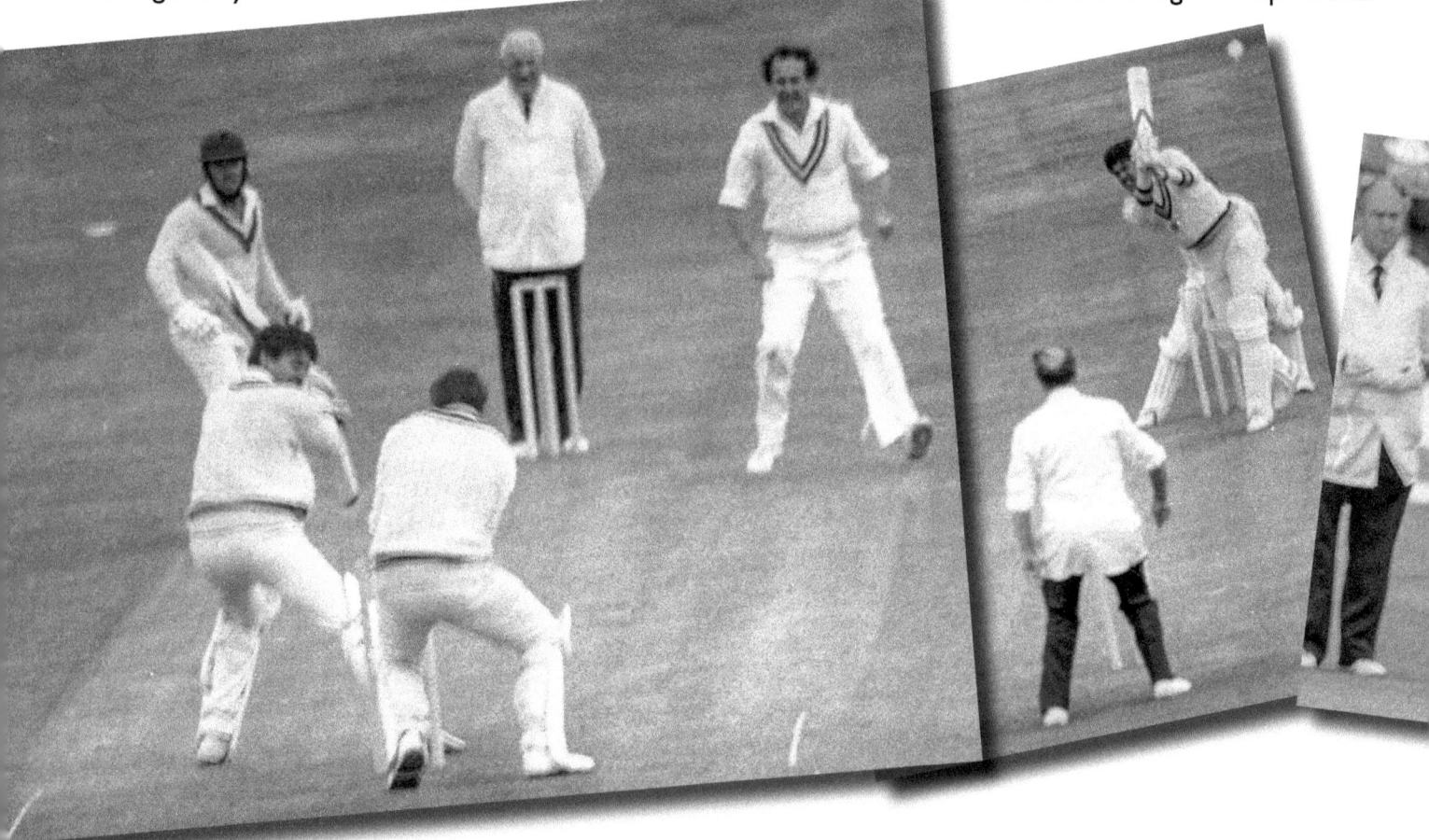

...Taking pictures of cricket requires a lot of patience, but you also need some specialist kit to do it successfully.

In the early days, when these images were taken, I didn't have the luxury of expensive long lenses, and was using a 500mm mirror lens which was cheap and fairly effective. There are several snags with using a mirror lens; first is that you are limited to a fixed F stop which is usually F/8, and secondly the focusing has to be absolutely spot on.

So what is a mirror lens?

The mirror lens, is also known as reflex or catadioptric lens, and was very popular in the 1970s and '80s, but now they have been replaced by modern conventional optics.

Telephoto mirror lenses were regarded as cool to own, because they were much more compact and much cheaper than the conventional telephoto lenses of the time, and are now much less common, although a couple of manufacturers make 300mm F/6.3 designs for certain cameras.

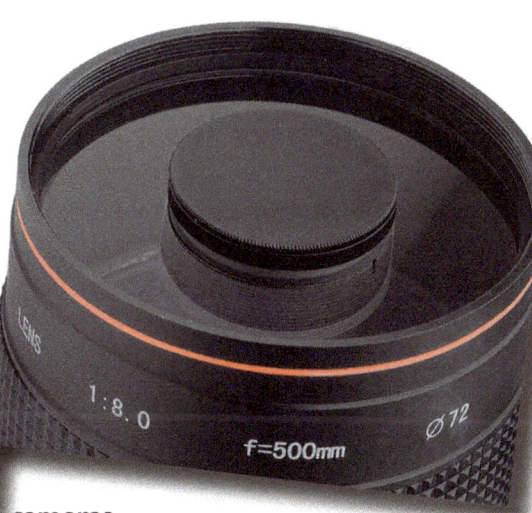

The basic design has been around for over 200 years and was originally developed for telescopes, as conventional refracting telephoto optics are inherently very long and heavy.

However, by using an arrangement of curved mirrors, an optically long telephoto lens could be fitted into a short space. Because the design uses both mirrors (catoptrics) and refracting optics (dioptrics) it means that lenses of this type are known as catadioptric, and often referred to as 'CAT's'

For the mirror aspect of the optics to work, you have to block the central area of the optical path to accommodate the secondary mirror.

You don't notice this in focused details; but contrasty, out-of-focus areas exhibit ring-like or 'doughnut' features, making the aesthetic quality of the blur produced in out-of-focus parts of an image, or bokeh, distracting.

Then, compared to a good conventional refracting lens design, you will notice lower contrast and sharpness.

As normal lenses are now quite cheap and light, with their computer-designed optics getting better with every change of design, the mirror lens fails to impress modern snappers.

Nevertheless, a bit like film cameras, there is some renewed interest in mirror lenses thanks to their affordability as used bargains, and because of their odd but distinctive characteristics...

...As we have heroes, so we have anti-heroes. This is a "not quite what it seems" story.

It's a story that shook the Scottish footballing world to its roots, and Swindon played a very significant role in the saga of the Hearts of Midlothian Football Club's attempt to take over Edinburgh rivals Hibernian Football Club.

My solicitor in 1989 was an enigmatic thirty-something Scotsman, who I had photographed with his car number plate HIBS 1 outside his office in Commercial Road.

He was described in a feature in the Scotsman newspaper as a product of the era, though there was a confusing twist. He was a Thatcherite, a Yuppie and, he says now, a socialist. He was also a trained pilot.

The solicitor was David Duff, who in 1987 bought the Edinburgh club he supported from the terraces as a lad, Hibernian; whose ground was at Easter Road in the east of the city.

I was invited to go to Easter Road to photograph a game and partake of the luxuries of the Directors Box, and eventually I took up the offer and made arrangements to fly to Edinburgh with David and his assistant Lynda Hobbs for the Hibs v Aberdeen mid-week match.

I booked a flight on British Airways to Turnhouse airport, and a room in the Post House in the Town Centre. My long-suffering wife was very sceptical, but reluctantly agreed, saying that I would never recoup the expense, but hey-ho.

On landing at Edinburgh, we went over to the flying school at the airport where David showed me the plane he was learning to fly, which I later found was part of his therapy to overcome the fear of flying. His dedication to the club was described, in a feature which I illustrated, as warranting a place in the *Guinness Book of Records* as soccer's most travelled fanatic.

The match was played in typical Scottish weather; and, at the half time break, I enjoyed the warmth and refreshments offered in the Directors Box...

...I returned to the box at the conclusion of the game, which I seem to remember Hibs lost, and made sure I grabbed a picture of David sitting in the stands before the floodlights were extinguished.

The deal with Wallace Mercer, the then owner of Hearts, could have made David almost a million pounds, according to a 2020 Scotsman newspaper report. The thought of an Edinburgh United team playing in maroon, not the beloved green of Hibs, and at Hearts ground, Tynecastle, was not on, so the attempted merger failed...

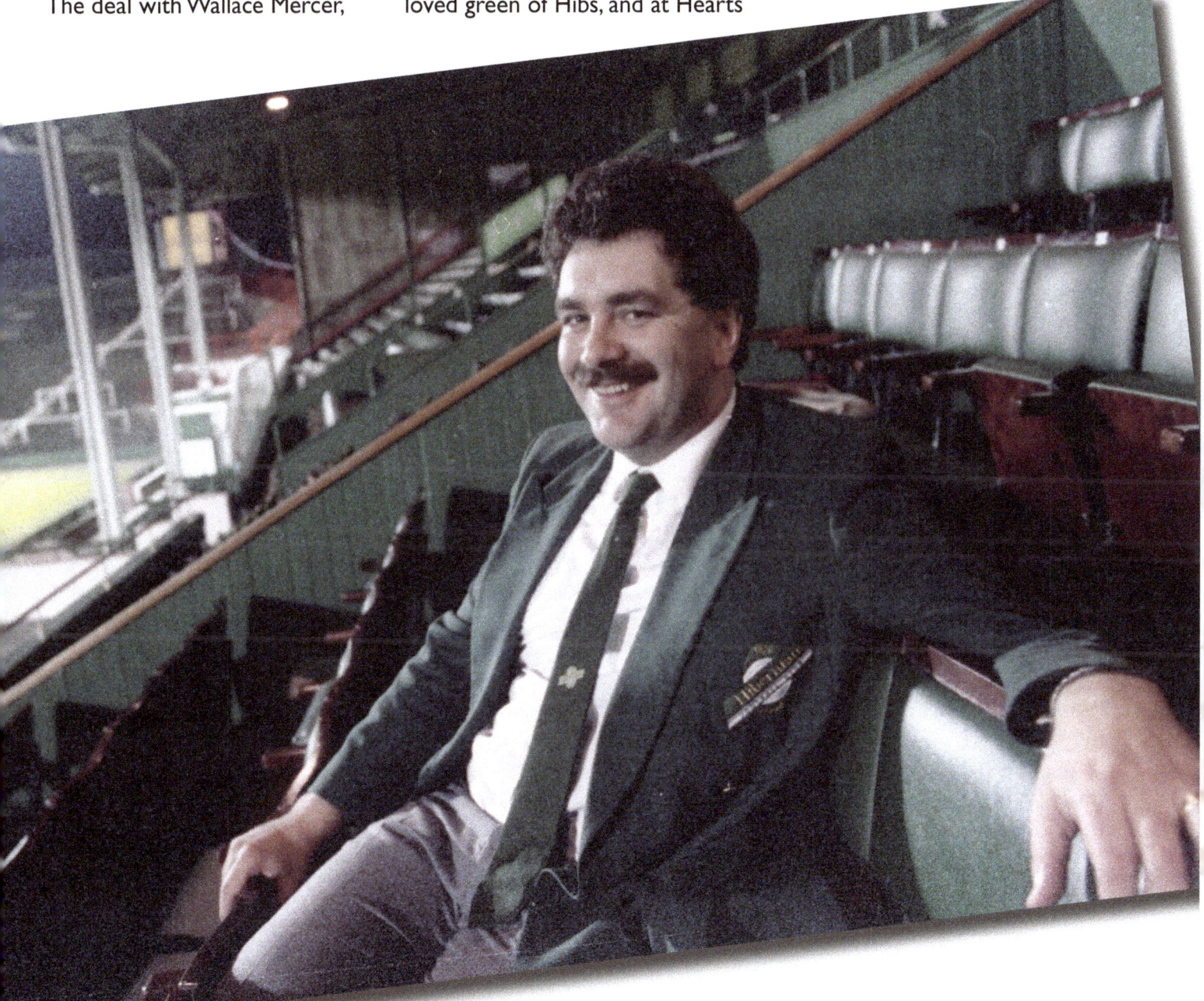

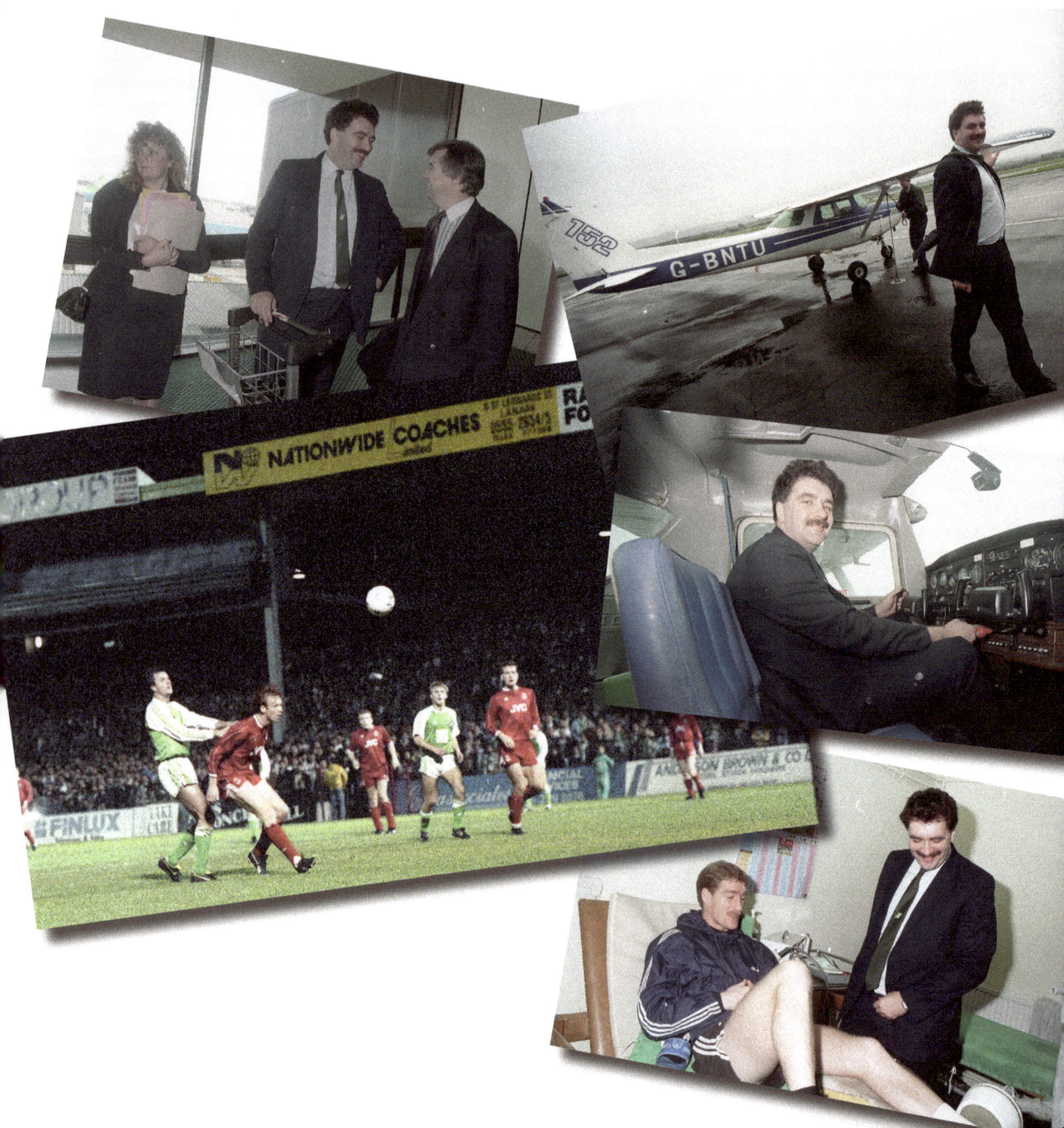

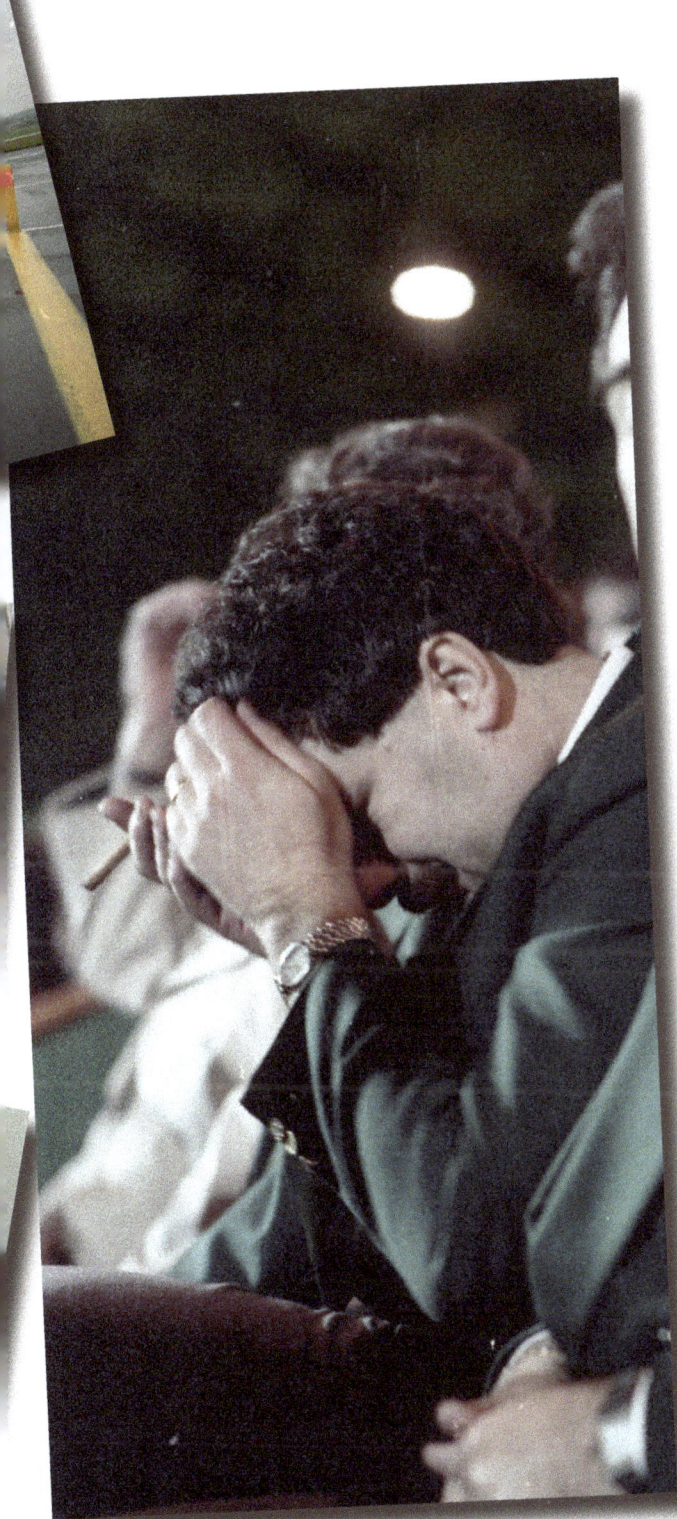

...Roll on a couple of years, and, as I was a client, I was one of the first to realise that all was not as it should be with David Duff, as the Law Society curtailed his Practice membership. He was arrested and charged with fraud, and in August 1993 appeared before Winchester Crown Court and was given a two-year sentence by Judge Ian Starforth Hill, QC.

His money-making exercises were described in court and published in the *Herald* (The Scottish Newspaper) as involving his personal assistant and lover, Lynda Hobbs, and Paul Hatch, who was in charge of the Phelps and Lawrence Fulham branch.

Mr Grunbar, prosecuting, said, "He stole money from his own firm by arranging for Hobbs and Hatch to apply for mortgages. False applications were backed up by letters and references, supplied by Duff, giving inflated salaries."

So where does my part of this story fit in?

The day David Duff was arrested I had a flurry of calls from frantic picture desks in Scotland as they hadn't any images of him in the ground.

They say "Everything comes to those who wait."

So what of David Duff now?

It's with some irony, according to the *Herald*, that he has turned to acting and appeared as a barman in the ITV drama Quiz. It's the story of Wiltshire's Major Charles Ingram who caused a major scandal when he was caught cheating on Who wants to be a Millionaire...

Sources: https://www.scotsman.com/sport/football/hibs/former-hibs-chairman-david-duff-speaks-first-time-then-hearts-owner-wallace-mercers-takeover-bid-it-wasnt-merger-it-was-destruction-2872541
https://www.heraldscotland.com/news/12725589.hibs-former-chief-jailed-for-two-years-for-fraud/
Football Today january 1990 from our archive.

...For the purposes of including a picture published in *The Times* newspaper on June 17th 1988 I am including the magnificent Littlecote House as one of the connections Swindon or Wiltshire has with the J Class racing super-yacht Velsheda.

Although with a Reading postcode and a Hungerford address, the former home of the Wills tobacco family, who had a factory in Swindon, is actually just in Wiltshire.

Sir Seton Wills, the last of the family to reside in the large Elizabethan country house and massive estate, was majority shareholder of Swindon Town between 1991 and 2007.

In 1985 the house was sold to the flamboyant entrepreneur Peter de Savary, who made it into an Elizabethan theme park which included the sport of jousting.

So how is this landlocked estate connected to one of the most beautiful sail racing boats ever built?...

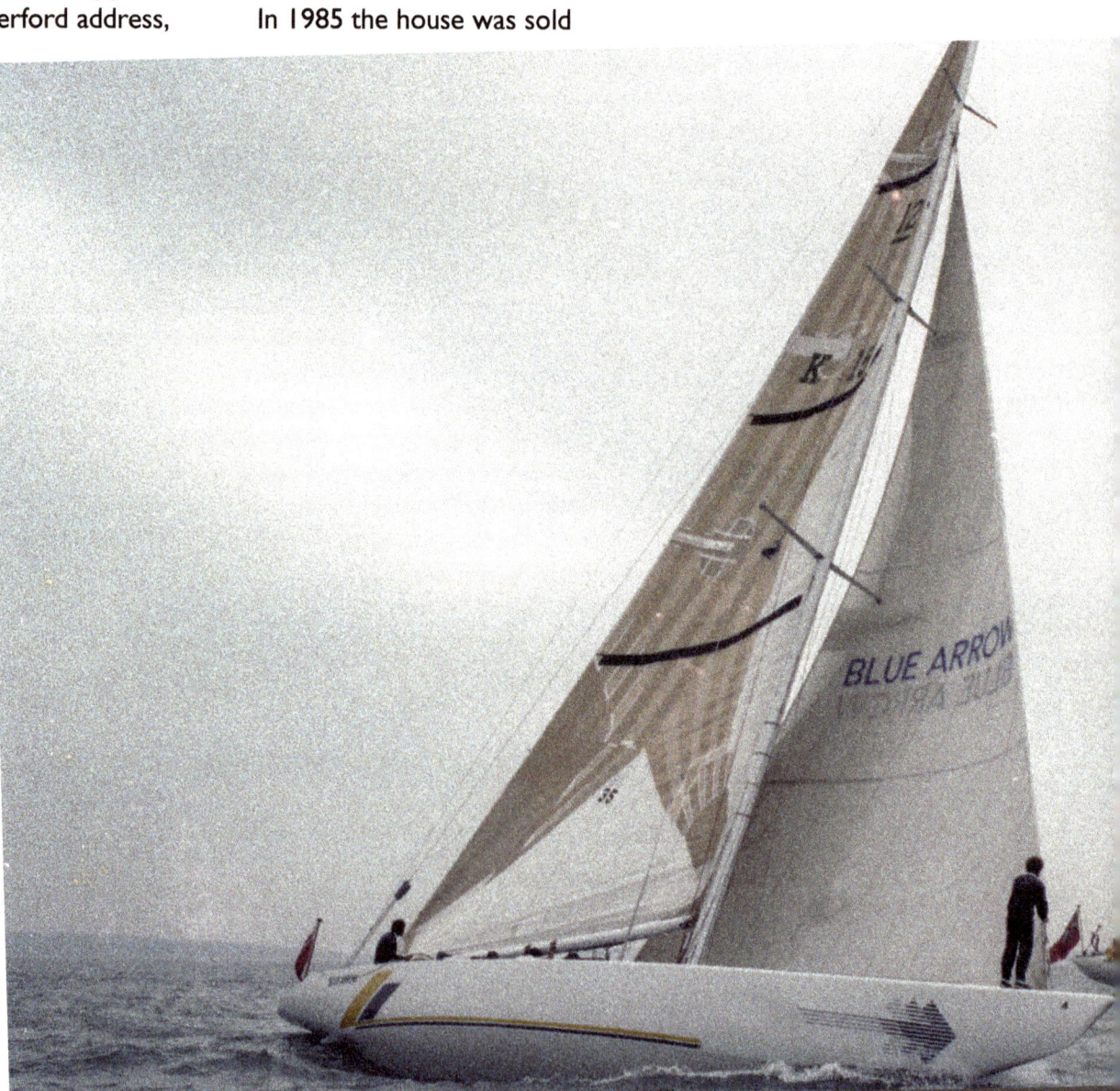

...One of Peter De Savary's enterprises was to sponsor the Blue Arrow Group's America Cup entry, a 12-metre racing yacht named Blue Arrow, in the world's most lucrative sailing race.

I was invited to the Solent to join the boat for a training and public relations day out on the water.

We were accompanied by a chase boat, which I was able to commandeer to get shots of Blue Arrow in full sail on the Solent.

About an hour or so into our sail I took advantage of the chase boat and did a few laps of the yacht, when the skipper of the chase boat pointed out a sailing yacht ahead, saying that was Velsheda, and to stay with him as Blue Arrow would soon catch it up...

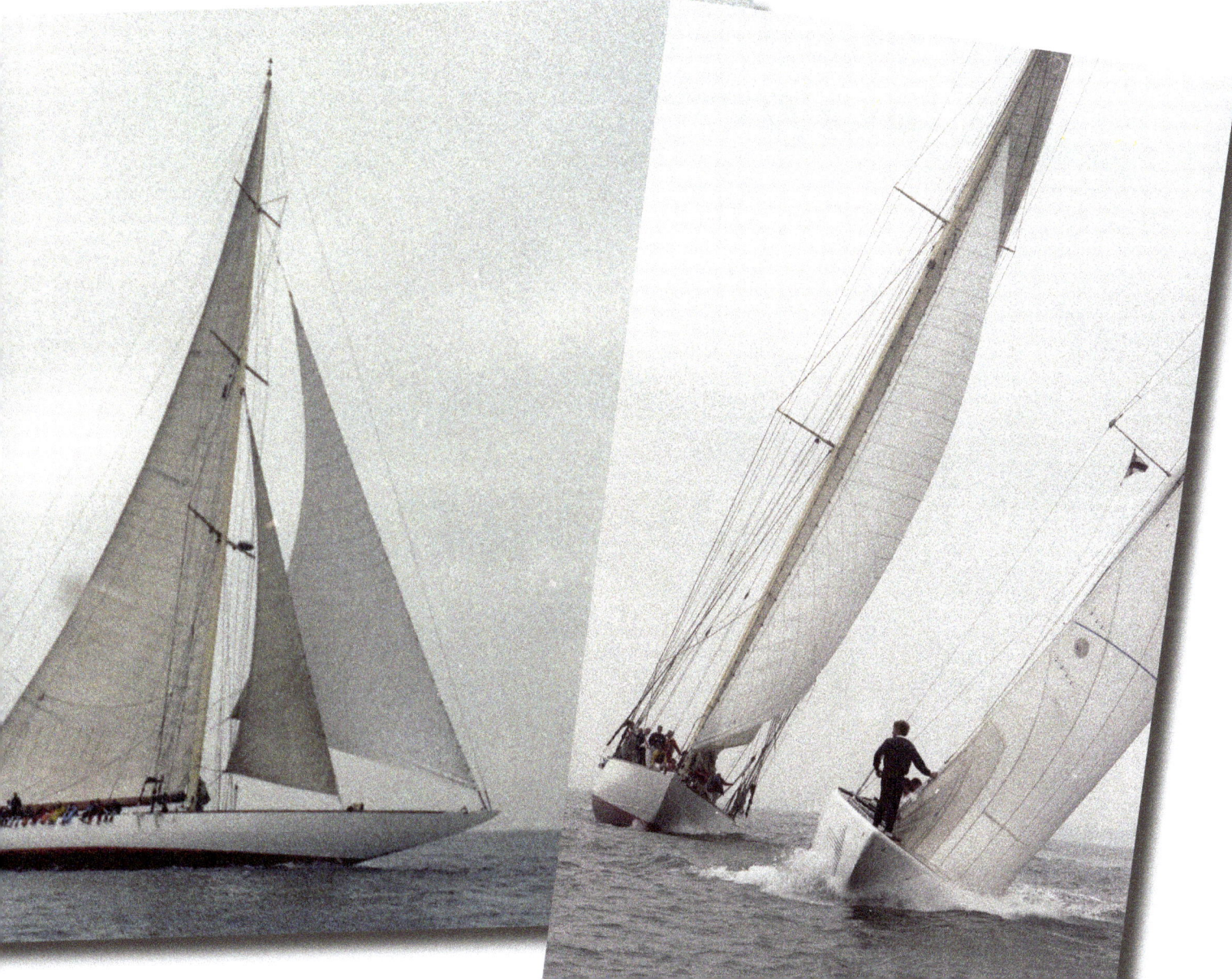

...So what is Velsheda and its somewhat distant connection with Swindon?

According to https://www.jclassyachts.com; Velsheda was designed by Charles Nicholson and built by Camper & Nicholson at Gosport in 1933 for Mr. W. L. Stephenson, owner of the Woolworth chain of shops; hence the slightly distant connection with the now long-gone distribution centre at Dorcan.,

The boat was named after Stephenson's three daughters, Velma, Sheila and Daphne. He built the boat never planning to compete for the America's Cup, as several other JK7 class boats had done, but raced in the JK7 class with the greatest names in classic yachting including King George V's boat "Britannia", "Endeavour" and "Shamrock" between 1933 and 1936.

In her second season she won more than 40 races, and achieved an outstanding record of success at regattas all along the south coast

Her design in the late 1930s was the most technically advanced design in sailing yachts.

Velsheda's masts were aluminium, which were made by bending plates and riveting them together, and her sails were made from a new material called Terylene.

But by 1937 she was laid up in a mud berth on the Hamble and became derelict, used only for overnight accommodation by sailing club members.

Velsheda was rescued in 1984 by Terry Brabant, who economically refitted her for charter work including a new steel mast and limited interior, but without an engine.

She sailed regularly along the UK south coast on charter, and occasionally ventured to the Mediterranean and Caribbean.

A second rebuild in 1996 gave her the tallest one-piece carbon mast in the world, and a comprehensive suite of racing sails were produced, developed from wind tunnel testing at Southampton University. She was re-launched in November 1997.

My sighting of the 1933 America's Cup reserve boat, Velsheda, made the day, and when the picture of the two boats made The Times, the PR people were quite happy too...

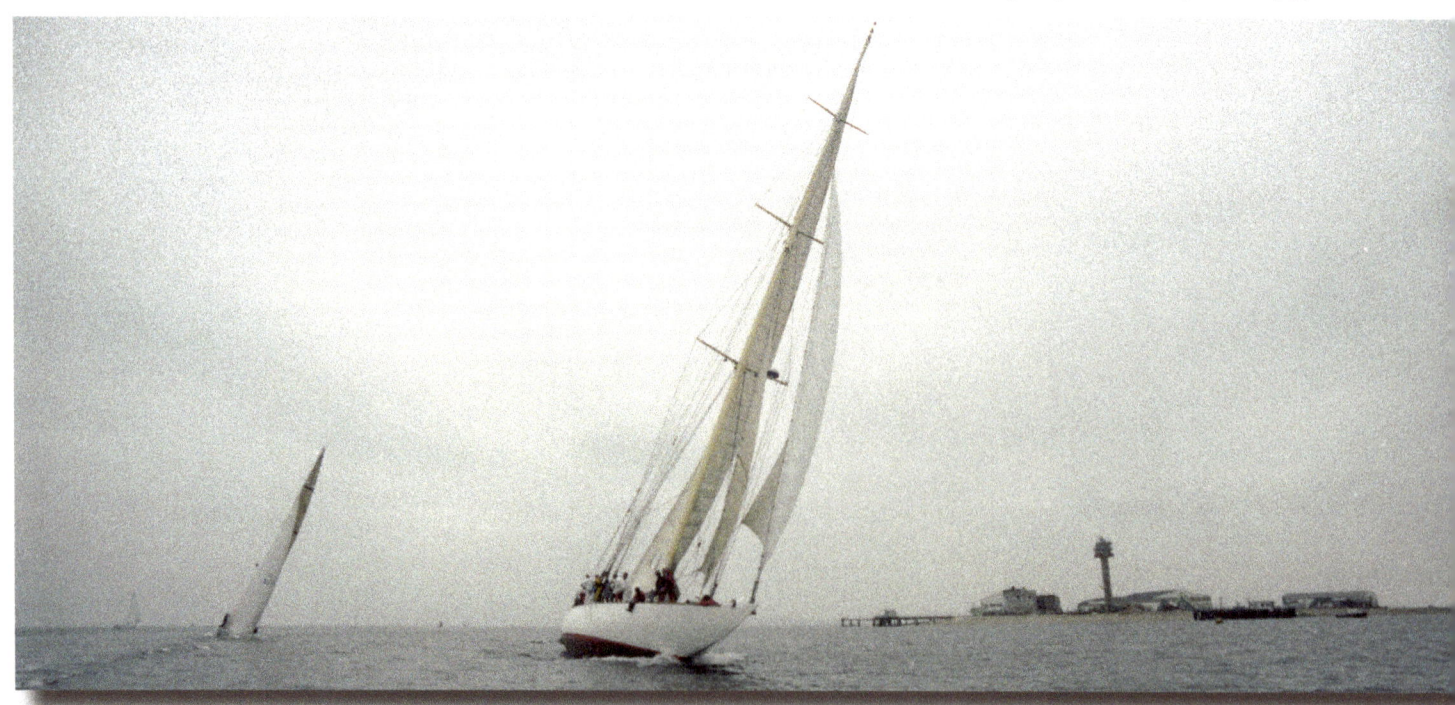

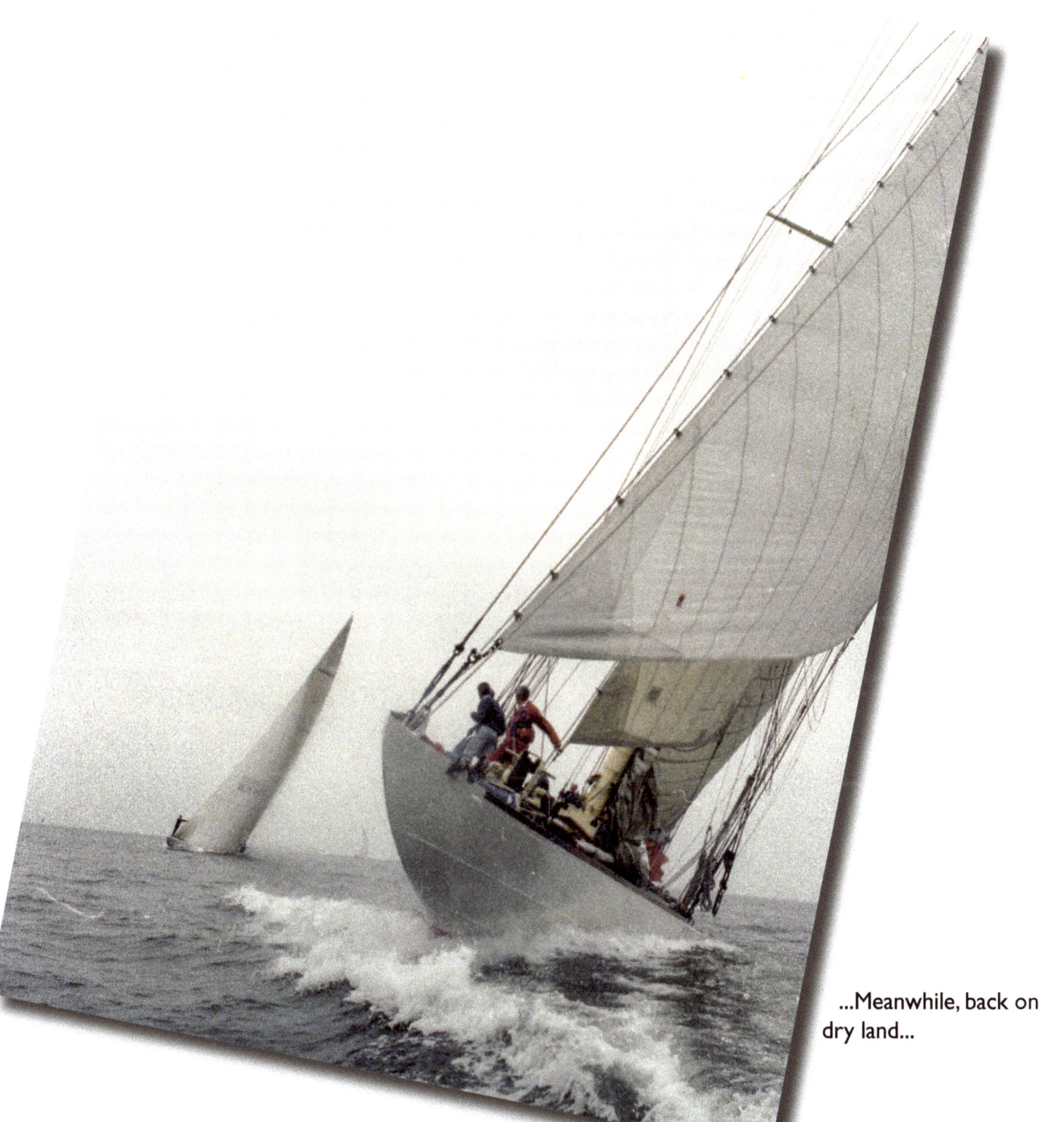

...Meanwhile, back on dry land...

...Sometimes it's not all that it seems, but sometime seeing is believing.

Ferreting through the cuttings books to research stories, I came across a cutting of rallycross:

The 1989 Autoglass trophy.

First stage first venue: Swindon. The tour attracted several of the world's finest rally drivers, such as the legendary Roger Clark in a Ford Sierra Cosworth (1); and, in a similar car, the winner of the event, again a legend in motor sport Jimmy McRae (3).

Where in Swindon could a 1.92 miles rallycross circuit be situated.

Believe it or not, the event took place on the old railworks site where A shop was, and what is now Churchward and Paddington Drive.

Note the old Princess Margaret Hospital in the background...

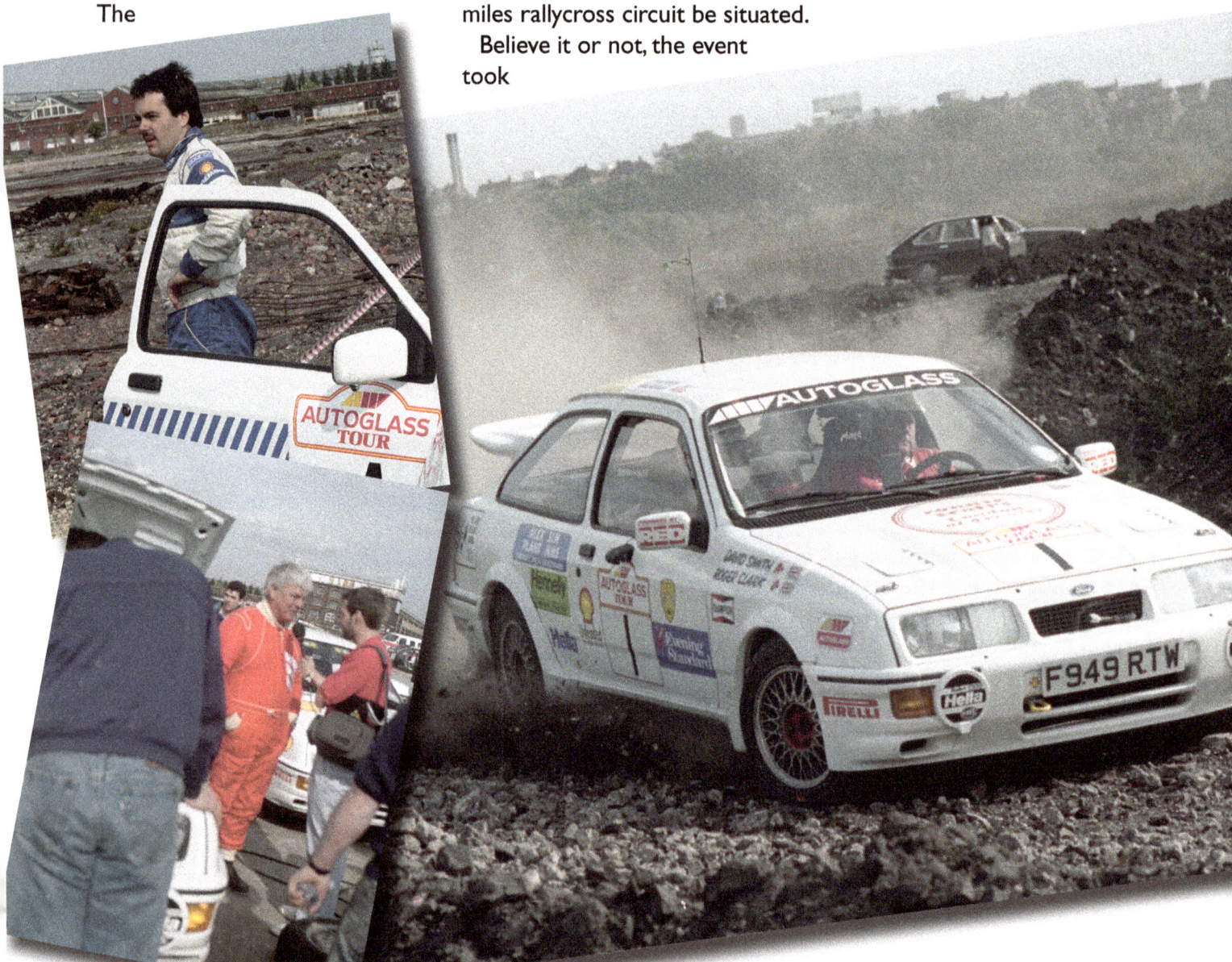

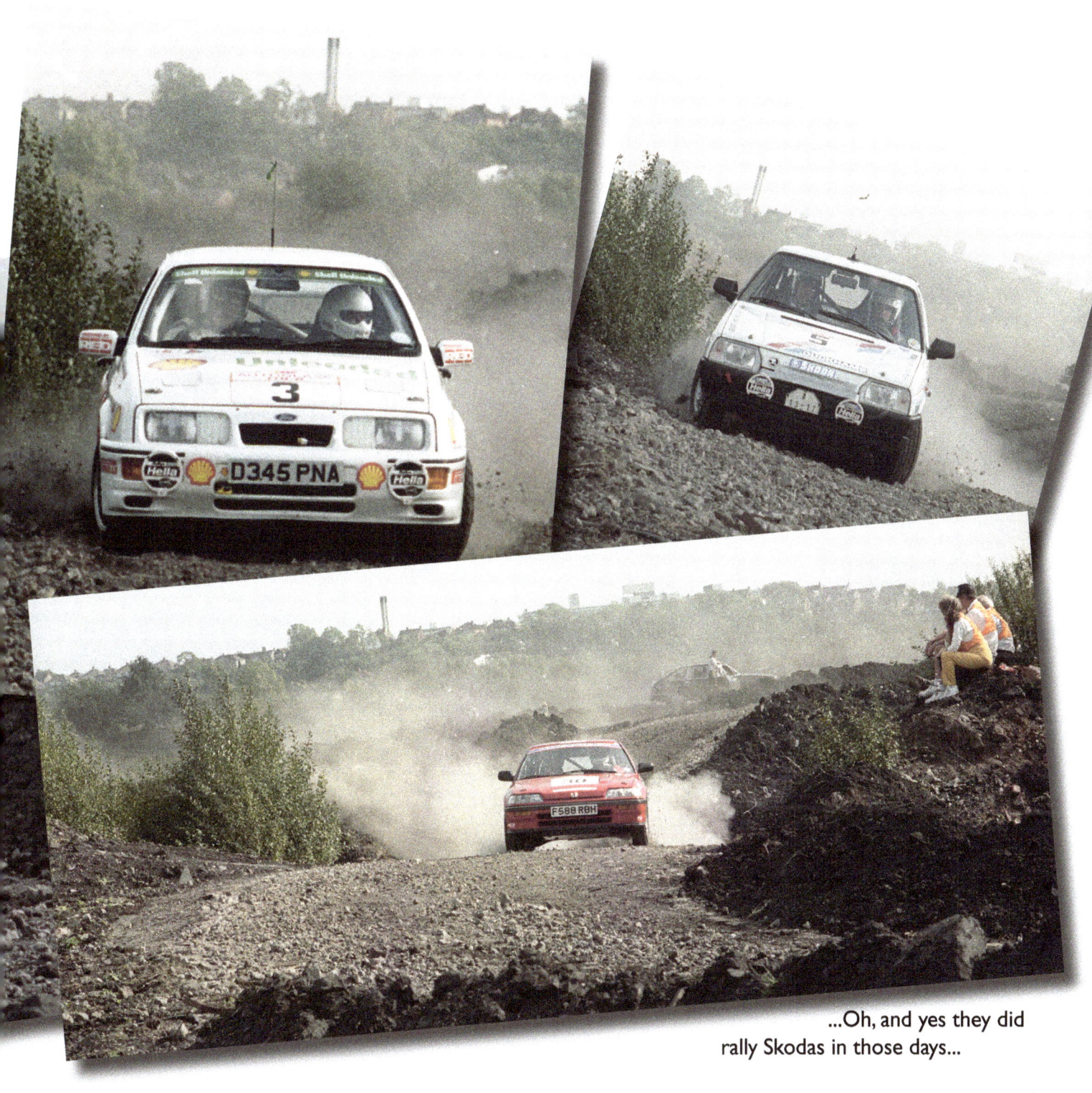

...Oh, and yes they did rally Skodas in those days...

...What we need is a bit of show biz to lighten up the pages.

Not so deep inside the archive there lies a file that reads Liz Hurley and Shane Warne at Cirencester Park - Cricket for Kids 9-6-2013.

I joined the very large A list press pack to see local resident Liz Hurley (who until 2015 lived just outside Cirencester at Ampney Knowle on her 72 acre farm) and her then beau, the Australian cricket star Shane Warne, host an international T20 charity cricket match at Cirencester Cricket Club in aid of two charities.

The Hop, Skip and Jump Foundation (which helps kids in the UK who suffer from learning difficulties) and the Shane Warne Charity (which helps underprivileged children in Australia) benefited from this A-lister event.

The Australian spin bowler captained the Australian side, who played against Michael Vaughan's England team.

Other cricket stars included Andrew Strauss, Darren Gough, Kevin Pietersen, and the famous moustached Aussie bowler Merv Hughes.

Australian captain Michael Clarke also took part in the match, which was umpired by former England captain David Gower.

The ceremony of the tossing of the coin at the start of the game brought Liz Hurley onto the pitch where she spun the coin and enabled play to commence.

The event in the park was attended by more than 3,000 spectators, who paid £45 for tickets to the sell-out event...

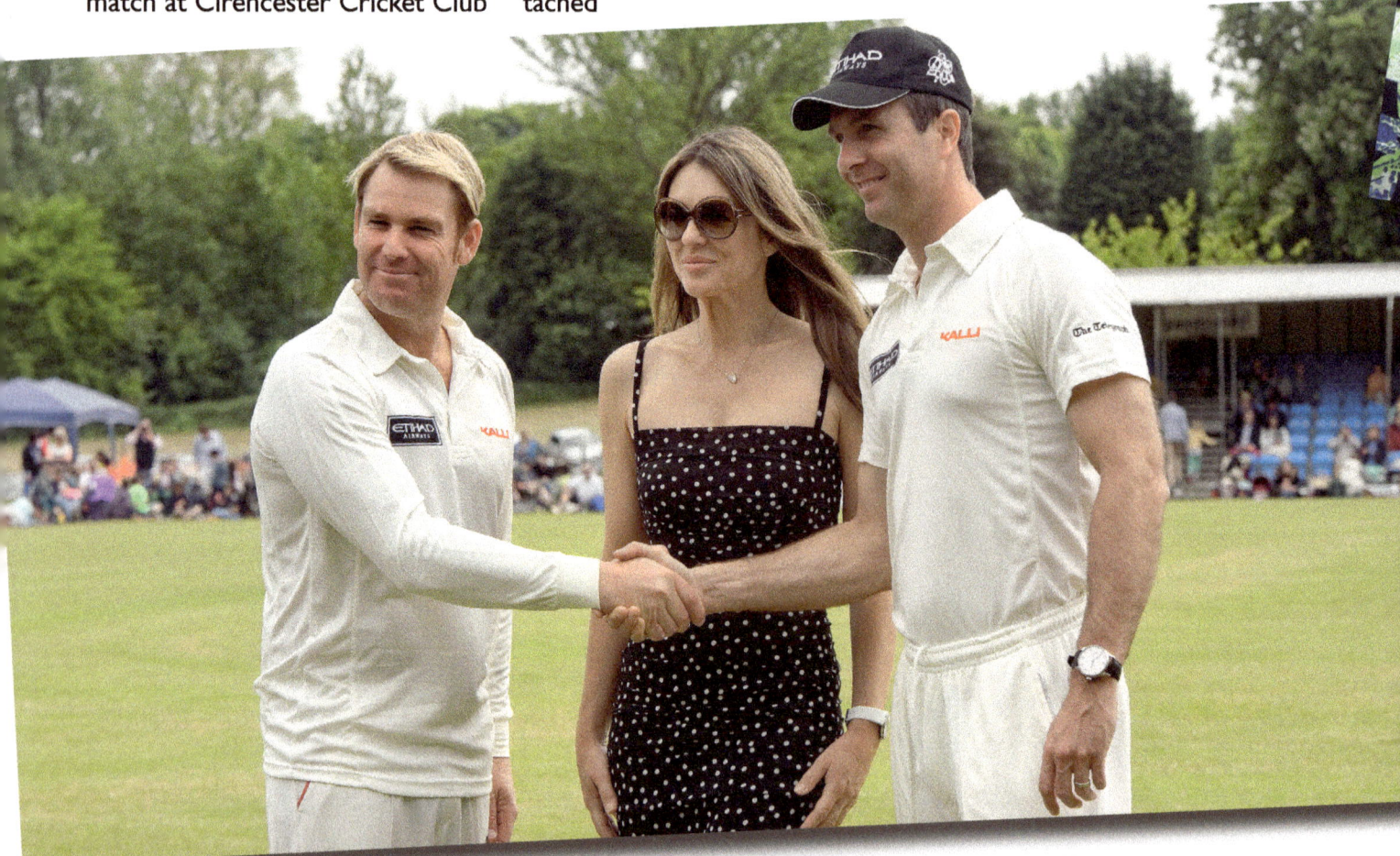

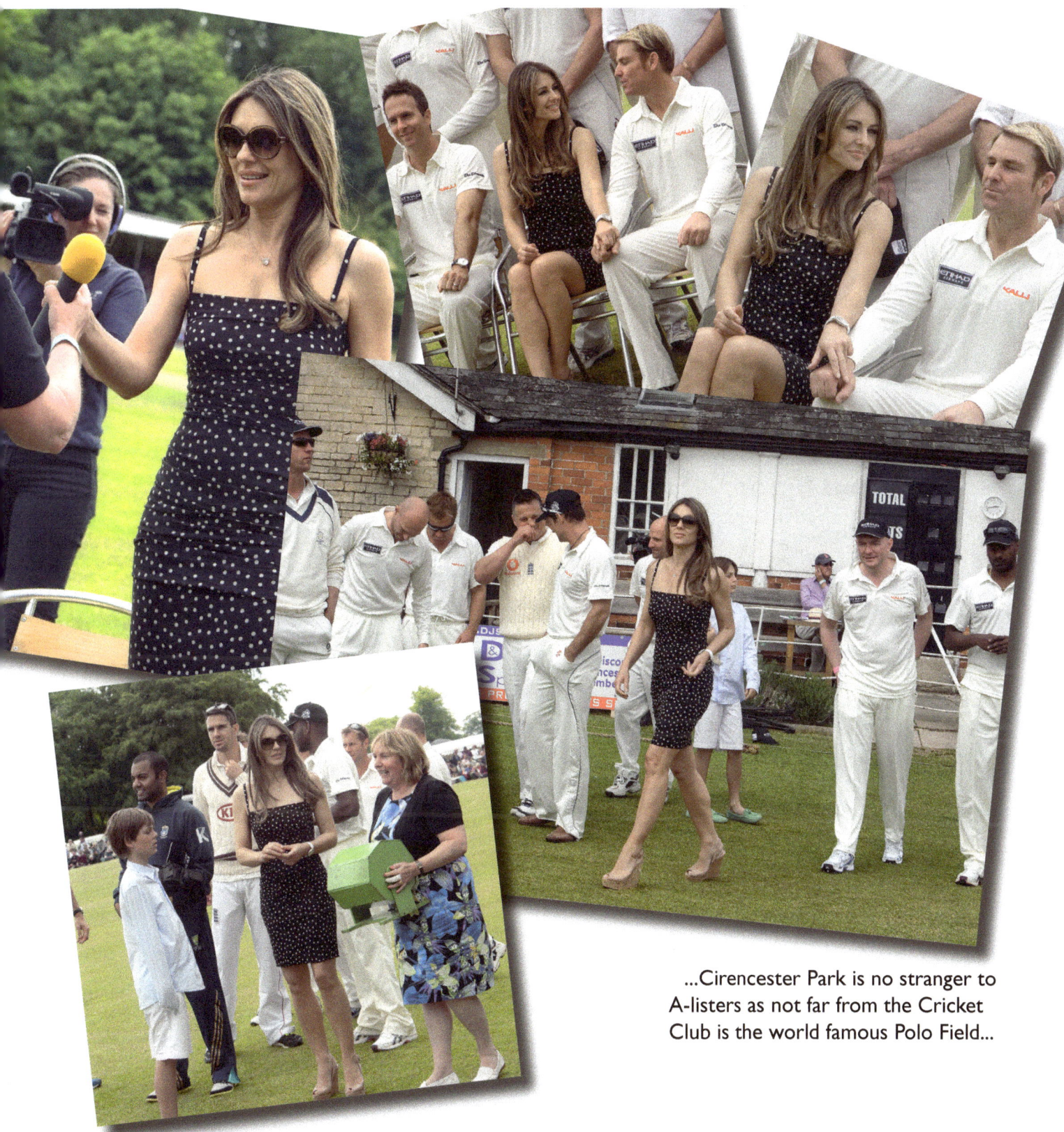

...Cirencester Park is no stranger to A-listers as not far from the Cricket Club is the world famous Polo Field...

...For about 12 years I followed the Royal Family as a freelance videographer, mainly covering events involving Prince Charles, Camilla, and the Princes William and Harry.

One of the highlights of the video year was the Dorchester Cup event at the delightful Cirencester Park Polo Ground, which lies in the woodland just off the Stroud Road.

On one of my first visits to the event I was lucky enough to film exclusively the first outing of the three royal princes playing as Team Highgrove.

Prince Harry had just turned 18 and was eligible to play in an adult polo team. He joined Prince William and their father Prince Charles for a not so private game.

As it was a private event there was no formal photocall, but the Royal press pack had descended and were all corralled at the western end of the field and were expecting some kind of group picture from the trio.

The shot sort of emerged during the warm-up when they gathered, shaking hands with the other players.

Obviously rehearsed, the three came together, turned the horses towards the pack, held it for a few seconds and then went about the warm-up. Blink and you would have missed it.

Fortunately I was just filming everything they were doing so managed to catch it on camera.

The images used here of that event are frame grabs, single frames taken from the video shot on the old 4x3 standard definition format, so not quite the quality of the still images...

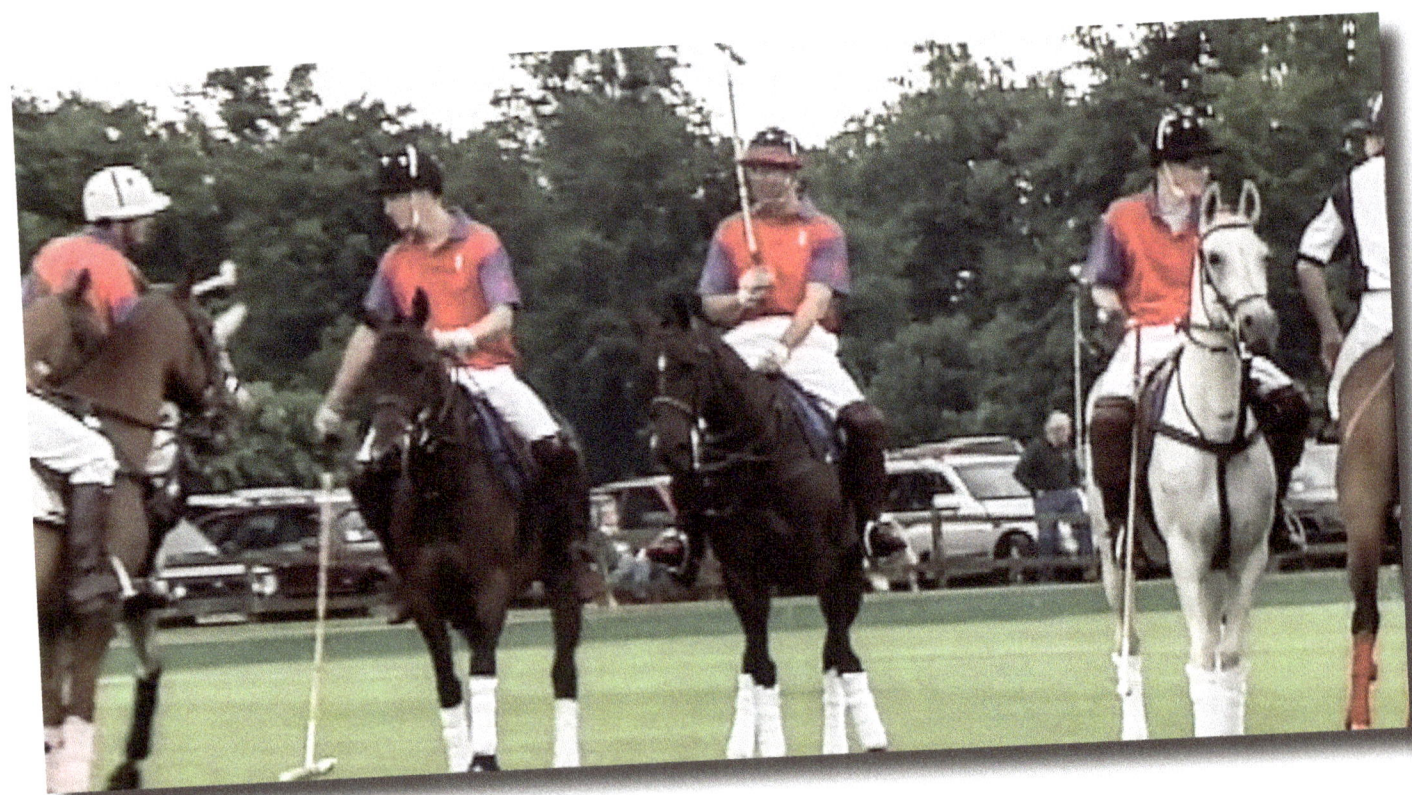

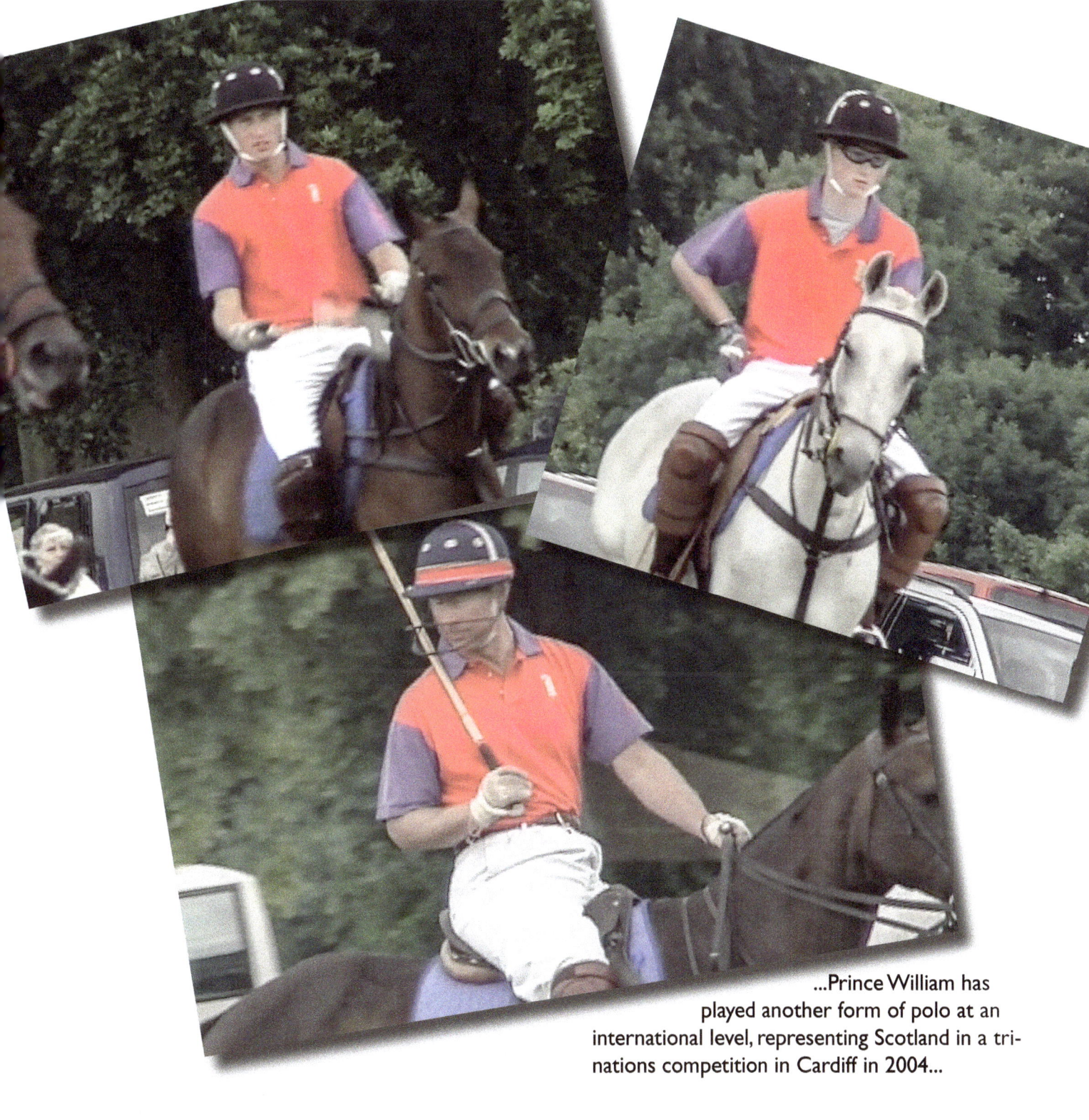

...Prince William has played another form of polo at an international level, representing Scotland in a tri-nations competition in Cardiff in 2004...

...The standing joke is, "Where are the horses?" when you attend a water polo game.

Swindon actually has a water polo team as an off-shoot of the Swindon Dolphins Swimming Club.

The matches that I photographed were held in the Milton Road Health Hydro, where the light was so awful for photography even the modern digital cameras of the time had difficulty getting a good image.

After several matches I sort of got used to the conditions.

As well as the lack of light, the humid atmosphere of an indoor pool causes havoc with cameras, and in particular lenses.

The lenses are usually much colder than the atmosphere inside the pool area, and so steam up very quickly, with water vapour getting between the elements of the lens.

The mirror and prism in the camera body also become steamed up, and it takes quite a while to get the camera serviceable.

In previous excursions photographing in such conditions, I have learned to warm the cameras up beforehand, so that the temperature of the kit is about the same as the pool area. This is done either by keeping the camera inside you coat for some time before you need to use it, or under the air from the car heater before wrapping it in a blanket or your coat to keep it warm...

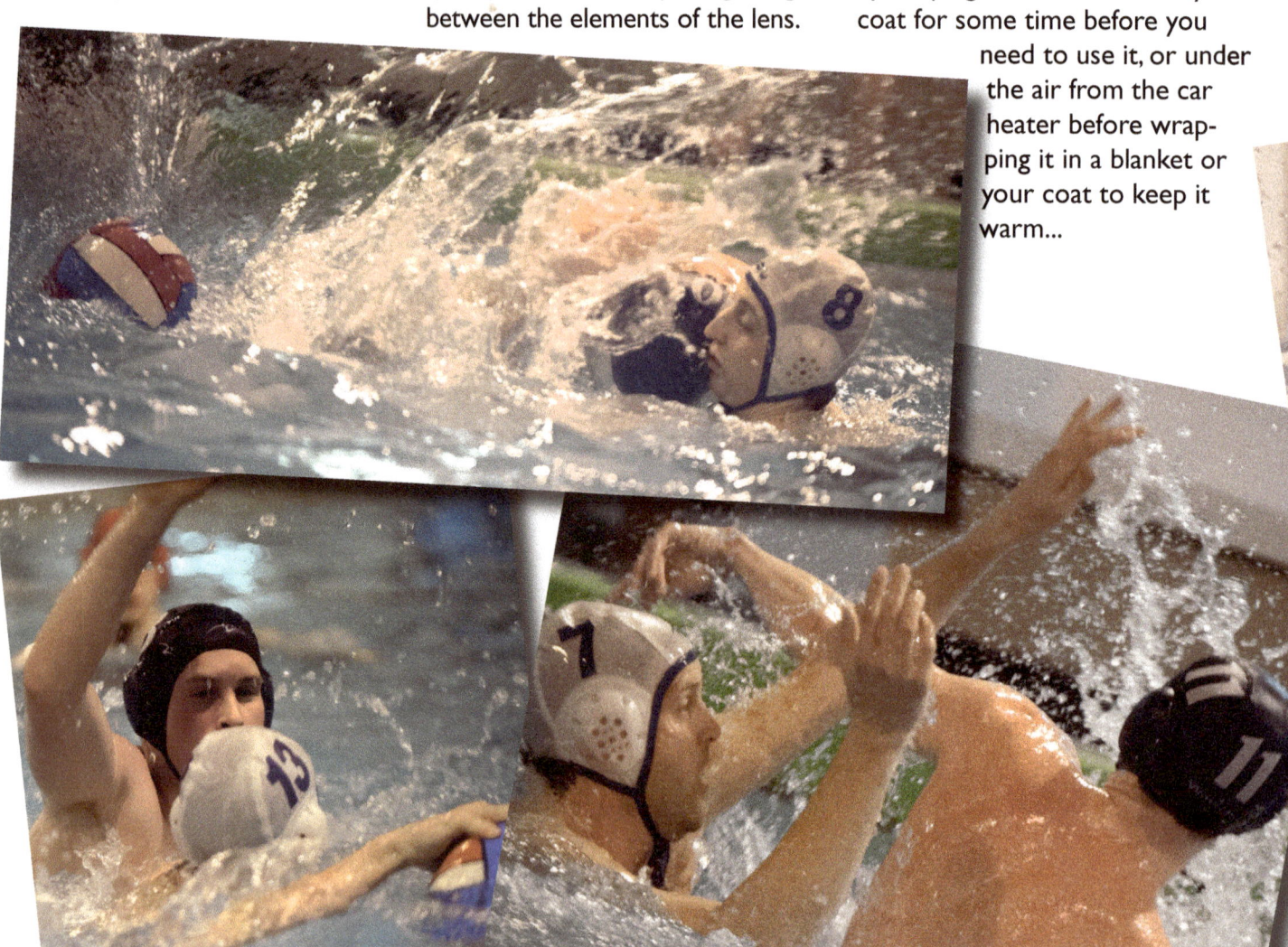

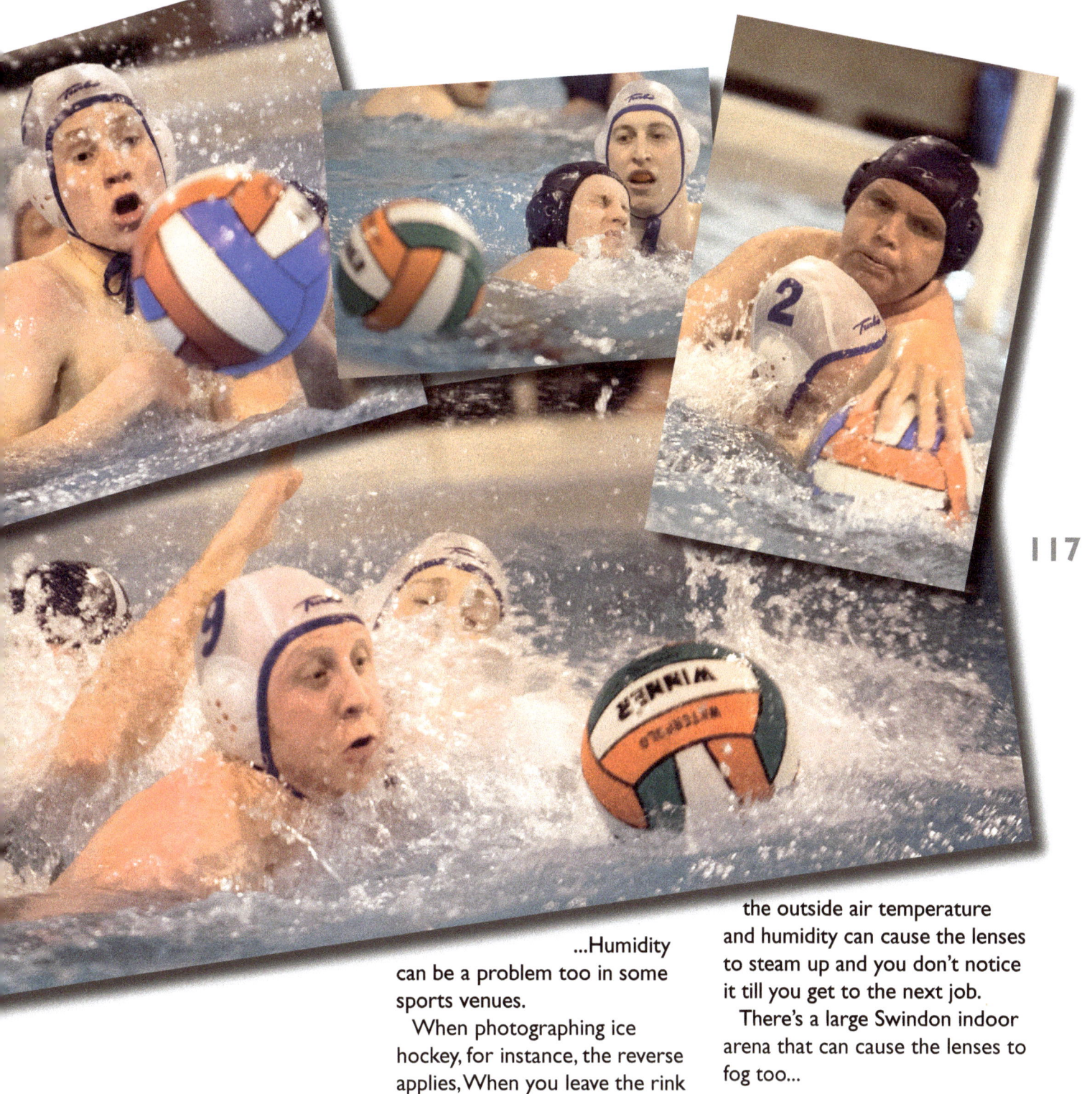

...Humidity can be a problem too in some sports venues.

When photographing ice hockey, for instance, the reverse applies. When you leave the rink the outside air temperature and humidity can cause the lenses to steam up and you don't notice it till you get to the next job.

There's a large Swindon indoor arena that can cause the lenses to fog too...

...Outside Swindon, just past the A419 at South Marston, is a sports complex which includes The Supermarine Rugby Club, the Swindon Sub Aqua Club and Swindon's second football club, Swindon Supermarine F. C.

Supermarine are some four leagues below the towns main football club as I write this piece, but under the chairmanship of their enigmatic leader, Jez Webb, they have proved to be a very good alternative venue for the Saturday football fix.

Jez took the club forward and in doing so created a football and sports complex that rivals many a higher league club, it's The Swindome complex which he helped construct in 2015...

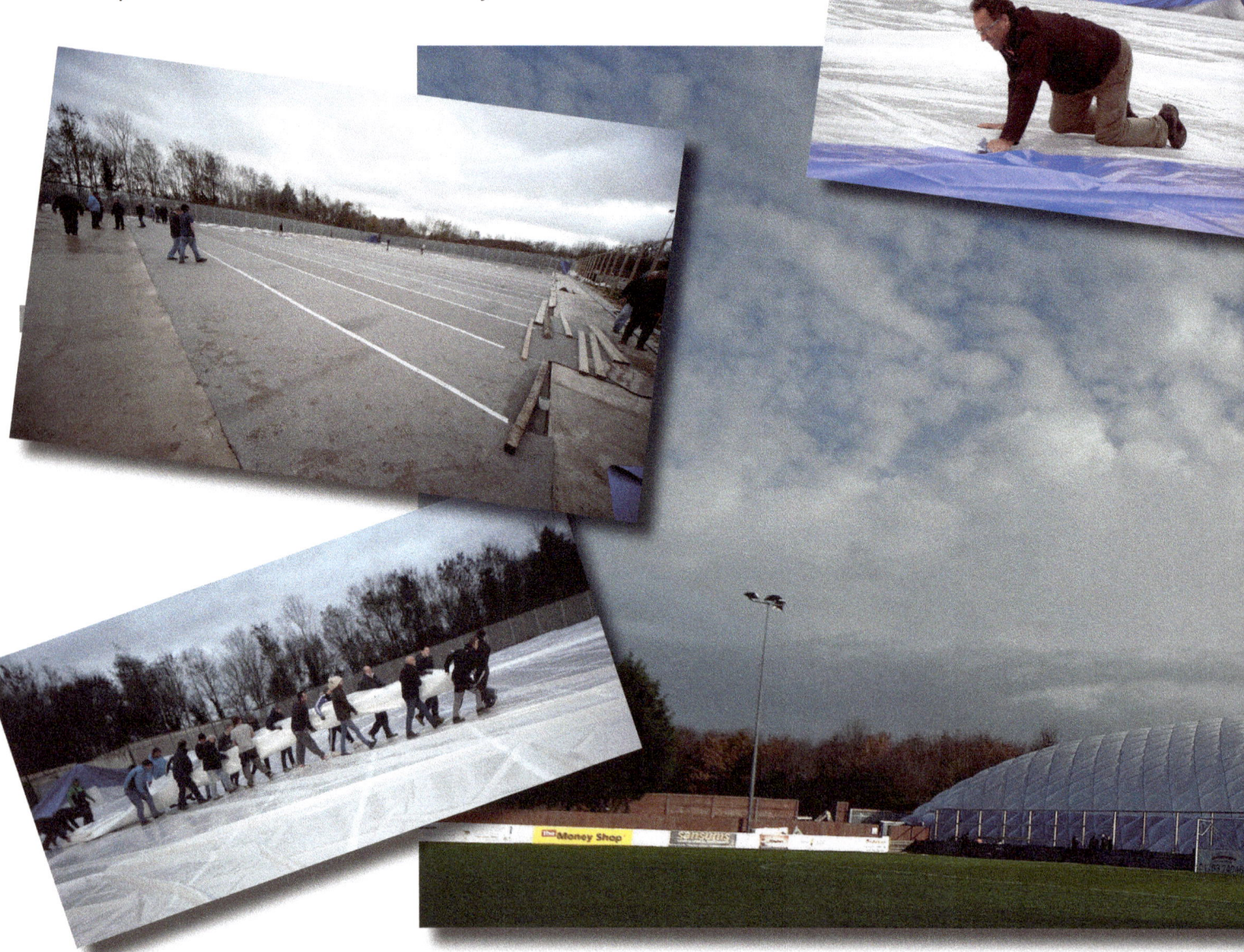

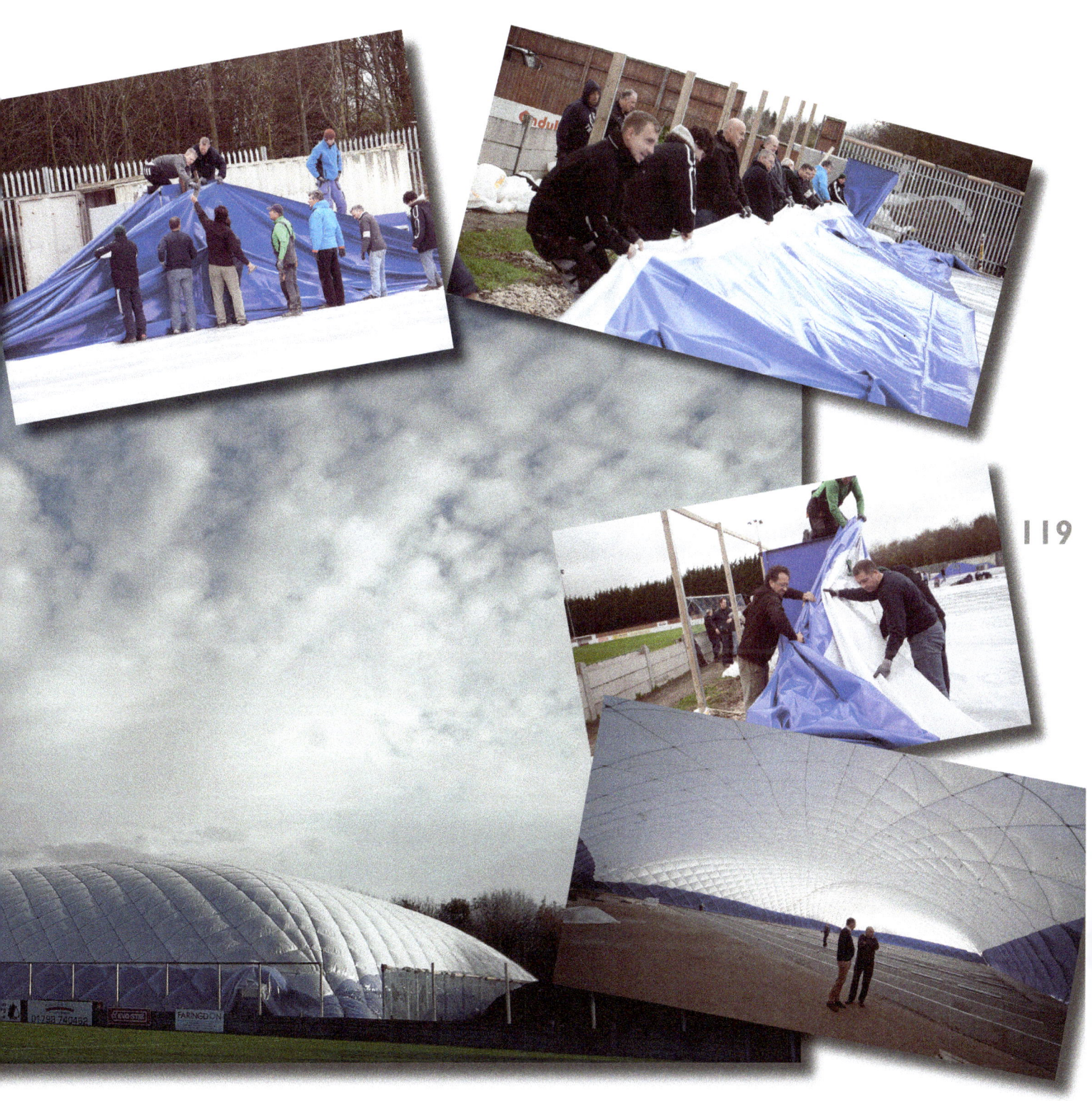

...For the uninitiated, this super sports facility is the town's first all-purpose indoor football facility. It's housed under a state of the art airdome covering the three modern third generation artificial football pitches, which can be converted to create one large pitch.

The club claims that its facility is one of the best artificial surfaces available for football hire in the UK, to quote their website, with a playing surface which was the most modern up to date surface known when it was built.

They have also installed a 12mm thick rubber shock pad underneath to give the user a comfortable and unique experience, and incorporated an in-house gym facility with treatment rooms, pitch side viewing areas, and changing room facilities.

The Dome had two opening ceremonies, both I think you could say were 'royal'...

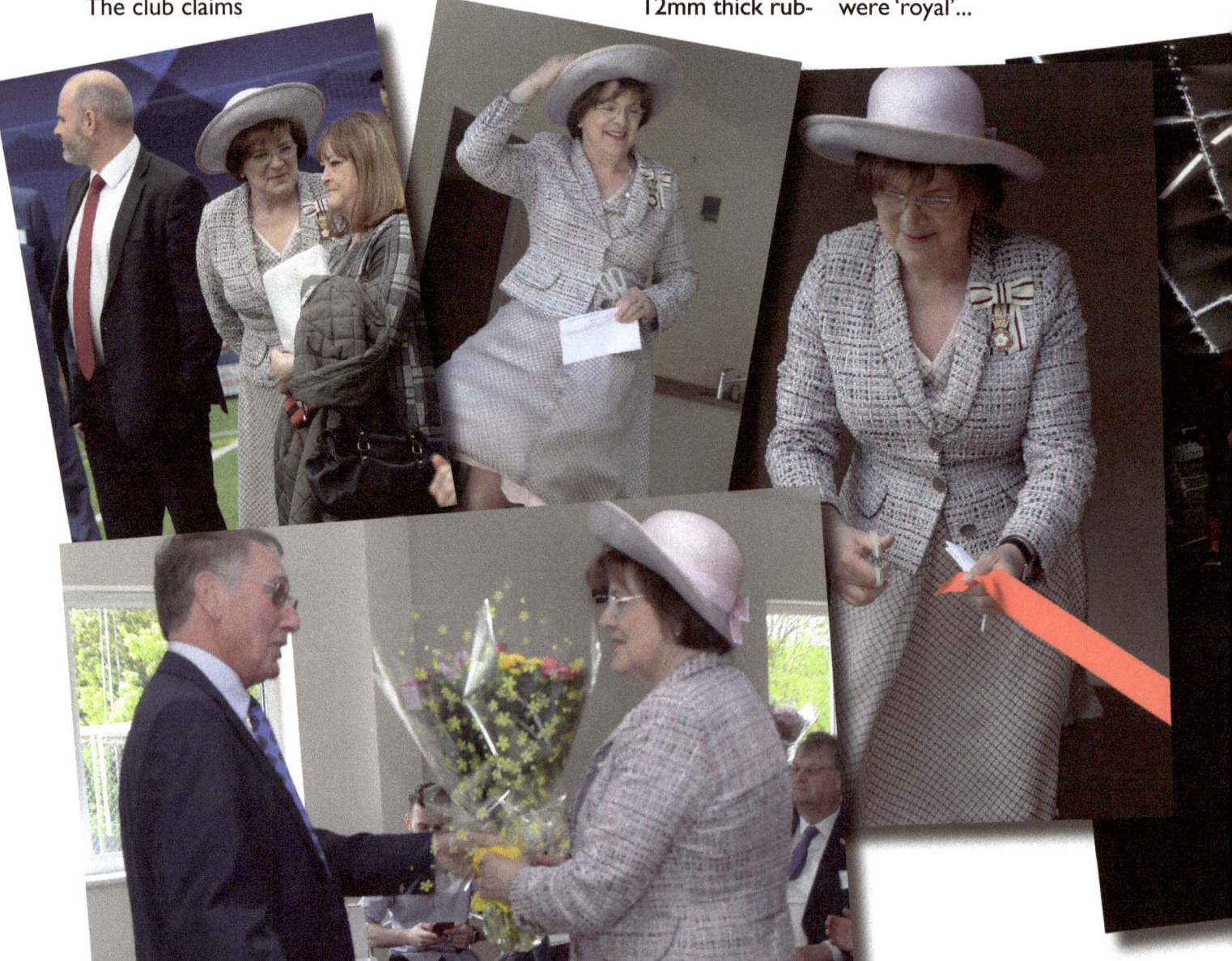

...The official opening was by the Queen's representative in Wiltshire, Lord-Lieutenant of Wiltshire Mrs. Sarah Rose Troughton who is a cousin of the Queen, on 5th May 2017; and then by football royalty in the form of World Cup hatrick hero Geoff Hurst. on the 8th July the following year...

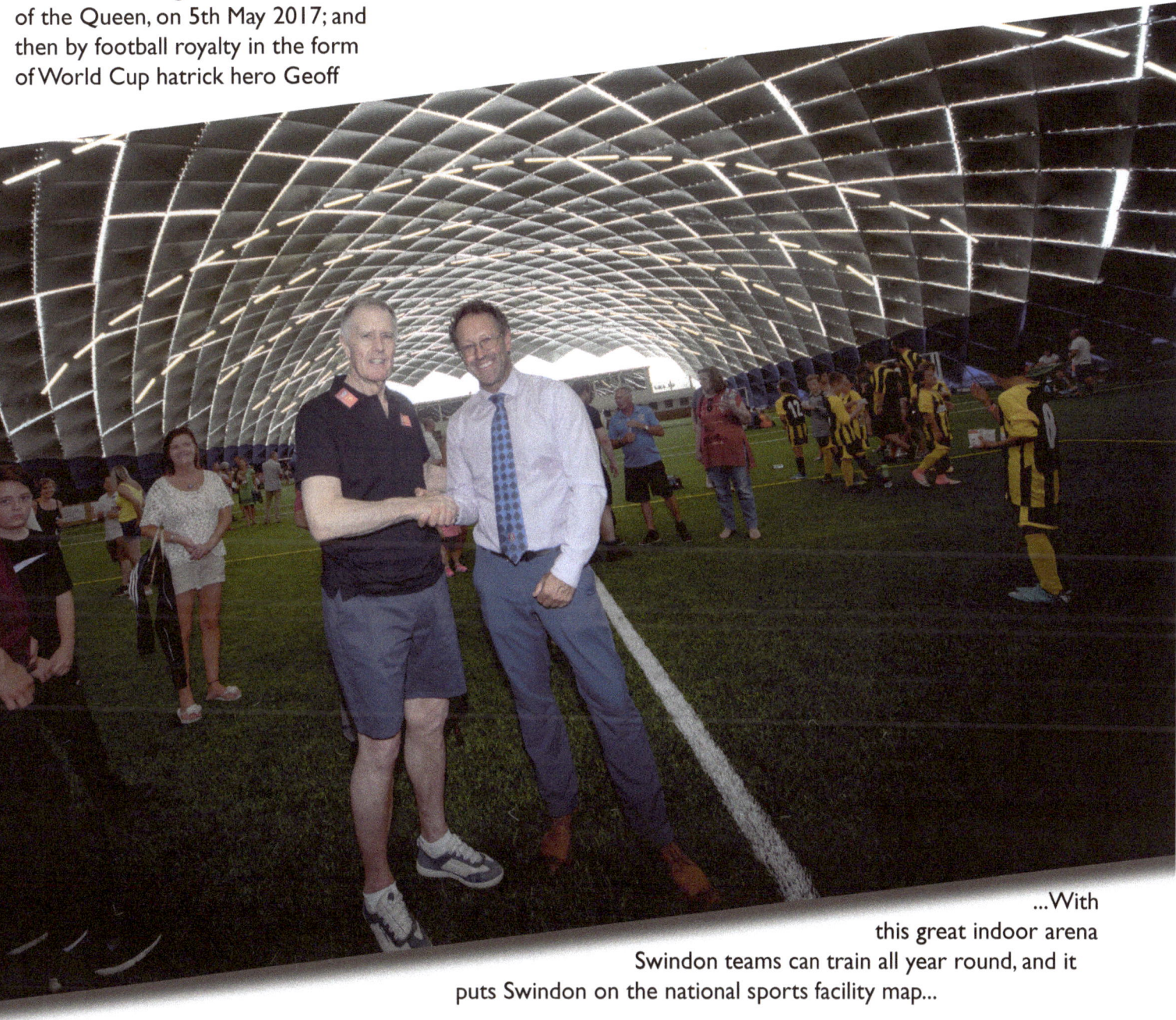

...With this great indoor arena Swindon teams can train all year round, and it puts Swindon on the national sports facility map...

...The Dome is situated behind the goal at the changing room end of the pitch at The Webbswood Stadium, in the Supermarine sports complex where Swindon Supermarine F.C, at the time of writing, play in the Southern League Premier Division South, having been formed by the union of Supermarine F.C. and Swindon Athletic F.C in 1992.

The annual pre-season friendly between Town and Marine has seen many famous names take their place in the away dugout, giving the media a chance to photograph new Swindon Town managers....

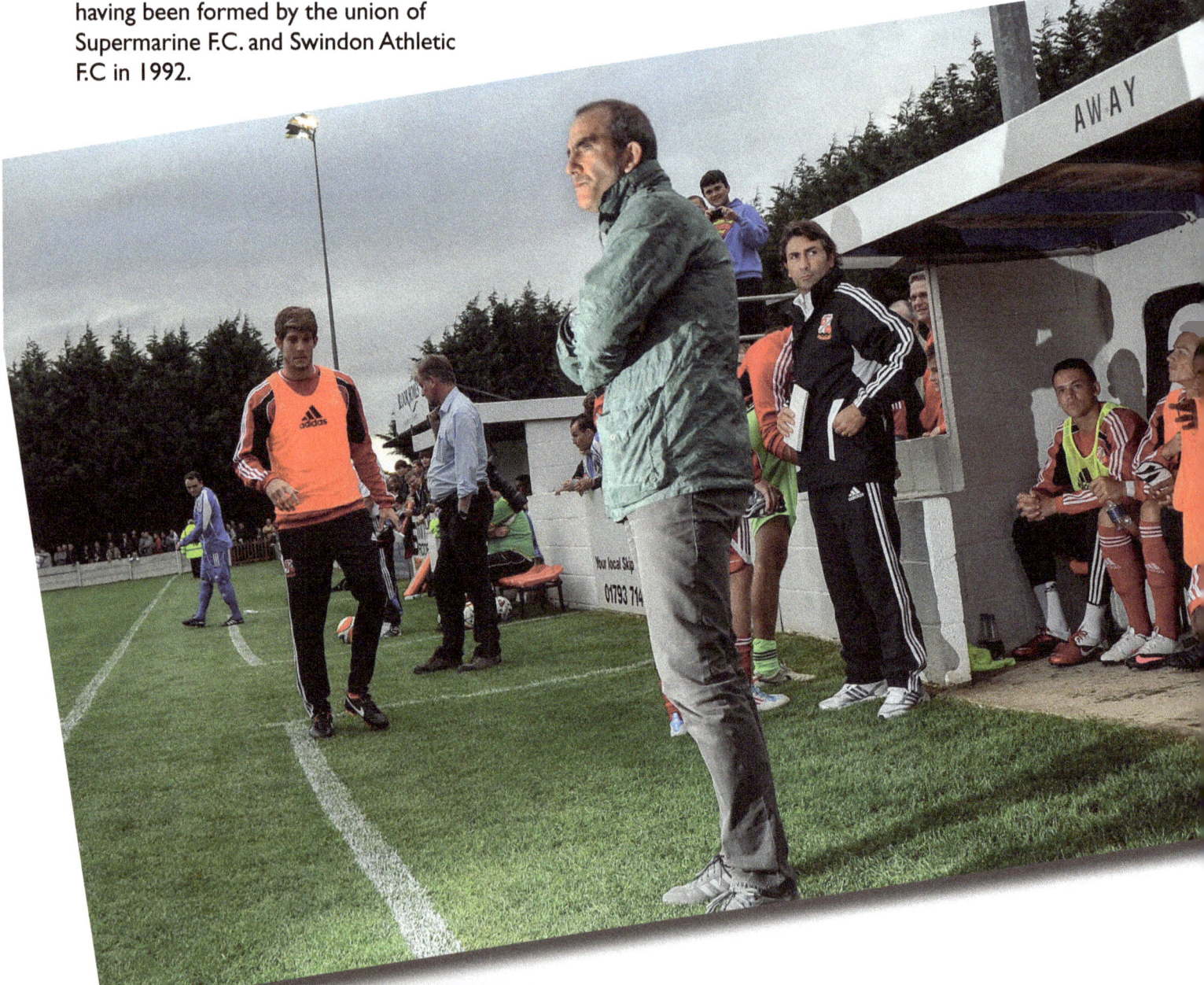

...I always try to avoid adding flash when there is enough daylight, as I find it kills the picture by blasting the subject.

You can overcome this by placing a flash gun off the camera, and firing it remotely with a radio trigger.

When you're photographing football managers in the technical area around the dug out, using a remote flash is a non starter; but sometimes in that situation you can get lucky, as I did when the enigmatic Paolo Di Canio made his first Swindon Town managerial outing to Supermarine for a pre-season friendly.

During the preliminaries of the game he stood in the technical area and was photographed by several members of the press using flash, including myself, as the Supermarine lights at the time were not the brightest and were quite directional.

When firing the camera on continuous the flash doesn't always keep up so you get un-flashed frames.

It was on one of these frames that I caught another photographer's flash illuminating Di Canio.

If you get this from the right angle the effect can be quite dramatic, but the chances are few and far between...

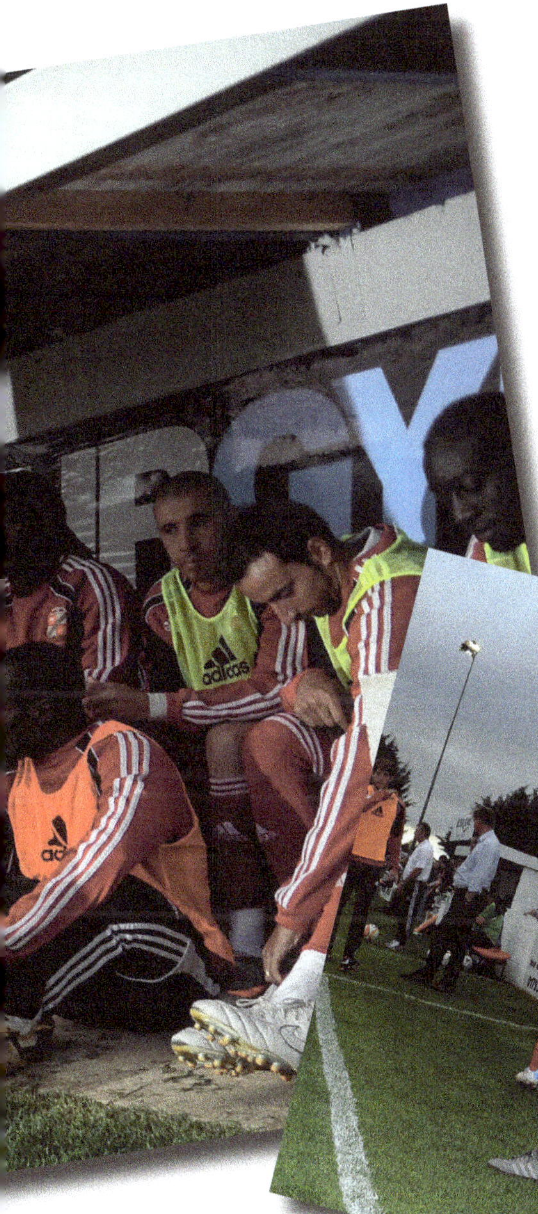

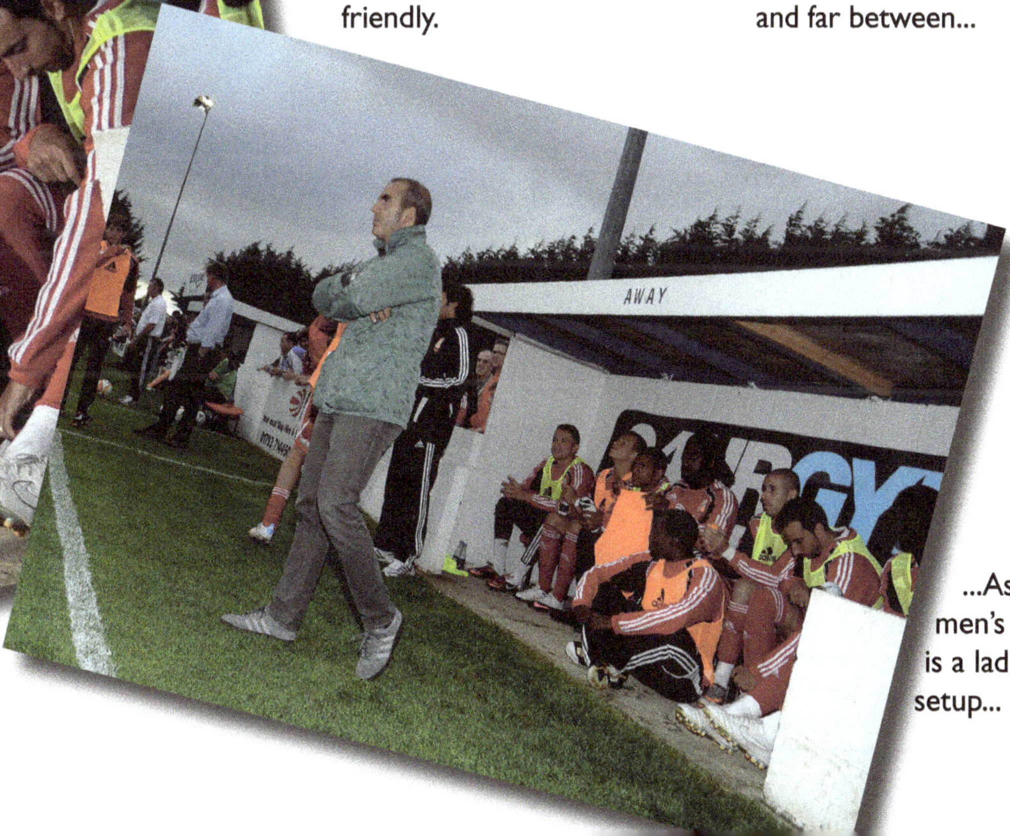

...As well as a men's team there is a ladies football setup...

...When I was young, and decidedly fitter than I am now, I refereed for a short period in the early nineteen seventies, and one thing that has changed since then is women's football.

When I refereed, if I officiated a ladies' game I would have been struck off the referees list, and now the women's game has obtained international status running almost parallel with men's football.

Supermarine, Swindon Town and Swindon Spitfires all run successful ladies' teams.

Believe me, the ladies play football as hard as any men's team, which makes for some good action images...

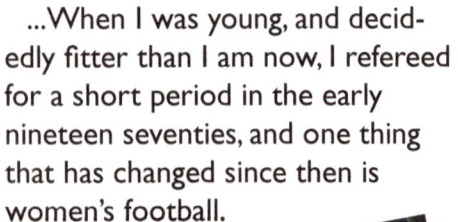

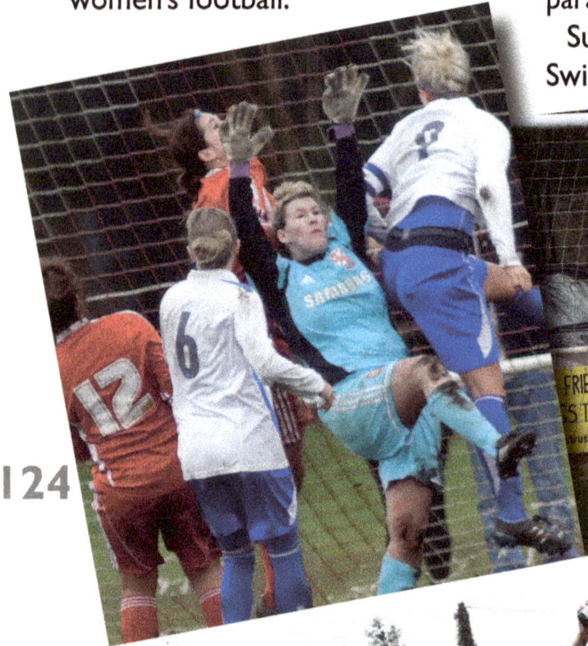

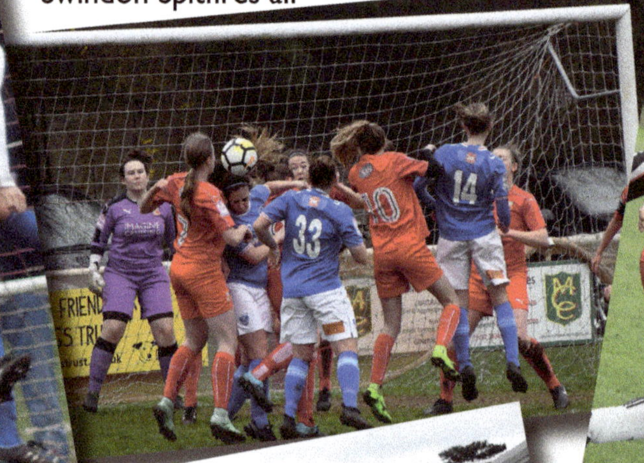

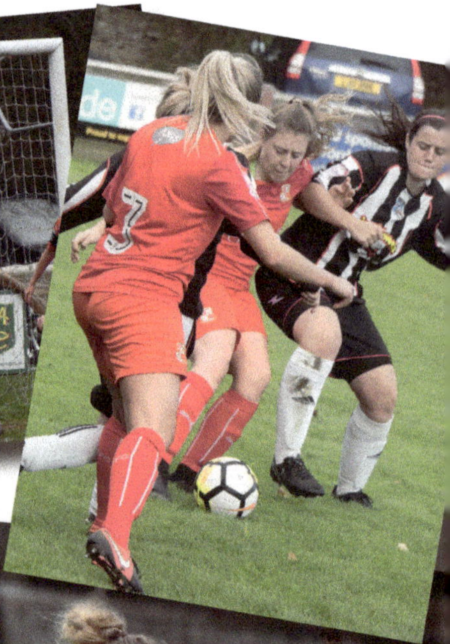

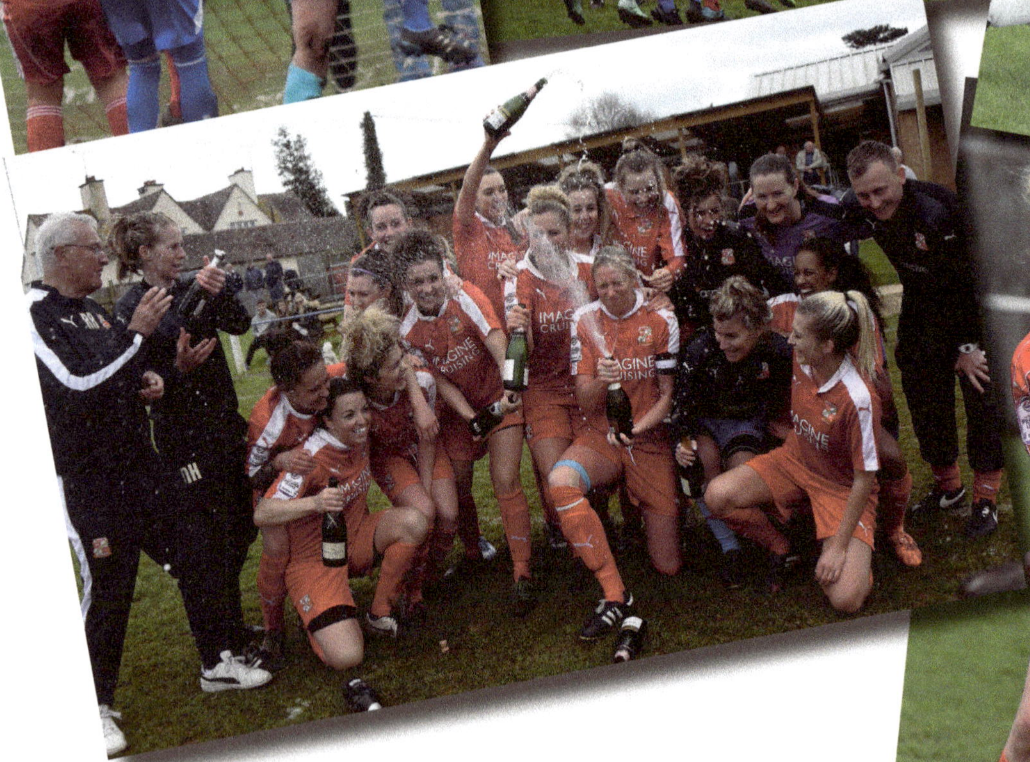

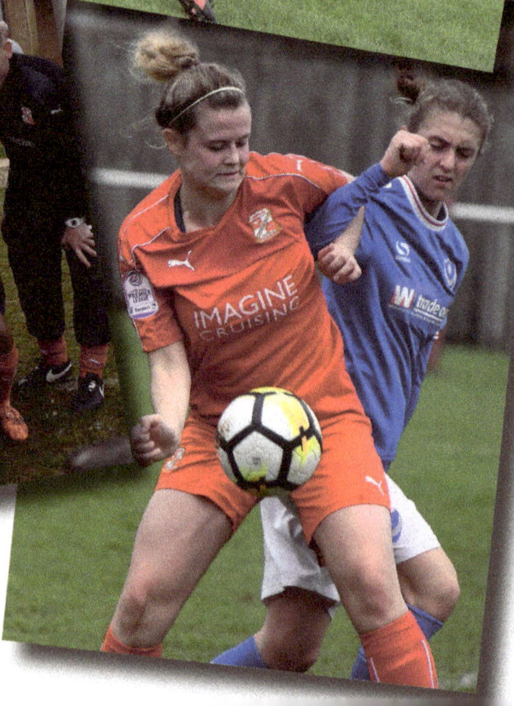

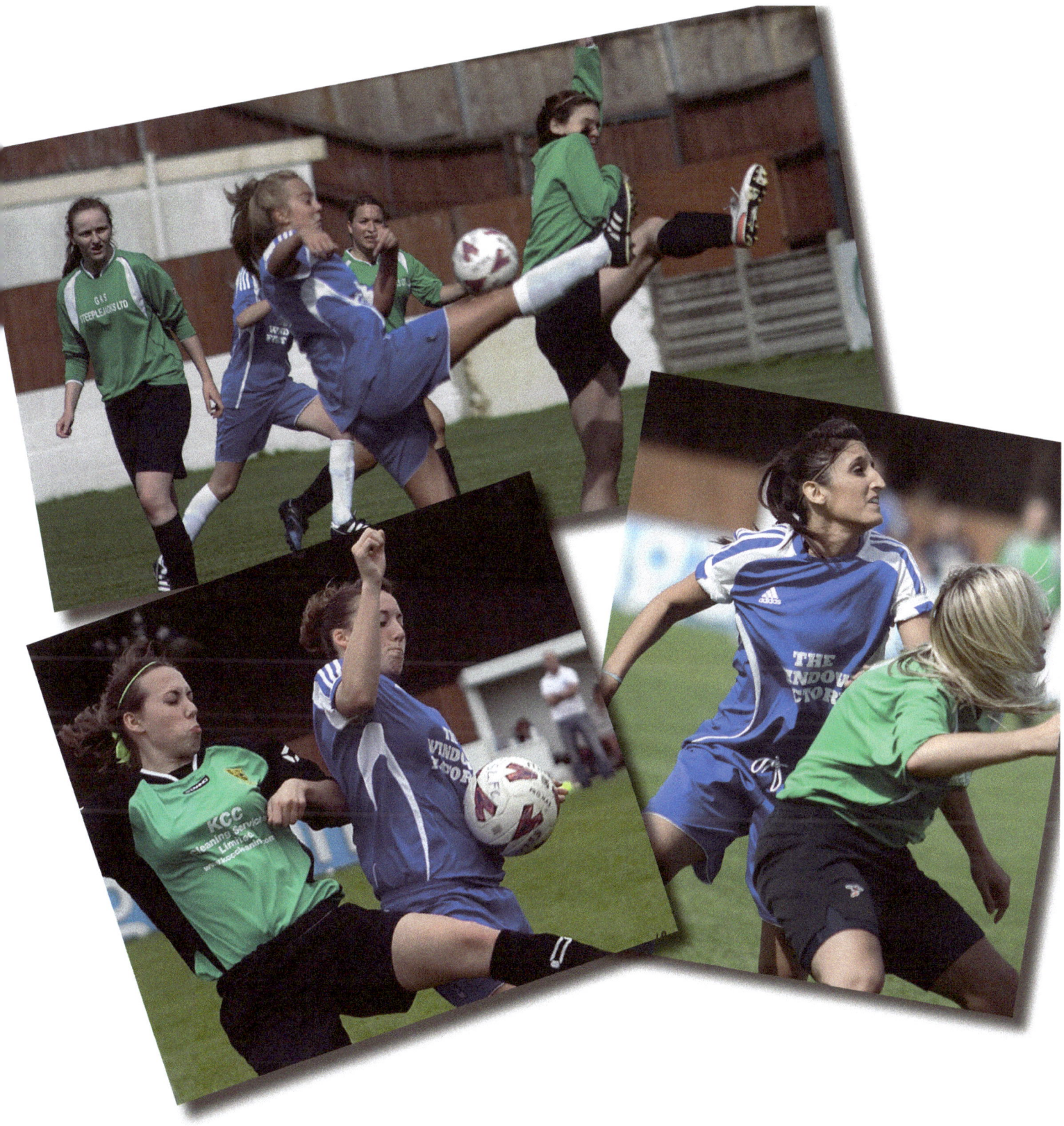

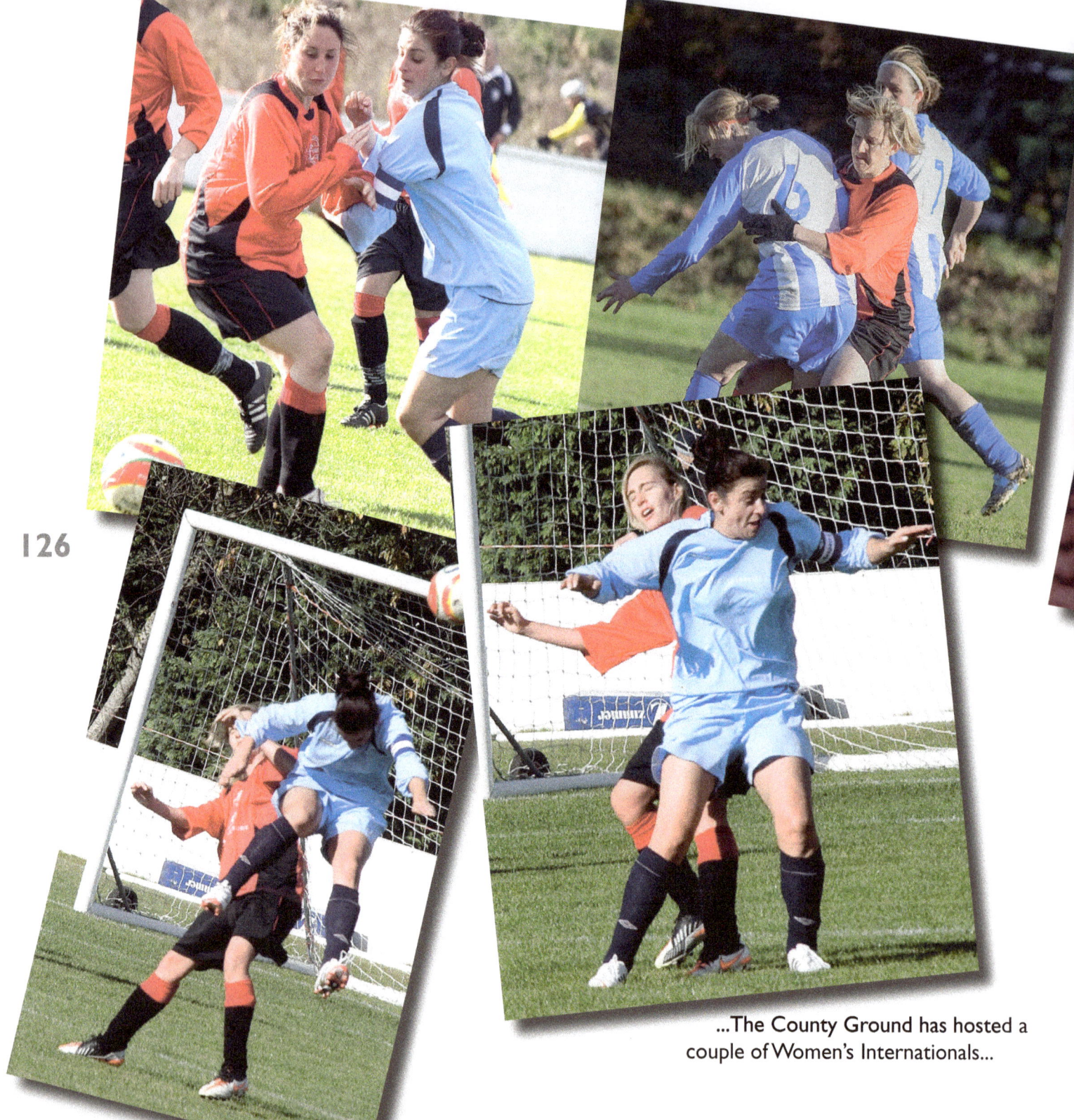

...The County Ground has hosted a couple of Women's Internationals...

...in 2011 the Lionesses defeated Slovenia 4-0 there...

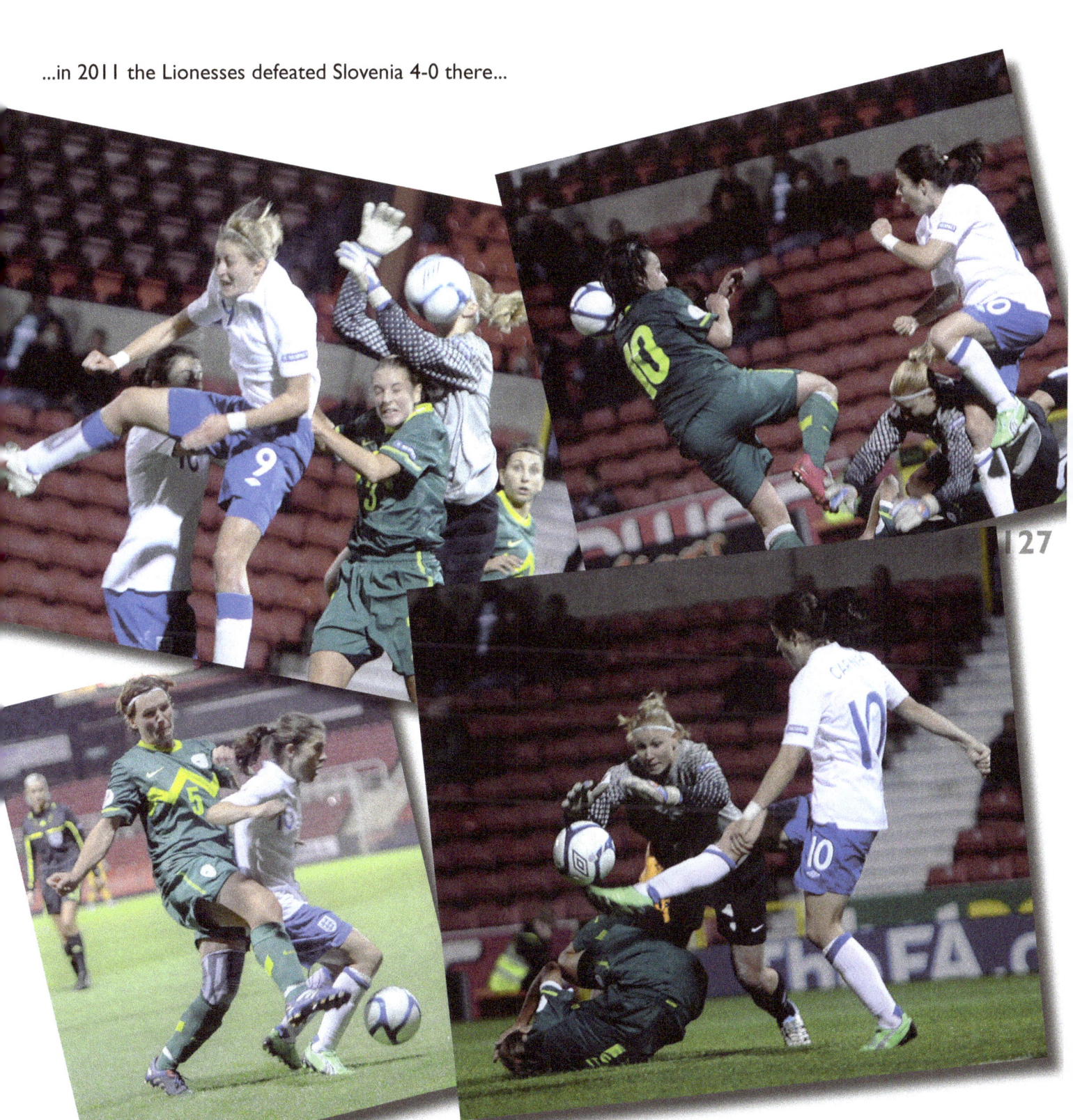

...Women not only play these sports but officiate too.

American football sees ladies in both playing and refereeing roles. In ice hockey there is often a lady official, and at both Swindon Town and Supermarine there have been woman officials.

I put this in because I wanted to show how sport has changed.

Being an observer, literally sitting on the sidelines, the changes have come, and not before time, as many of these lady officials are as good if not better than their male equivalents.

Teenager Chloe Smart from Oxford, who is a class 5 referee (that is refereeing to Senior County league) gives out a booking during a Swindon Town Ladies match.

Ice hockey referee Jo Johnson (Tottman) was the first woman to officiate men's games in the UK, and was the referee in the Sochi Olympic ladies ice hockey final.

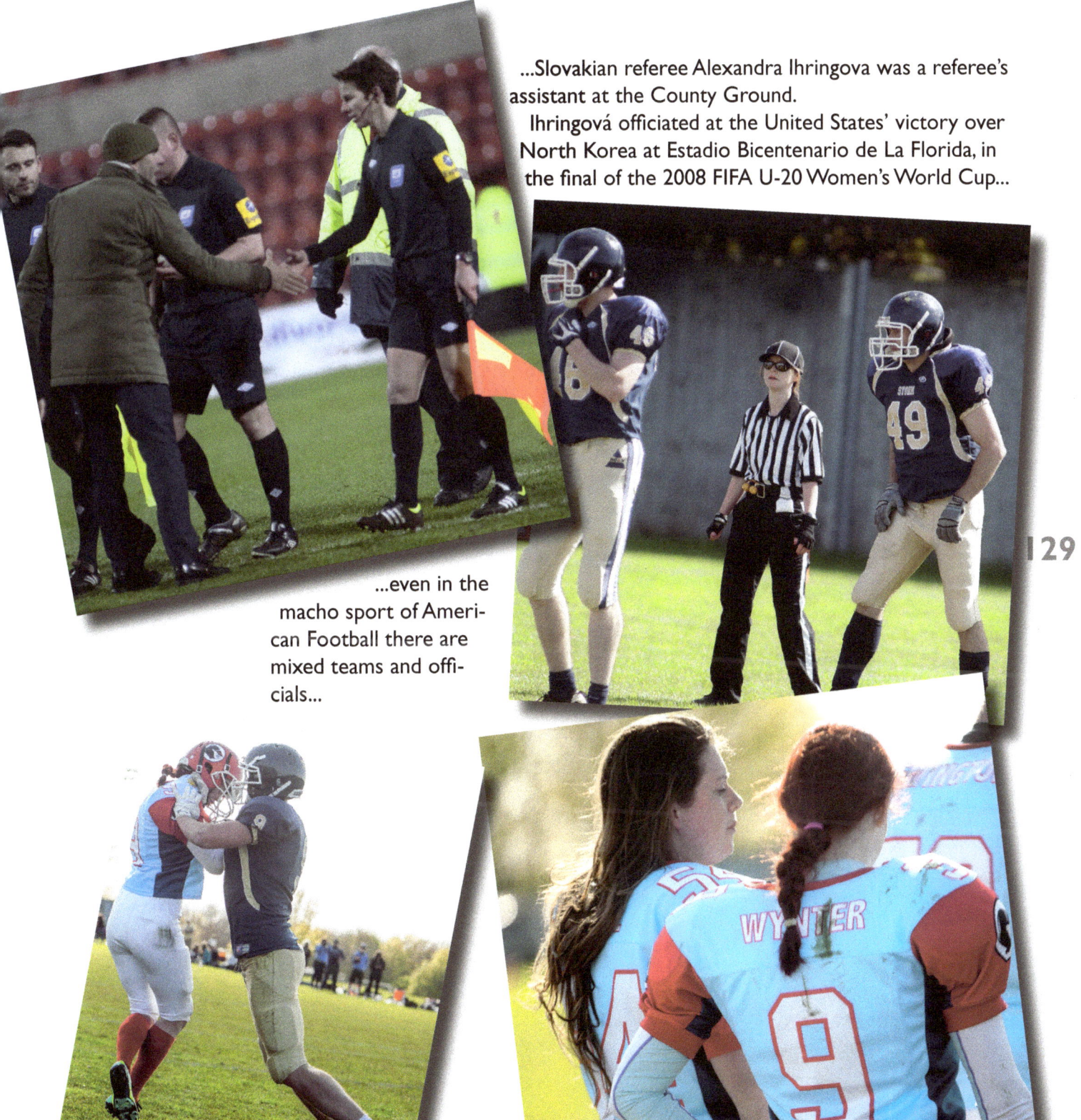

...Slovakian referee Alexandra Ihringova was a referee's assistant at the County Ground.

Ihringová officiated at the United States' victory over North Korea at Estadio Bicentenario de La Florida, in the final of the 2008 FIFA U-20 Women's World Cup...

...even in the macho sport of American Football there are mixed teams and officials...

...In the heady days of Swindon's short tenure in the Premier League, when film was king and your knowledge of taking photographs had to be masterful, Swindon played Everton at the County Ground on Saturday 16th October 1993.

Typical of that season, Everton scored in the first few minutes and duly celebrated.

As I said film was master, and to process that film took time, and the newspapers needed their pictures at half time to get them into the editions that covered Swindon.

To enable this we would work a shift system where we would start with four snappers around the pitch. We would collect the cassettes of film from our photographers and the national boys, who had hired our darkroom facility, of the first ten minutes of play, and dash them back to the office for processing. Each of the national photographers would have their own marked envelope, and our films were all piled in together with the first inch of film sticking out of the cassette for a speedy loading of the processor when back at base.

On this occasion I was the person doing the first run, and when I got to one of my photographers, Darren Jack, he said, "I think I have a very good celebration shot."

Knowing his skill I tagged the film by notching the leader with a small rip, and back at the office I put his film through first...

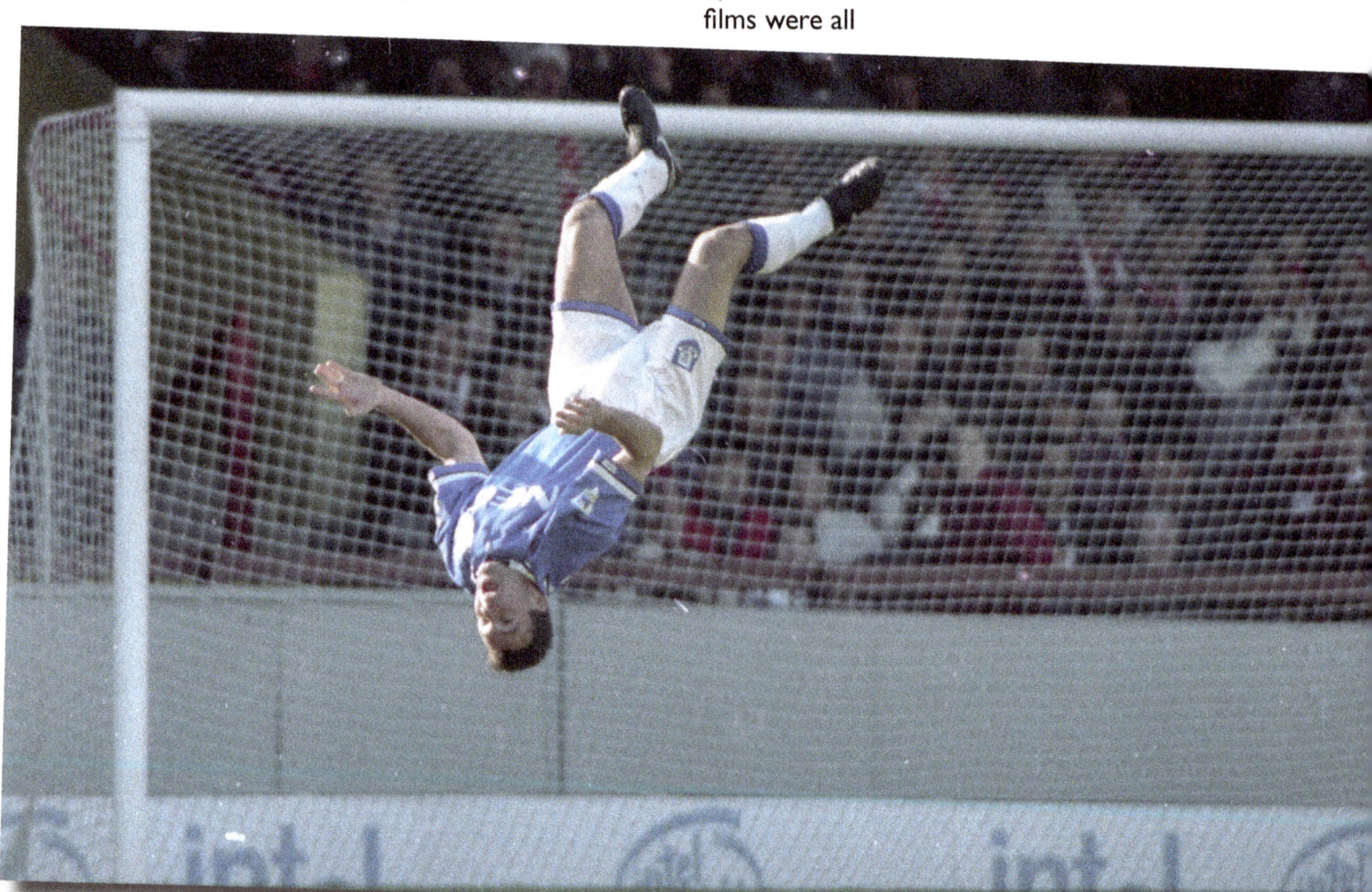

...About ten minutes later out came the film, and Darren was right; he did have a superb celebration shot of Everton's Peter Beagrie doing a back flip in the centre of an empty goal.

Having printed the image I rang round all the sport picture desks and they all said send the picture, even though some had their own snappers there, but the Sunday Mirror declined saying that they would take their man's picture.

To transmit the pictures I needed a NGA union wireman who sorted out the connections with the telephone exchange and the paper's wire rooms. With tongue in cheek I told him to send Darren's picture to the Mirror first.

Come Monday I purchased the papers to see what had been used, and almost all the papers had our picture on the back page; including the Sunday Mirror.

Later that week I had cause to call a very good friend and mentor, the late George Phillips, who had been covering the game for the Mirror Group of papers.

"You know what happened on Saturday don't you? They saw Darren's picture and scrapped the layout of the back page. They then rebuilt the page around it!".

Without the luxury of the image being instantly available to see on the back of the camera, photographers of the film era had to know what they had taken, and in this case it proved essential as the film went through first and was sent first.

As I mentioned at the start of this book timing is essential. In this case being first made it onto the back pages!..

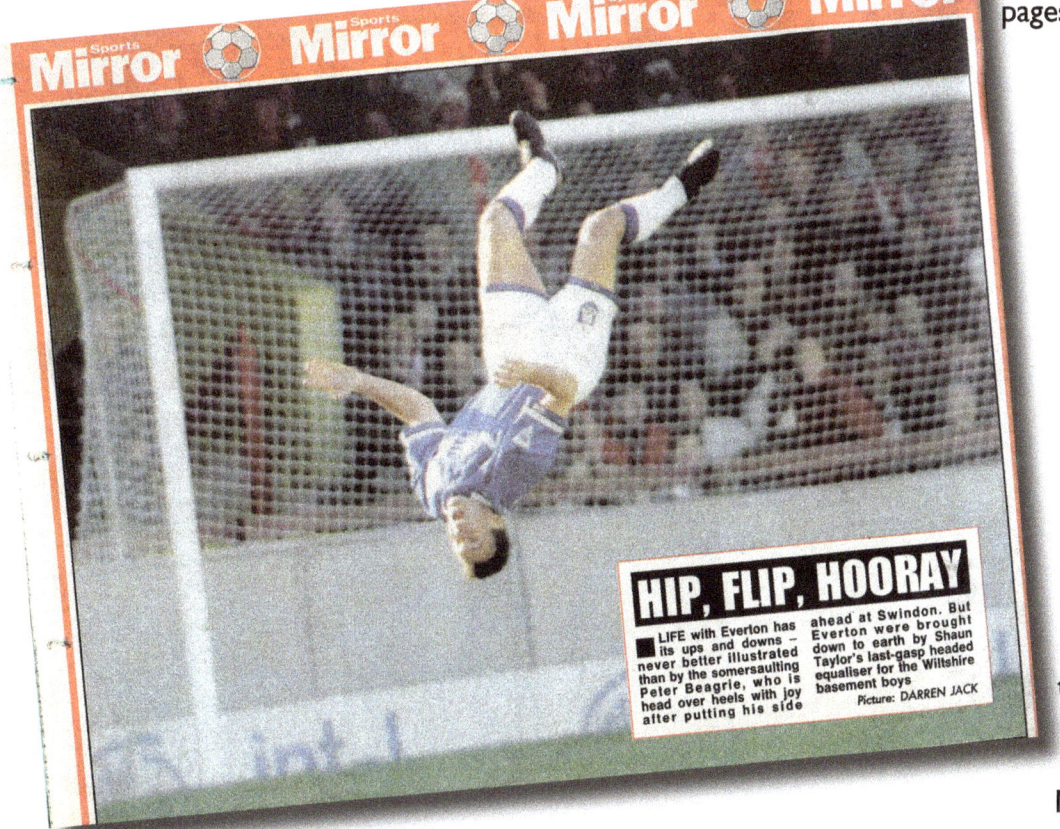

...In 2021, as I retire, there is a new era starting at the County Ground: enter Clem Morfuni...

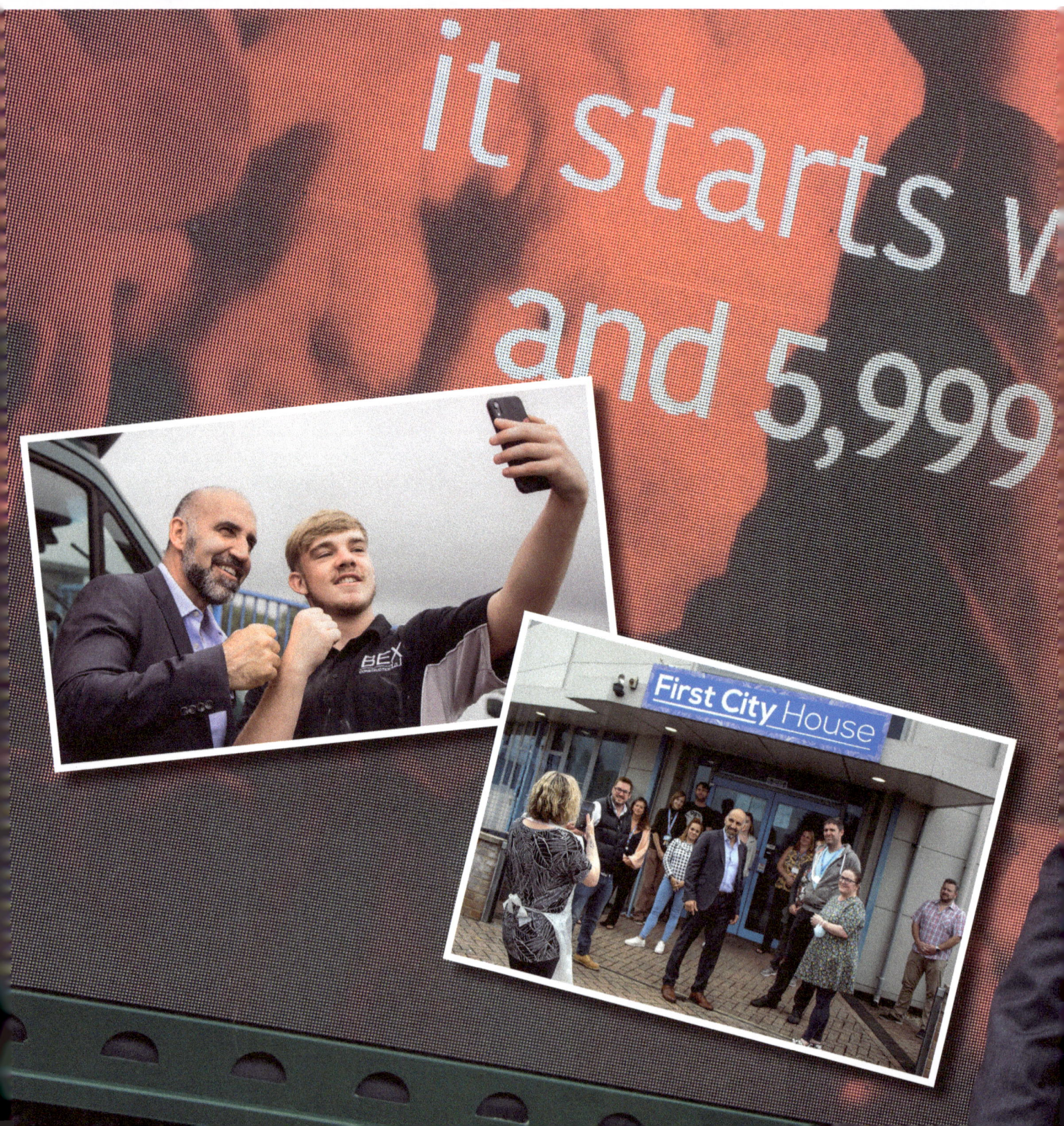

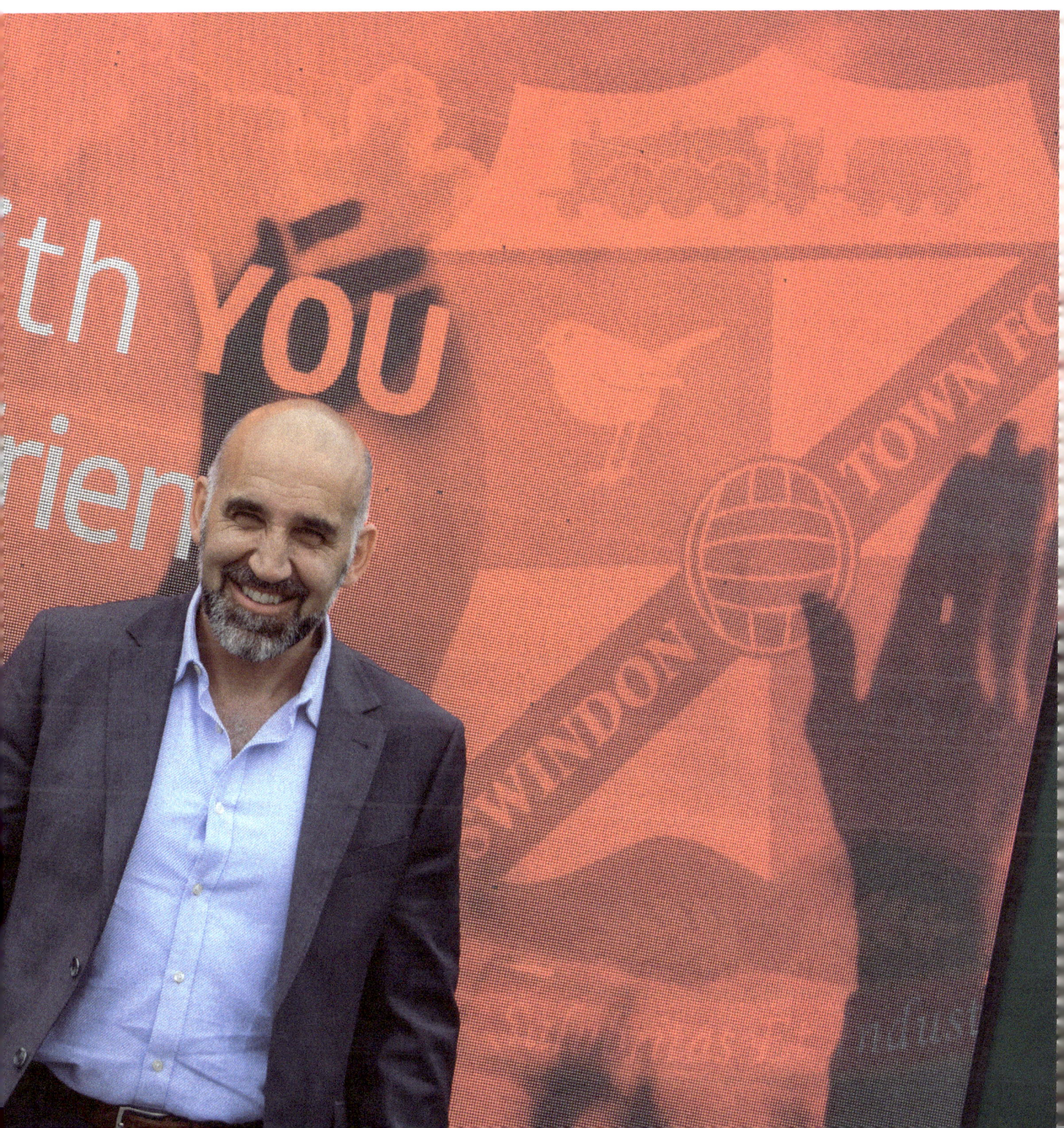

I must thanks a group of people who have helped me with this meander:

Firstly the photographers:
Richard Wintle
Sarah Johnson
Neil Atkinson
Clint Randall
Darren Jack
Rachel Davis

Those who filed and indexed the material over the years:
Pat Wintle,
Julie Chamberlain,
Sarah Wintle,

The many who helped and advised to put this together:

Darryl Moody,
Dawn Heavens and the Local Studies Team at central Library
Ross Wintle,

My publisher:
John Chandler.

My heartfelt thanks go out to my wife, who has proofed this missive, after putting up with me being in my office for hours during the evenings, and repeatedly telling me the scanner in the other office had finished!

Right now let's start on volume 4 ; The Little Black Book.

www.ingramcontent.com/pod-product-compliance
Lightning Source LLC
Chambersburg PA
CBHW040546220526
45473CB00017B/3038